TALES OF THE ALHAMBRA

WASHINGTON IRVING

TALES
OF
THE ALHAMBRA

MIGUEL SÁNCHEZ, EDITOR
GRANADA

© Miguel Sánchez, Editor-Marqués de Mondéjar, 44-Granada
Introduction and notes: Ricardo Villa-Real
Depósito legal: M. 27.344-1977
ISBN: 84-7169-026-8
Illustrations: Offo-Madrid
Impression: GREFOL, S.A.,
Pol. II, La Fuensanta, Móstoles (Madrid)
Printed in Spain

INTRODUCTION

*O*NCE *upon a time, when the world was still a leisurely place for those who could afford to pay for their leisure, long before tramcars grated or limousines hooted their way along the Calle de los Reyes Católicos, long before uniformed curators or printed entrance tickets had established their dominion within the precincts of the Alhambra, two friends, both diplomats by profession, the one an American, the other a Russian, set off on horseback from Seville and came to Granada. If that, to the modern reader, should bear too much resemblance to a fairy-tale, then it serves as a fitting introduction to a book of fairy-tales; for of such, by and large, consists «The Alhambra» by Washington Irving.*

The story of his friendship with the Russian, of their adventurous journey together, of their first encounter on the outskirts of the city with a self-appointed cicerone who conducted them to a «recommended» lodging forms a diverting introduction to this book. The modern visitor to Spain may experience, even across the gulf of a century, a certain kinship of feeling with the humorous, observant and often naïve American. And once the bond of sympathy is established one cannot help envying Irving's good fortune. The further one reads of his stay in the Alhambra, of his passing conversations with the picturesque inhabitants of that «old enchanted palace», of his hours of solitude in cool Moorish

7

patios, *the more one realizes that all the dreams of the modern tourist were transformed into living experience by a romantic American, more than a century ago. Who would not wish to be conducted privately through the Alhambra by the informative Mateo Jiménez? Or which of us has not dreamed of moonlit, solitary reveries in the Salón de Embajadores, gazing from Moorish balconies upon the Sacro-Monte and the Albaicín? Who in fact is «so dull of soul» that he would not, for a single night, exchange the comfort of his modern hotel for the enchantments of Boabdil's palace?*

Romanticism is indeed more than a mere literary mode that passed out of fashion in the last century. It is the living experience of all who have come to appreciate the dream world behind the landscape, the fantasy that lurks behind form, the eternal mystery couched in a woman's eyes.

Spain and Granada in particular have always evoked the fervour of the Romantics. One recalls certain poems from Hugo's «Orientales», Fauriel's «Chants populaires», Chateaubriand's «Le Dernier Abencerrage» and the first-fruits of all Granadine mythology, Pérez de Hita's «Civil Wars of Granada». If, for the Northern European on the one hand, the Spaniard has always been a figure of romance, daring and passion, the Spaniard in his turn has conjured up similar visions of the Granadine Moors. The gallant flower of Moorish Knighthood, symbolised in the story of the Abencerrage, rides out from the stronghold of Granada on his fiery Arab charger, clad in flowing burnous and brilliant turban, the name of his lady inscribed upon the pennon of his lance, to challenge the Christian invaders to single and mortal combat.

* * *

Thus here to Granada, where two great civilisations once blended to the death, have trekked thousands of sentimental pilgrims from Europe, Africa and America to evoke in the Alhambra the elusive memories of a more picturesque past. Irving was one of the first story-tellers in the Romantic age, and his work has outlived a century. Let that suffice as a judgement of his literary talents.

Irving's life, like his books, was an adventurous one. Born in 1783, the son of a New York merchant, he was trained for the bar. But like many other excellent writers before and after him, he abandoned the legal profession; thereupon he joined his brothers in the family business. When that collapsed, he turned seriously to literature. But during the next twenty years he also played a part of some prominence in the diplomatic world. After living in England as Secretary to the American Embassy, he was appointed Ambassador to Spain. Here he became one of the most noteworthy travellers of the Peninsula. His journey from Sevilla to Granada, mentioned in the opening paragraph, took place in the spring of 1829.

Irving's literary output was both varied and prolific. Under the title of «Salmagundi or the Whim-Whams of Launcelot and Others», he published a series of miscellaneous essays which brought him certain fame as a humorous essayist. But Irving's genius depends not so much on his descriptive or reflective powers—for at times he tends to prolixity and overemployment of the adjective—so much as on his consummate abilities as a story-teller. He is the raconteur par excellence; his true métier lies in the short story. With history, legend or biography Irving finds himself equally at home. His biographical portraits are varied, amusing and informative—«The Adventures of Captain Bonneville» (1837); «Mohamed and his Successors» (1839); «Oliver Goldsmith (1849); and «The Life of Washington» (1859).

Naturally one does not expect to find an exact historian of the academic type in Irving; the spirit of the age and the author's character bred the opposite tendency. As an admirer of Sir Walter Scott Irving consciously confuses history and legend. The result is a delightful, often unique blend of vivacity, understanding and humour, spiced with a whimsicality that rivals that of his great compatriot Mark Twain.

Irving's humorous powers are displayed to the full in his «History of New York from the Beginning of the World to the End of the Dutch Dynasty», which he relates through his genial mouthpiece, Dietrich Knickerbocker, that incomparable collector of comic chronicles. Better known to most of us, perhaps, is «The Legend of Sleepy Hollow», with the unforgetable figure of the angular village schoolmaster, Mr. Ichabod, pursued on his shambling nag by the gruesome Plantom Hussar.

Here in Spain Irving is chiefly known for his «Chronicle of the Conquest of Granada» (1829), and the present volume, «Tales of the Alhambra», which first appeared under the title «The Alhambra; a Series of Tales and Sketches of the Moors and Spaniards». The first edition of the book was the English one of 1832, printed by Messrs. Colburn and Bentley of London. Several months later came the Philadelphia publication of Lea and Carey. The same year it was published in Paris by A. and W Galignani, under the title of «The Alhambra, or the New Sketch Book: in One Volume». Wherever it appeared, it met with immediate success.

It is only fitting that this latest edition should be produced in Granada, the city that inspired the book. To illustrate Irving's stories we offer you thirty-two engravings of the Romantic period; and for your further illumination, a few notes in English. And now, dear reader, the rest is yours; browse to your heart's content, evoke your own memories or dreams of Granada and the Alhambra, and the splendour that is past; and may you derive from it as much pleasure and appreciation as did Washington Irving, more than a century ago.

R. VILLA-REAL

TO DAVID WILKIE, ESQ. R. A. [1]

MY DEAR SIR;

You may remember, that in the rambles we once took together about some of the old cities of Spain, particularly Toledo and Seville, we remarked a strong mixture of the Saracenic with the Gothic, remaining from the time of the Moors, and were more than once struck with scenes and incidents in the streets, which reminded us of passages in the «Arabian Nights». You then urged me to write something that should illustrate those peculiarities, «something in the Haroun Alraschid style», that should have a dash of that Arabian spice which pervades everything in Spain. I call this to your mind to show you that you are, in some degree, responsible for the present work, in which I have given a few «arabesque» sketches from the life and tales founded on popular traditions, which were chiefly struck-off during a residence in one of the most Morisco-Spanish places in the Peninsula.

I inscribe these pages to you as a memorial of the pleasant scenes we have witnessed together in that land of adventure, and as a testimonial of an esteem for your worth which is only exceeded by admiration of your talents.

Your friend and fellow-traveller,

THE AUTHOR

May, 1832

[1] English painter. This dedication appeared in the original publication.

THE ALHAMBRA

A SERIES OF TALES AND SKETCHES
OF THE MOORS AND SPANIARDS

THE JOURNEY

I N the spring of 1829, the author of this work whom curiosity had brought into Spain, made a rambling expedition from Seville to Granada in company with a friend, a member of the Russian Embassy at Madrid. Accident had thrown us together from distant regions of the globe and a similarity of taste led us to wander together among the romantic mountains of Andalusia. Should these pages meet his eye, wherever thrown by the duties of his station, whether mingling in the pageantry of courts or meditating on the truer glories of nature, may they recall the scenes of our adventurous companionship and with them the remembrance of one in whom neither time nor distance will obliterate the remembrance of his gentleness and worth!

And here, before setting forth, let me indulge in a few previous remarks on Spanish scenery and Spanish travelling. Many are apt to picture Spain to their imaginations as a soft southern region, decked out with all the luxuriant charms of voluptuous Italy. On the contrary, though there are exceptions in some of the maritime provinces, yet, for the greater part, it is a stern, melancholy country with rugged mountains and long sweeping plains destitute of trees and indescribably silent and lonesome, partaking of the savage and solitary character of Africa. What adds to this silence and loneliness is the absence of singing-birds, a natural consequence of the want of groves and hedges. The vulture and the eagle are seen wheeling about the mountain cliffs and soaring over the plains, and groups of shy bustards stalk about the heaths, but the myriads of smaller birds which animate the whole face of other countries are met with in but few provinces in Spain, and in those chiefly among the orchards and gardens which surround the habitations of man.

In the interior provinces the traveller occasionally traverses great tracts cultivated with grain as far as the eye can reach, waving, at times with verdure, at other times naked and sun-burnt, but he looks round in vain for the hand that has tilled the soil. At length he perceives some village on a steep hill or rugged crag with mouldering battlements and ruined watch-tower, a stronghold in old times against civil war or Moorish inroad, for the custom among the peasantry of congregating together for mutual protection is still kept up in most parts of Spain, in consequence of the maraudings of roving free-booters.

But though a great part of Spain is deficient in the garni-ture of groves and forests and the softer charms of ornamental cultivation, yet its scenery has something of a high and lofty character to compensate the want. It partakes something of the attributes of its people, and I think that I better understand the proud, hardy, frugal and abstemious Spaniard, his manly defiance of hardships and contempt of effeminate indulgences, since I have seen the country he inhabits.

There is something, too, in the sternly simple features of the Spanish landscape that impresses on the soul a feeling of sublimity. The inmense plains of the Castiles and of La Man-cha, extending as far as the eye can reach, derive an interest from their very nakedness and immensity, and have something of the solemn grandeur of the ocean. In ranging over these boundless wastes, the eye catches sight here and there of a straggling herd of cattle attended by a lonely herdsman, motionless as a statue with his long slender pike tapering up like a lance into the air or beholds a long train of mules slowly moving along the waste like a train of camels in the desert, or a single herdsman armed with blunderbuss and stiletto, and prowling over the plain. Thus the country, the habits, the very looks of the people, have something of the Arabian character. The general insecurity of the country is evinced in the universal use of weapons. The herdsman in the field, the shepherd in the plain, has his musket and his knife. The wealthy villager rarely ventures to the market-town without his *trabuco,* and perhaps a servant on foot with a blunderbuss on his shoulder, and the most petty journey is undertaken with the preparation of a warlike enterprise.

The dangers of the road produce also a mode of travelling, resembling on a diminutive scale the caravans of the East. The *arrieros* or carriers congregate in convoys and set off in large and well-armed trains on appointed days, while additional travellers swell their number and contribute to their strength. In this primitive way is the commerce of the country carried on. The muleteer is the general medium of traffic and the legitimate traverser of the land, crossing the Peninsula from the Pyrenees and the Asturias to the Alpujarras, the *Serranía de Ronda,* and even to the gates of Gibraltar. He lives frugally and hardily; his *alforjas* of coarse cloth hold his scanty stock of provisions, a leathern bottle hanging at his saddle-bow contains wine or water, for a supply across barren mountains and thirsty plains. A mulecloth spread upon the ground is his bed at night and his pack-saddle is his pillow. His low but clean-limbed and sinewy form betokens strength; his complexion is dark and sunburnt; his eye resolute but quiet in its expression, except when kindled by sudden emotion; his demeanour is frank, manly and courteous, and he never passes you without a grave salutation: «¡*Dios guarde a usted!*» «¡*Vaya usted con Dios, caballero!*» «God guard you! God be with you, cavalier!»

As these men have often their whole fortune at stake upon the burden of their mules, they have their weapons at hand, slung to their saddles and ready to be snatched out for desperate defence. But their united numbers render them secure against petty bands of marauders, and the solitary *bandolero,* armed to the teeth and mounted on his Andalusian steed, hovers about them, like a pirate about a merchant convoy, without daring to make an assault.

The Spanish muleteer has an inexhaustible stock of songs and ballads, with which to beguile his incessant wayfaring. The airs are rude and simple, consisting of but few inflexions. These he chants forth with a loud voice and long, drawling cadence, seated sideways on his mule who seems to listen with infinite gravity and to keep time with its paces to the tune. The couplets thus chanted, are often old traditional romances about the Moors or some legend of a saint or some love-ditty or, what is still more frequent, some ballad about a bold *contrabandista* or hardy *bandolero,* for the smuggler and the robber are poetical heroes among the common people of Spain. Often the song of the muleteer is composed at the instant and relates to some local scene or some incident of the journey. This talent for singing and improvising is frequent in Spain and is said to have been inherited from the Moors. There is something wildly pleasing in listening to these ditties among the rude and lonely scenes that they illustrate, accompanied, as they are, by the occasional jingle of the mulebell.

It has a most picturesque effect also to meet a train of muleteers in some mountain-pass. First you hear the bells of the leading mules, breaking with their simple melody the stillness of the airy height, or perhaps the voice of the muleteer, admonishing some tardy or wandering animal, or chanting, at the full stretch of his lungs, some traditionary ballad. At length you see the mules slowly winding along the cragged defile, sometimes descending precipitous cliffs, so as to present themselves in full relief against the sky, sometimes toiling up the deep arid chasms below you. As they approach, you descry their gay decorations of worsted tufts, tassels and saddle-cloths, while, as they pass by, the ever-ready *trabuco* slung behind the packs and saddles gives a hint of the insecurity of the road.

The ancient kingdom of Granada, into which we are about to penetrate, is one of the most mountainous regions of Spain. Vast *sierras* or chains of mountains, destitute of shrub or tree and mottled with variegated marbles and granites, elevate their sunburnt summits against a deep-blue sky, yet in their rugged bosoms lie engulfed the most verdant and fertile valleys, where the desert and the garden strain for mastery, and the very rock is, as it were, compelled to yield the fig, the orange and the citron, and to blossom with the myrtle and the rose.

In the wild passes of these mountains the sight of walled towns and villages, built like eagles' nests among the cliffs and surrounded by Moorish battlements, or of ruined watch-towers perched on lofty peaks, carries the mind back to the chivalric days of Christian and Moslem warfare, and to the romantic struggle for the conquest of Granada. In traversing these lofty *sierras,* the traveller is often obliged to alight, and lead his horse up and down the steep and jagged ascents and descents, resembling the broken steps of a staircase. Sometimes the road winds along dizzy precipices, without parapet to guard him from the gulfs below, and then will plunge down steep dark and dangerous declivities. Sometimes it straggles through rugged *barrancos* or ravines, worn by winter torrents, the obscure path of the *contrabandista,* while ever and anon the ominous cross, the monument of robbery and murder, erected on a mound of stones at some lonely part of the road, admonishes the traveller that he is among the haunts of banditti, perhaps at that very moment under the eye of some lurking *bandolero.*

Sometimes, in winding through the narrow valleys, he is start-led by a hoarse bellowing, and beholds above him, on some green fold of the mountain side, a herd of fierce Andalusian bulls, destined for the combat of the arena. There is something awful in the contemplation of these terrific animals, clothed with tremendous strength, and ranging their native pastures in untamed wildness, strangers almost to the face of man. They know no one but the solitary herdsman who attends upon them, and even he at times dares not venture to approach them. The low bellowing of these bulls, and their menacing aspect as they look down from their rocky height, give additional wildness to the savage scenery around.

I have been betrayed unconsciously into a longer disquisi-tion than I had intended on the general features of Spanish tra-velling, but there is a romance about all the recollections of the Peninsula that is dear to the imagination.

It was on the first of May that my companion and myself set forth from Seville on our route to Granada. We had made all due preparations for the nature of our journey which lay through mountainous regions where the roads are little better than mere mule-paths, and too frequently beset by robbers. The most valuable part of our luggage had been forwarded by the *arrieros;* we retained merely clothing and necessaries for the journey and money for the expenses of the road, with a sufficient surplus of the latter to satisfy the expectations of robbers should we be assailed, and to save ourselves from the rough treatment that awaits the too wary and empty-handed traveller. A couple of stout hired steeds were provided for the conveyance of a sturdy Biscayan lad of about twenty years of age, who was to guide us through the perplexed mazes of the mountain roads, to take care of the horses, to act occasio-nally as our valet, and at all times as our guard, for he had a formidable *trabuco* or carbine to defend us from *rateros* or so-litary footpads, about which weapon he made much vain-glorious boast, though, to the discredit of his generalship, I must say that it generally hung unloaded behind his saddle. He was, however, a faithful, cheery, kindhearted creature, full of saws and proverbs as that miracle of squires the renowned Sancho himself, whose name we bestowed upon him, and, like a true Spaniard, though treated by us with companionable familiarity, he never for a moment, in his utmost hilarity, overstepped the bounds of respectful decorum.

Thus equipped and attended, we set out on our journey with a genuine disposition to be pleased. With such a disposition, what a country is Spain for a traveller, where the most miserable inn is as full of adventure as an enchanted castle and every meal is in itself an achievement! Let others repine at the lack of turnpike-roads and sumptuous hotels, and all the elaborate comforts of a country cultivated into tameness and the common-place, but give me the rude mountain scramble, the roving, haphazard manners that give such a true game flavour to romantic Spain!

Our first evening's entertainment had a relish of the kind. We arrived after sunset at a little town among the hills after a fatiguing journey over a wide houseless plain, where we had been repeatedly drenched with showers. In the inn were a party of *migueletes* who were patrolling the country in pursuit of robbers. The appearance of foreigners like ourselves was unusual in this remote town; mine host, with two or three old gossiping comrades in brown cloaks, studied our passports in a corner of the *posada,* while an *alguacil* took notes by the dim light of a lamp. The passports were in foreign languages and perplexed them, but our squire Sancho assisted them in their studies and magnified our importance with the grandiloquence of a Spaniard. In the meantime, the magnificent distribution of a few cigars had won the hearts of all around us; in a little while the whole community seemed put in agitation to make us welcome. The *corregidor* himself waited upon us, and a great rush-bottomed arm chair was ostentatiusly bolstered into our room by our landlady, for the accommodation of that important personage. The commander of the patrol took supper with us, a lively, talking, laughing *andaluz* who had made a campaign in South America, and recounted his exploits in love and war with much pomp of phrase, vehemence of gesticulation and mysterious rolling of the eye. He told us that he had a list of all the robbers in the country and meant to ferret out every mother's son of them; he offered us at the same time some of his soldiers as an escort. «One is enough to protect you, *señores;* the robbers know me and know my men; the sight of one is enough to spread terror through a whole *sierra.*» We thanked him for his offer, but assured him in his own strain that with the protection of our redoubtable squire, Sancho, we were not afraid of all the *ladrones* of Andalusia.

While we were supping with our drawcansir friend, we heard the notes of a guitar and the click of castanets, and presently a chorus of voices singing a popular air. In fact, mine host had gathered together the amateur singers and musicians and the rustic belles of the neighbourhood, and on going forth, the court-yard or *patio* of the inn presented a scene of true Spanish festivity. We took our seats with mine host and hostess and the commander of the patrol under the archway of the court; the guitar passed from hand to hand, but a jovial shoemaker was the Orpheus of the place. He was a pleasant-looking fellow, with huge black whiskers; his sleeves were rolled up to his elbows. He touched the guitar with masterly skill and sang little amorous ditties with an expressive leer at the women, with whom he was evidently a favourite. He afterwards danced a *fandango* with a buxom Andalusian damsel, to the great delight of the spectators. But none of the females present could compare with mine host's pretty daughter, Pepita, who had slipped away and made her toilette for the occasion, and had covered her head with roses, and who distinguished herself in a *bolero* with a handsome young dragoon. We had ordered our host to let wine and refreshment circulate freely among the company, yet, though there was a motley assembly of soldiers, muleteers and villagers, no one exceeded the bounds of sober enjoyment. The scene was a study for a painter; the picturesque group of dancers, the troopers in their half military dresses, the peasantry wrapped in their brown cloaks; nor must I omit to mention the old meagre *alguacil* in a short black cloak, who took no notice of anything going on, but sat in a corner diligently writing by the dim light of a huge copper lamp that might have figured in the days of Don Quixote.

I am not writing a regular narrative and do not pretend to give the varied events of several days, rambling over hill and dale, moor and mountain. We travelled in true *contrabandista* style, taking everything, rough and smooth, as we found it, and mingling with all classes and conditions in a kind of vagabond companionship. It is the true way to travel in Spain. Knowing the scanty larders of the inns, and the naked tracts of country, which the traveller has often to traverse, we had taken care, on starting to have the *alforjas* or saddle-bags of our squire well stocked with cold provisions, and his *bota* or leathern bottle which was of portly dimensions, filled to the neck with choice Valdepeñas wine. As this was a munition for our campaign more important than even his *trabuco,* we exhorted him to have an eye to it and I will do him the justice to say that his namesake, the trencher-loving Sancho himself, could not excel him as a provident purveyor. Though the *alforjas* and *bota* were repeatedly and vigorously assailed throughout the journey, they appeared to have a miraculous property of being never empty, for our vigilant squire took care to sack everything that remained from our evening repast at the inns to supply our next day's luncheon.

What luxurious noontide repasts have we made, on the green sward by the side of a brook ot fountain, under a shady tree, and then what delicious *siestas* on our cloaks, spread out on the herbage!

We paused one day at noon for a repast of the kind. It was in a pleasant little green meadow, surrounded by hills covered with olive-trees. Our cloaks were spread on the grass under an elm-tree by the side of a bubbling rivulet, our horses were tethered where they might crop the herbage and Sancho produced his *alforjas* with an air of triumph. They contained the contributions of four day's journeying, but had been signally enriched by the foraging of the previous evening in a plenteous inn at Antequera. Our squire drew forth the heterogeneous contents, one by one, and these seemed to have no end. First came forth a shoulder of roasted kid, very little the worse for wear, then an entire partridge, then a great morsel of salted codfish wrapped in paper, then the residue of a ham, then the half of a pullet, together with several rolls of bread and a rabble rout of oranges, figs, raisins, and walnuts. His *bota* also had been recruited with some excellent wine of Malaga. At every fresh apparition from his larder, he would enjoy our ludicrous surprise, throwing himself back on the grass and shouting with laughter. Nothing pleased the simple-hearted varlet more than to be compared for his devotion to the trencher to the renowned squire of Don Quixote. He was well versed in the history of Don Quixote and, like most of the common people of Spain, firmly believed it to be a true history.

«All that, however, happened a long time ago, *señor?*» said he to me one day with an inquiring look.

«A very long time», was the reply.

«I dare say more than a thousand years?»—still looking dubiously.

«I dare say, not less.»

The squire was satisfied.

As we were making a repast, above described, and diverting ourselves with the simple drollery of our squire, a solitary beggar approached us, who had almost the look of a pilgrim. He was evidently very old with a grey beard and supported himself on a staff, yet age had not bowed him down; he was tall and erect, and had the wreck of a fine form. He wore a round Andalusian hat, a sheep-skin jacket, and leathern breeches, gaiters and sandals. His dress, though old and patched, was decent, his demeanour manly and he addressed us with that grave courtesy that is to be remarked in the lowest Spaniard. We were in a favourable mood for such a visitor, and in a freak of capricious charity gave him some silver, a loaf of fine wheaten bread, and a goblet of our choice wine of Malaga. He received them thankfully, but without any grovelling tribute of gratitude. Tasting the wine, he held it up to the light with a slight beam of surprise in his eye, then quaffing it off at a draught, «It is many years», said he, «since I have tasted such wine. It is a cordial to an old man's heart». Then, looking at the beautiful wheaten loaf, «¡bendito sea tal pan!» «blessed be such bread!» So saying, he put it in his wallet. We urged him to eat it on the spot. «No, señores», replied he, «the wine I had to drink or leave, but the bread I must take home to share with my family.»

Our man Sancho sought our eye and reading permission there gave the old man some of the ample fragments of our repast, on condition, however, that he should sit down and make a meal.

He accordingly took his seat at some little distance from us, and began to eat slowly and with a sobriety and decorum that would have become an *hidalgo*. There was altogether a measured manner and a quiet self-possession about the old man that made me think he had seen better days; his language too, though simple, had occasionally something picturesque and almost poetical in the phraseology. I set him down for some broken-down cavalier. I was mistaken; it was nothing but the innate courtesy of a Spaniard, and the poetical turn of thought and language often to be found in the lowest classes of this clear-witted people. For fifty years, he told us, he had been a shepherd, but now he was out of employ, and destitute. «When I was a young man», said he, «nothing could harm or trouble me. I was always gay, but now I am seventy-nine years of age and a beggar, and my heart begins to fail me.»

Still he was not a regular mendicant; it was not until recently that want had driven him to this degradation, and he gave a touching picture of the struggle between hunger and pride, when abject destitution first came upon him. He was returning from Malaga without money; he had not tasted food for some time and was crossing one of the great plains of Spain, where there were but few habitations. When almost dead with hunger, he applied at the door of a *venta* or country inn. «*¡Perdone usted, por Dios hermano!*» (Excuse us, brother, for God's sake!) was the reply—the usual mode in Spain of refusing a beggar. «I turned away», said he, «with shame greater than my hunger, for my heart was yet too proud. I came to a river with high banks and deep rapid current, and felt tempted to throw myself in. «What should such an old, worthless, wretched man as I live for?» But when I was on the brink of the current, I thought on the Blessed Virgin and turned away. I travelled on until I saw a country-seat at a little distance from the road and entered the outer gate of the court-yard. The door was shut, but there were two young *señoras* at a window. I approached and begged:—«*¡Perdone usted, por Dios, hermano!*» (Excuse us, brother, for God's sake!) and the window closed. I crept out of the court-yard, but hunger overcame me and my heart gave way. I thought my hour at hand, so I laid myself down at the gate, commended myself to the Holy Virgin and covered my head to die. In a little while afterwards, the master of the house came home; seeing me lying at his gate, he uncovered my head, had pity on my grey hairs, took me into his house and gave me food. So, *señores,* you see that one should always put confidence in the protection of the Virgin.»

The old man was on his way to his native place, Archidona, which was close by on the summit of a steep and rugged mountain. He pointed to the ruins of its old Moorish castle: «That castle», he said, «was inhabited by a Moorish king at the time · of the wars of Granada. Queen Isabella invaded it with a great army, but the king looked down from his castle among the clouds and laughed her to scorn! Upon this the Virgin appeared to the queen and guided her and her army up a mysterious path in the mountains, which had never before been known. When the Moor saw her coming, he was astonished and springing with his horse from a precipice was dashed to pieces! «The marks of his horse's hoof», said the old man, «are to be seen in the margin of the rock to this day. And see, *señores,* yonder is the road by which the queen and her army mounted; you see it like a riband up the mountain side, but the miracle is that, though it can be seen at a distance, when you come near it disappears!»

The ideal road to which he pointed was undoubtedly a sandy ravine of the mountain, which looked narrow and defined at a distance, but became broad and indistinct on an approach.

As the old man's heart warmed with wine and wassail, he went on to tell us a story of the buried treasure left under the castle by the Moorish king. His own house was next to the foundations of the castle. The curate and notary dreamed three times of the treasure and went to work at the place pointed out in their dreams. His own son-in-law heard the sound of their pick-axes and spades at night. What they found, nobody knows; they became suddenly rich, but kept their own secret. Thus the old man had once been next door to fortune, but was doomed never to get under the same roof.

I have remarked that the stories of treasure buried by the Moors, which prevail throughout Spain, are most current among the poorest people. It is thus kind nature consoles with shadows for the lack of substantials. The thirsty man dreams of fountains and running-streams, the hungry man of ideal banquets and the poor man of heaps of hidden gold. Nothing certainly is more magnificent than the imagination of a beggar.

The last travelling sketch I shall give is an evening scene at the little city of Loja. This was a famous belligerent frontier post in the time of the Moors and repulsed Ferdinand from its walls. It was the stronghold of old Aliatar, the father-in-law of Boabdil, when that fiery veteran sallied forth with his son -in-law on their disastrous inroad, that ended in the death of the chieftain and the capture of the monarch. Loja is wildly situated in a broken mountain-pass on the banks of the Genil among rocks and groves, meadows and gardens. The people seem still to retain the bold fiery spirit of the olden time. Our inn was suited to the place. It was kept by a young and handsome Andalusian widow, whose trim *basquiña* of black silk, fringed with bugles, set off the play of a graceful form and round pliant limbs. Her step was firm and elastic, her dark eye was full of fire, and the coquetry of her air and varied ornaments of her person showed that she was accustomed to be admired.

She was well matched by a brother, nearly about her own age; they were perfect models of the Andalusian *majo* and *maja*. He was tall, vigorous and well-formed, with a clear olive-complexion, a dark beaming eye and curling chestnut whiskers that met under his chin. He was gallantly dressed in a short green velvet jacket, fitted to his shape, profusely decorated with silver buttons, with a white handkerchief in each pocket. He had breeches of the same, with rows of buttons from the hips to the knees, a pink silk handkerchief round his neck, gathered through a ring, on the bosom of a neatly planted shirt, a sash round the waist to match, *botines* or spatterdashes of the finest russet-leather, elegantly worked and open at the calf to show his stocking, and russet-shoes, setting off a well-shaped foot.

As he was standing at the door, a horseman rode up and entered into low and earnest conversation with him. He was dressed in similar style and almost with equal finery, a man about thirty, square-built, with strong Roman features, handsome, though slightly pitted with the small-pox, with a free, bold and somewhat daring air. His powerful black horse was decorated with tassels and fanciful trappings, and a couple of broad-mouthed blunderbusses hung behind the saddle. He had the air of one of those *contrabandistas* that I have seen in the mountains of Ronda and evidently had a good understanding with the brother of mine hostess, nay, if I mistake not, he was a favoured admirer of the widow. In fact, the whole inn and its inmates had something of a *contrabandista* aspect, and the blunderbuss stood in a corner beside the guitar. The horseman I have mentioned passed his evening in the *posada* and sang several bold mountain romances with great spirit. As we were at supper, two poor Asturians put in in distress, begging food and a night's lodging. They had been waylaid by robbers as they came from a fair among the mountains, robbed of a horse which carried all their stock in trade, stripped of their money and most of their apparel, beaten for having offered resistance and left almost naked in the road. My companion, with a prompt generosity natural to him ordered them a supper and a bed, and gave them a sum of money to help them forward towards their home.

As the evening advanced, the *dramatis personnœ* thickened. A large man about sixty years of age, of powerful frame, came strolling in to gossip with mine hostess. He was dressed in the ordinary Andalusian costume, but had a huge sabre tucked under his arm, wore large moustaches, and had something of a

29

lofty swaggering air. Every one seemed to regard him with great deference.

Our man Sancho whispered to us that he was Don Ventura Rodríguez, the hero and champion of Loja, famous for his prowess and the strength of his arm. In the time of the French invasion he surprised six troopers who were asleep. He first secured their horses, them attacked them with his sabre, killed some and took the rest prisoners. For this exploit the king allows him a *peseta* (the fifth of a *duro* or dollar) per day, and has dignified him with the title of *Don*.

I was amused to notice his swelling language and demeanour. He was evidently a thorough Andalusian, boastful as he was brave. His sabre was always in his hand or under his arm. He carries it always about with him as a child does her doll, calls it his Santa Teresa and says that when he draws it, «*¡tiembla la tierra!*»—the earth trembles.

I sat until a late hour listening to the varied themes of this motley group who mingled together with the unreserve of a Spanish *posada*. We had *contrabandista* songs, stories of robbers, *guerrilla* exploits and Moorish legends. The last were from our handsome landlady who gave a poetical account of the *infiernos* or infernal regions of Loja —dark caverns, in which subterranean streams and waterfalls make a mysterious sound. The common people say that there are money-coiners shut up there from the time of the Moors and that the Moorish kings kept their treasures in those caverns.

Were it the purport of this work, I could fill its pages with the incidents and scenes of our rambling expedition, but other themes invite me. Journeying in this manner, we at length emerged from the mountains and entered upon the beautiful *vega* of Granada. Here we took our last midday's repast under a grove of olive-trees, on the borders of a rivulet, with the old Moorish capital in the distance and animated by the ruddy towers of the Alhambra, while far above in the snowy summits of the Sierra Nevada shone like silver. The day was without a cloud and the heat of the sun tempered by cool breezes from the mountains; after our repast, we spread our cloaks and took our last *siesta,* lulled by the humming of bees among the flowers and the notes of ring-doves from the neighbouring olive trees. When the sultry hours were past, we resumed our journey and, after passing between hedges of aloes and Indian figs, and through a wilderness of gardens, arrived about sunset at the gates of Granada.

* * *

To the traveller imbued with a feeling for the historical and poetical, the Alhambra of Granada is as much an object of veneration as is the Kaaba or sacred house of Mecca to all true Moslem pilgrims. How many legends and traditions, true and fabulous, how many songs and romances, Spanish and Arabian, of love and war and chivalry are associated with this romantic pile! The reader may judge therefore of our delight when, shortly after our arrival in Granada, the Governor of the Alhambra gave us his permission to occupy his vacant apartments in the Moorish palace. My companion was soon summoned away by the duties of his station, but I remained for several months, spellbound in the old enchanted pile. The following papers are the result of my reveries and researches during that delicious thraldom. If they have the power of imparting any of the witching charms of the place to the imagination of the reader, he will not repine at lingering with me for a season in the legendary halls of the Alhambra.

GOVERNMENT OF THE ALHAMBRA

THE Alhambra is an ancient fortress or castellated palace of the Moorish kings of Granada, where they held dominion over this their boasted terrestrial paradise and made their last stand for empire in Spain. The palace occupies but a portion of the fortress, the walls of which, studded with towers, stretch irregularly round the whole crest of a lofty hill that overlooks the city and forms a spur of the Sierra Nevada or Snowy Mountain.

In the time of the Moors the fortress was capable of containing an army of forty thousand men within its precincts and served occasionally as a stronghold of the sovereigns against their rebellious subjects. After the kingdom had passed into the hands of the Christians, the Alhambra continued as a royal demesne and was occasionally inhabited by the Castilian monarchs. The Emperor Charles V. began a sumptuous palace within its walls, but was deterred from completing it by repeated shocks of earthquakes [1]. The last royal residents were Philip V. and his beautiful queen Elizabetta of Parma early in the eighteenth century. Great preparations were made for their reception. The palace and gardens were placed in a state

[1] The true reason for the interruption in construction was a Morisco revolt, for the Moriscoes used to contribute 80.0000 ducats yearly for this purpose, in exchange for certain privileges. *(Ed. note.)*

of repair and a new suite of apartments erected and decorated by artists brought from Italy. The sojourn of the sovereigns was transient, and after their departure the palace once more became desolate. Still the place was maintained with some military state. The governor held it immediately from the crown, its jurisdiction extended down into the suburbs of the city and was independent of the Captain General of Granada. A considerable garrison was kept up, the governor had his apartments in the front of the old Moorish palace and never descended into Granada without some military parade. The fortress in fact was a little town of itself, having several streets of houses within its walls, together with a Franciscan convent and a parochial church.

The desertion of the court, however, was a fatal blow to the Alhambra. Its beautiful halls became desolate and some of them fell to ruin, the gardens were destroyed and the fountains ceased to play. By degrees the dwellings became filled up with a loose and lawless population; *contrabandistas* who availed themselves of its independent jurisdiction to carry on a wide and daring course of smuggling, and thieves and rogues of all sorts, who made this their place of refuge from whence they might depredate upon Granada and its vicinity. The strong arm of government at length interfered; the whole community was thoroughly sifted; none were suffered to remain but such as were of honest character and had legitimate right to a residence; the greater part of the houses were demolished and a mere hamlet left, with the parochial church and the Franciscan convent. During the recent troubles in Spain, when Granada was in the hands of the French, the Alhambra was garrisoned by their troops, and the palace was occasionally inhabited by the French commander. With that enlightened taste which has ever distinguished the French nation in their conquests, this monument of Moorish elegance and grandeur was rescued from the absolute ruin and desolation that were overwhelming it [1]. The roofs were repaired, the saloons and galleries protected from the weather, the gardens cultivated, the water-courses restored, the fountains once more made to throw up their sparkling showers, and Spain may thank her invaders for having preserved to her the most beautiful and interesting of her historical monuments.

On the departure of the French they blew up several towers of the outer wall, and left the fortifications scarcely tenable. Since that time the military importance of the post is at an end. The garrison is a handful of invalid soldiers whose principal duty is to guard some of the outer towers which serve occasionally as a prison of state, and the governor, abandoning the lofty hill of the Alhambra, resides in the centre of Granada, for the more convenient dispatch of his duties. I cannot conclude this brief notice of the state of the fortress without bearing testimony to the honourable exertions of its present commander, Don Francisco de Serna, who is tasking all the limited resources at his command to put the palace in a state of repair and by his judicious precautions has for some time arrested its too certain decay. Had his predecessors discharged the duties of their station with equal fidelity, the Alhambra might yet have remained in almost its pristine beauty; were government to second him with means equal to his zeal, this edifice might still be preserved to adorn the land and to attract the curious and enlightened of every clime for many generations.

[1] This was far from being the case; the French commander, prior to evacuating the Alhambra, mined it and would have blown it up but for the presence of mind of a Spanish ex-soldier who cut the fuse. The depredations of Napoleon's troops in Spain are a shocking episode in the history of war, exceeded only by the barbarities inflicted on the civil population, inmortalized in Goya's «Disasters of War». *(Ed. note.)*

INTERIOR OF THE ALHAMBRA

T HE Alhambra has been so often and so minutely described
by travellers that a mere sketch will probably be sufficient
for the reader to refresh his recollection. I will give therefore
a brief account of our visit to it the morning after our arrival
in Granada.

Leaving our *posada* of La Espada, we traversed the renowned square of the Bibarrambla, once the scene of Moorish
jousts and tournaments, now a crowded market-place. From
thence we proceeded along the Zacatín, the main street of
what in the time of the Moors was the Great Bazaar, where
the small shops and narrow alleys still retain the Oriental character. Crossing an open place in front of the Palace of the
Captain-General, we ascended a confined and winding street,
the name of which reminded us of the chivalric days of Granada. It is called the *calle* or street of the Gomeres from a
Moorish family famous in chronicle and song. This street led
up to a massive gateway of Grecian architecture built by Charles V., forming the entrance to the domains of the Alhambra.

At the gate were two or three ragged and superannuated
soldiers, dozing on a stone bench, the successors of the Zegríes
and the Abencerrages, while a tall meagre varlet whose rusty-
brown cloak was evidently intended to conceal the ragged state
of his nether garments was lounging in the sunshine and gossiping with an ancient sentinel on duty. He joined us as we

entered the gate and offered his services to show us the fortress.

I have a traveller's dislike to officious ciceroni and did not altogether like the garb of the applicant.

«You are well acquainted with the place, I presume?»

«*Ninguno más; pues, Señor, soy hijo de la Alhambra.*»— (Nobody better; in fact, Sir, I am a son of the Alhambra!)

The common Spaniards have certainly a most poetical way of expressing themselves. «A son of the Alhambra!» The appellation caught me at once; the very tattered garb of my new acquaintance assumed a dignity in my eyes. It was emblematic of the fortunes of the palace and befitted the progeny of a ruin.

I put some further questions to him and found that his title was legitimate. His family had lived in the fortress from generation to generation ever since the time of the conquest. His name was Mateo Jiménez. «Then perhaps», said I «you may be a descendant from the great Cardinal Jiménez?»— «*¡Dios sabe!* God knows, *señor!* It may be so. We are the oldest family in the Alhambra.— *Cristianos viejos,* old Christians, without any taint of Moor or Jew. I know we belong to some great family or other, but I forget which. My father knows all about it; he has the coat of arms hanging up in his cottage up in the fortress.» —There is not any Spaniard, however poor, but has some claim to high pedigree. The first title of this ragged worthy, however, had completely captivated me; so I gladly accepted the services of the «son of the Alhambra».

We now found ourselves in a deep narrow ravine, filled with beautiful groves with a steep avenue and various footpaths winding through it, bordered with stone seats and ornamented with fountains. To our left we beheld the towers of the Alhambra beetling above us; to our right on the opposite side of the ravine we were equally dominated by rival towers on a rocky eminence. These, we were told, were the Torres Bermejas, or Vermilion Towers, so called from their ruddy hue. No one knows their origin. They are of a date much anterior to the Alhambra; some suppose them to have been built by the Romans, others by some wandering colony of Phoenicians. Ascending the steep and shady avenue, we arrived at the foot of a huge square Moorish tower forming a kind of barbican, through which passed the main entrance to the fortress. Within the barbican was another group of veteran invalids, one mounting guard at the portal, while the rest wrapped in their tattered cloaks slept on the stone benches. This portal is called the Gate of Justice from the tribunal held within its porch during the Moslem domination, for the immediate trial of petty causes, a custom common to the oriental nations and occasionally alluded to in the Sacred Scriptures.

The great vestibule or porch of the gate is formed by an immense Arabian arch of horseshoe form, which springs to half the height of the tower. On the key-stone of this arch is engraven a gigantic hand. Within the vestibule on the keystone of the portal is sculptured in like manner a gigantic key. Those who pretend to some knowledge of Mahometan symbols affirm that the hand is the emblem of doctrine and the key of faith; the latter, they add, was emblazoned on the standard of the Moslems when they subdued Andalusia, in opposition to the Christian emblem of the Cross. A different explanation, however, was given by the legitimate son of the Alhambra, and one more in unison with the notions of the common people who attach something of mystery and magic to everything Moorish and have all kinds of superstitions connected with this old Moslem fortress.

According to Mateo it was a tradition handed down from the oldest inhabitants and which he had from his father and grandfather that the hand and key were magical devices on which the fate of the Alhambra depended. The Moorish king who built it was a great magician or, as some believed, had sold himself to the devil and had laid the whole fortress under a magic spell. By this means it had remained standing for several hundred years in defiance of storms and earthquakes, while almost all other buildings of the Moors had fallen to ruin and disappeared. This spell, the tradition went on to say, would last until the hand on the outer arch should reach down and grasp the key, when the whole pile would tumble to pieces and all the treasures buried beneath it by the Moors would be revealed.

Notwithstanding this ominous prediction, we ventured to pass through the spell-bound gateway, feeling some little assurance against magic art in the protection of the Virgin, a statue of whom we observed above the portal.

After passing through the barbican, we ascended a narrow lane winding between walls and came on an open esplanade within the fortress, called the Plaza de los Aljibes or Place of the Cisterns from great reservoirs which undermine it, cut in the living rock by the Moors, for the supply of the fortress. Here also is a well of immense depth, furnishing the purest and coldest of water, another monument of the delicate taste of the Moors who were indefatigable in their exertions to obtain that element in its crystal purity.

In front of this esplanade is the splendid pile commenced by Charles V., intended, it is said, to eclipse the residence of the Moslem kings. With all its grandeur and architectural merit, it appeared to us like an arrogant intrusion and, passing by it, we entered a simple unostentatious portal, opening into the interior of the Moorish palace.

The transition was almost magical; it seemed as if we were at once transported into other times and another realm, and were treading the scenes of Arabian story. We found ourselves in a great court, paved with white marble and decorated at each end with light Moorish peristyles; it is called the Court of the Alberca. In the centre was an immense basin or fish-pond, a hundred and thirty feet in length by thirty in breadth, stocked with gold-fish and bordered by hedges of roses. At the upper end of this court rose the great Tower of Comares.

From the lower end we passed through a Moorish archway into the renowned Court of Lions. There is no part of the edifice that gives us a more complete idea of its original beauty and magnificence than this, for none has suffered so little from the ravages of time. In the centre stands the fountain famous in song and story. The alabaster basins still shed their diamond drops, and the twelve lions which support them cast forth their crystal streams as in the days of Boabdil. The court is laid out in flower-beds and surrounded by light Arabian arcades of open filigree-work, supported by slender pillars of white marble. The architecture, like that of all the other parts of the palace, is characterized by elegance rather than grandeur, bespeaking a delicate and graceful taste and a disposition to indolent enjoyment. When one looks upon the fairy tracery of the peristyles and the apparently fragile fretwork of the walls, it is difficult to believe that so much has survived the wear and tear of centuries, the shocks of earthquakes, the violence of war and the quiet, though no less baneful, pilferings of the tasteful traveller, it is almost sufficient to excuse the popular tradition that the whole is protected by a magic charm.

On one side of the court a portal, richly adorned, opens into a lofty hall paved with white marble and called the Hall of the Two Sisters. A *cúpula* or lantern admits a tempered light from above and a free circulation of air. The lower part of the walls is encrusted with beautiful Moorish tiles, on some of which are emblazoned the escutcheons of the Moorish monarchs; the upper part is faced with the fine stucco-work invented at Damascus, consisting of large plates, cast in moulds and artfully joined, so as to have the appearance of having been laboriously sculptured by the hand into light relievos and fanciful arabesques, intermingled with texts of the Koran and poetical inscriptions in Arabian and Cufic characters. These decorations of the walls and *cúpula* are richly gilded and the interstices pencilled with lapis-lazuli, and other brilliant and enduring colours. On each side of the hall are recesses for ottomans and couches. Above an inner porch is a balcony which communicated with the women's apartment. The latticed *jalousies* still remain, from whence the dark-eyed beauties of the harem might gaze unseen upon the entertainments of the hall below.

It is impossible to contemplate this once favourite abode of Oriental manners without feeling the early associations of Arabian romance, and almost expecting to see the white arm of some mysterious princess beckoning from the balcony or some dark eye sparkling through the lattice. The abode of beauty is here, as if it had been inhabited but yesterday; but where are the Zoraydas and Lindaraxas?

On the opposite side of the Court of Lions is the Hall of the Abencerrages, so called from the gallant cavaliers of that illustrious line, who were here perfidiously massacred. There are some who doubt the whole truth of this story, but our humble attendant Mateo pointed out the very wicket of the portal through which they are said to have been introduced, one by one, and the white marble fountain in the centre of the hall where they were beheaded. He showed us also certain broad ruddy stains in the pavement, traces of their blood which, according to popular belief, can never be effaced. Finding we listened to him with easy faith, he added that there was often heard at night in the Court of Lions, a low, confused sound, resembling the murmuring of a multitude, with now and then a faint tinkling, like the distant clank of chains. These noises are probably produced by the bubbling currents and tinkling falls of water, conducted under the pavement through pipes and channels to supply the fountains; but, according to the legend of the son of the Alhambra, they are made by the spirits of the murdered Abencerrages who nightly haunt the scene of their suffering and invoke the vengeance of Heaven on their destroyer.

From the Court of Lions we retraced our steps through the Court of the Alberca or Great Fish-pool, crossing which, we proceeded to the Tower of Comares, so called from the name of the Arabian architect. It is of massive strength and lofty height, domineering over the rest of the edifice and over-hanging the steep hill side which descends abruptly to the banks of the Darro. A Moorish archway admitted us into a vast and lofty hall which occupies the interior of the tower and was the grand audience-chamber of the Moslem monarchs, thence called the Hall of Ambassadors. It still bears the traces of past magnificence. The walls are richly stuccoed and decorated with arabesques; the vaulted ceiling of cedar wood, almost lost in obscurity from its height, still gleams with rich gilding and the brilliant tints of the Arabian pencil. On three sides of the saloon are deep windows cut through the immense thickness of the walls, the balconies of which look down upon the verdant valley of the Darro, the streets and convents of the Albaicín, and command a prospect of the distant *vega*.

I might go on to describe minutely the other delighful apartments of this side of the palace: the *Tocador* or toilet of the queen, an open belvedere on the summit of a tower, where the Moorish *sultanas* enjoyed the pure breezes from the mountain and the prospect of the surrounding paradise; the secluded little *patio* or garden of Lindaraxa, with its alabaster fountain, its thickets of roses and myrtles, of citrons and oranges; the cool halls and grottoes of the baths, where the glare and heat of day are tempered into a soft mysterious light and a pervading freshness. But I forbear to dwell minutely on those scenes; my object is merely to give the reader a general introduction into an abode where, if so disposed, he may linger and loiter with me through the remainder of this work, gradually becoming familiar with all its localities.

An abundant supply of water, brought from the mountains by old Moorish aqueducts, circulates throughout the palace, supplying its baths and fish-pools, sparkling in jets within its halls or murmuring in channels along the marble pavements. When it has paid its tribute to the royal pile and visited its gardens and pastures, it flows down the long avenue leading to the city, tinkling in rills, gushing in fountains and maintaining a perpetual verdure in those groves that embower and beautify the whole hill of the Alhambra.

Those only who have sojourned in the ardent climates of the South can appreciate the delights of an abode combining the breezy coolness of the mountain with the freshness and verdure of the valley.

While the city below pants with the noontide heat and the parched *vega* trembles to the eye, the delicate airs from the Sierra Nevada play through these lofty halls, bringing with them the sweetness of the surrounding gardens. Everything invites to that indolent repose, the bliss of southern climes, and while the half-shut eye looks out from shaded balconies upon the glittering landscape, the ear is lulled by the rustling of groves and the murmur of running streams.

THE TOWER OF COMARES

THE reader has had a sketch of the interior of the Alhambra and may be desirous of a general idea of its vicinity. The morning is serene and lovely, the sun has not gained sufficient power to destroy the freshness of the night; we will mount to the summit of the Tower of Comares and take a bird's eye view of Granada and its environs.

Come then, worthy reader and comrade, follow my steps into this vestibule, ornamented with rich tracery, which opens to the Hall of Ambassadors. We will not enter the hall, however, but turn to the left to this small door opening in the wall. Have a care! Here are steep winding steps and but scanty light; yet up this narrow, obscure and winding staircase the proud monarchs of Granada and their queens have often ascended to the battlements of the Tower to watch the approach of Christian armies or to gaze on the battles in the *vega*. At length we are on the terraced roof and may take breath for a moment, while we cast a general eye over the splendid panorama of city and country, of rocky mountain, verdant valley and fertile plain, of castle, cathedral, Moorish towers and Gothic domes, crumbling ruins and blooming groves.

Let us approach the battlements and cast our eyes immediately below. See, on this side we have the whole plan of the Alhambra laid open to us and can look down into its Court of the Alberca with its great tank or fish-pool, bordered with flowers;

and yonder is the Court of Lions, with its famous fountains and its light Moorish arcades and in the centre of the pile is the little garden of Lindaraxa, buried in the heart of the building, with its roses and citrons and shrubbery of emerald green.

That belt of battlements, studded with square towers, straggling round the whole brow of the hill, is the outer boundary of the fortress. Some of the towers, you may perceive, are in ruins and their massive fragments are buried among vines, fig-trees and aloes.

Let us look on this northern side of the tower. It is a giddy height; the very foundations of the tower rise above the groves of the steep hillside. And see, a long fissure in the massive walls shows that the tower has been rent by some of the earth-quakes which from time to time have thrown Granada into consternation and which, sooner or later, must reduce this crumbling pile to a mere mass of ruin. The deep, narrow glen below us, which gradually widens as it opens from the mountains, is the valley of the Darro; you see the little river winding its way under embowered terraces and among orchards and flower-gardens. It is a stream famous in old times for yielding gold and its sands are still sifted occasionally in search of the precious ore. Some of those white pavilions which here and there gleam from among groves and vineyards were rustic retreats of the Moors to enjoy the refreshment of their gardens.

The airy palace, with its tall white towers and long arcades, which breasts yon mountain among pompous groves and hanging gardens is the Generalife, a summer palace of the Moorish kings, to which they resorted during the sultry months to enjoy a still more breezy region than that of the Alhambra. The naked summit of the height above it, where you behold some shapeless ruins, is the Silla del Moro or Seat of the Moor, so called from having been a retreat of the unfortunate Boabdil during the time of an insurrection, where he seated himself and looked down mournfully upon his rebellious city.

A murmuring sound of water now and then rises from the valley. It is from the aqueduct of yon Moorish mill nearly at the foot of the hill. The avenue of trees beyond is the Alameda along the bank of the Darro, a favourite resort in evenings and a rendez-vous of lovers in the summer nights, when the guitar may be heard at a late hour from the benches along its walks. At present, there are but a few loitering monks to be seen there and a group of water-carriers from the fountain of Avellano.

You start! It is nothing but a hawk that we have frightened from his nest. This old tower is a complete breeding-place for vagrant birds; the swallow and martlet abound in every chink and cranny, and circle about it the whole day long, while at night, when all other birds have gone to rest, the moping owl comes out of its lurking-place and utters its boding cry from the battlements. See how the hawk we have dislodged sweeps away below us, skimming over the tops of the trees and sailing up to the ruins above the Generalife.

Let us leave this side of the tower and turn our eyes to the west. Here you behold in the distance a range of mountains bounding the Vega, the ancient barrier between Moslem Granada and the land of the Christian. Among their heights you may still discern warrior towns, whose grey walls and battlements seem of a piece with the rocks on which they are built; while here and there is a solitary *atalaya* or watch-tower, mounted on some lofty point and looking down, as it were from the sky, into the valleys on either side. It was down the defiles of these mountains by the pass of Lope that the Christian armies descended into the Vega. It was round the base of yon grey and naked mountain, almost insulated from the rest and stretching its bold rocky promontory into the bosom of the plain that the invading squadrons would come bursting into view with flaunting banners and the clangour of drums and trumpets. How changed is the scene! Instead of the glittering line of mailed warriors, we behold the patient train of the toilful muleteer, slowly moving along the skirts of the mountain. Behind that promontory is the eventful bridge of Pinos, renowned for many a bloody strife between Moors and Christians, but still more renowned as being the place where Columbus was overtaken and called back by the messenger of Queen Isabella, just as he was departing in despair, to carry his project of discovery to the court of France.

Behold another place famous in the history of the discoverer. Yon line of walls and towers gleaming in the morning sun in the very centre of the Vega, is the city of Santafé, built by the Catholic sovereigns during the siege of Granada, after a conflagration had destroyed their camp. It was to these walls that Columbus was called back by the heroic queen, and within them the treaty was concluded that led to the discovery of the western world.

Here, towards the south, the eye revels in the luxuriant beauties of the Vega; a blooming wilderness of grove and garden and teeming orchard, with the Xenil winding through it in silver links and feeding innumerable rills, conducted through ancient Moorish channels which maintain the landscape in perpetual verdure. Here are the beloved bowers and gardens and rural retreats, for which the Moors fought with such desperate valour. The very farm-houses and hovels which are now inhabited by the boors, retain traces of arabesques and other tasteful decorations which show them to have been elegant residences in the days of the Moslems.

Beyond the enbowered region of the Vega you behold to the south a line of arid hills, down which a long train of mules is slowy moving. It was from the summit one of those hills that the unfortunate Boabdil cast back his last look upon

Granada and gave vent to the agony of his soul. It is the spot famous in song and story, «The last sigh of the Moor».

Now raise your eyes to the snowy summit of yon pile of mountains shining like a white summer cloud in the blue sky. It is the Sierra Nevada, the pride and delight of Granada, the source of her cooling breezes and perpetual verdure, of her gushing fountains and perennial streams. It is this glorious pile of mountains that gives to Granada that combination of delights so rare in a southern city: the fresh vegetation and the temperate airs of a northern climate, with the vivifying ardour of a tropical sun and the cloudless azure of a southern sky. It is this aërial treasury of snow which, melting in proportion to the increase of the summer heat, sends down rivulets and streams through every glen and gorge of the Alpujarras, diffusing emerald verdure and fertility throughout a chain of happy and sequestered valleys.

Those mountains may well be called the glory of Granada. They dominate the whole extent of Andalusia and may be seen from its most distant parts. The muleteer hails them, as he views their frosty peaks from the sultry level of the plain, and the Spanish mariner on the deck of his bark far, far off on the bosom of the blue Mediterranean watches them with a pensive eye, thinks of delightful Granada and chants in low voice some old romance about the Moors.

But enough—the sun is high above the mountains, and is pouring his full fervour upon our heads. Already the terraced roof of the tower is hot beneath our feet; let us abandon it and descend and refresh ourselves under the arcades by the Fountain of the Lions.

REFLECTIONS
ON THE
MOSLEM DOMINATION IN SPAIN

ONE of my favourite resorts is the balcony of the central window of the Hall of Ambassadors in the lofty tower of Comares. I have just been seated there, enyoying the close of a long brilliant day. The sun, as he sank behind the purple mountains of Alhama, sent a stream of effulgence up the valley of the Darro, that spread a melancholy pomp over the ruddy towers of the Alhambra, while the Vega covered with a slight sultry vapour that caught the setting ray spread out in the distance like a golden sea. Not a breath of air disturbed the stillness of the hour; and though the faint sound of music and merriment now and then arose from the gardens of the Darro, it but rendered more impressive the monumental silence of the pile which overshadowed me. It was one of those hours and scenes in which memory asserts an almost magical power and, like the evening sun beaming on these mouldering towers, sends back her retrospective rays to light up the glories of the past.

As I sat watching the effect of the declining daylight upon this Moorish pile, I was led into a consideration of the light, elegant and voluptuous character prevalent throughout its internal architecture and to contrast it with the grand but gloomy solemnity of the Gothic edifices, reared by the Spanish con-' querors. The very architecture thus bespeaks the opposite and irreconciliable natures of the two warlike people who so long battled here for the mastery of the Peninsula. By degrees I fell into a course of musing upon the singular fortunes of the Arabian or Morisco Spaniards, whose whole existence is as a tale that is told and certainly forms one of the most anomalous yet splendid episodes in history. Potent and durable as was their dominion, we scarcely know how to call them. They are a nation, as it were, without a legitimate country or a name. A remote wave of the great Arabian inundation, cast upon the shores of Europe, they seemed to have all the impetus of the first rush of the torrent. Their career of conquest from the rock of Gibraltar to the cliffs of the Pyrenees was as rapid and brillant as the Moslem victories of Syria and Egypt. Nay, had they not been checked on the plains of Tours, all France, all Europe, might have been overrun with the same facility as the empires of the East, and the crescent might at this day have glittered on the fanes of Paris and of London.

Repelled within the limits of the Pyrenees, the mixed hordes of Asia and Africa, that formed this great irruption, gave up the Moslem principle of conquest and sought to establish in Spain a peaceful and permanent dominion. As conquerors, their heroism was only equalled by their moderation, and in both, for a time, they excelled the nations with whom they contended. Severed from their native homes, they loved the land given them as they supposed by Allah and strove to embellish it with everything that could administer to the happiness of man. Laying the foundations of their power in a system of wise and equitable laws, diligently cultivating the arts and sciences, and promoting agriculture, manufactures and commerce, they gradually formed an empire unrivalled for its prosperity by any of the empires of Christendom, and diligently drawing round them the graces and refinements that marked the Arabian empire in the East at the time of its greatest civilisation, they diffused the light of Oriental knowledge through the western regions of benighted Europe.

The cities of Arabian Spain became the resort of Christian artisans, to instruct themselves in the useful art. The Universities of Toledo, Cordova, Seville, and Granada [1], were sought by the pale student from other lands to acquaint himself with the sciences of the Arabs and the treasure lore of antiquity; the lovers of the gay sciences resorted to Cordova and Granada to imbibe the poetry and music of the East, and the steel-clad warriors of the North hastened thither to accomplish themselves in the graceful exercises and courteous usages of chivalry.

If the Moslem monuments in Spain, if the mosque of Cordova, the alcazar of Seville and the Alhambra of Granada, still bear inscriptions fondly boasting of the power and permanence of their dominion, can the boast be derided as arrogant and vain? Generation after generation, century after century, had passed away and still they maintained possession of the land. A period had elapsed longer than that which has passed since England was subjugated by the Norman Conqueror and the descendants of Musa and Taric might as little anticipate being driven into exile, across the same straits traversed by their triumphant ancestors, as the descendants of Rollo and William their veteran peers may dream of being driven back to the shores of Normandy.

With all this, however, the Moslem empire in Spain was but a brilliant exotic that took no permanent root in the soil it embellished. Severed from all their neighbours in the West

[1] A *medersa* or *madraza,* amongst the Arabs, signified a school or college. Those cited by the author were renowned throughout the Spain of the period. The *madraza* of Granada occupied the site of the Old Town Hall *(Ayuntamiento Viejo)* which stands directly opposite the Royal Chapel. *(Ed. note.)*

by impassable barriers of faith and manners, and separated by seas and deserts from their kindred of the East, they were an isolated people. Their whole existence was a prolonged, though gallant and chivalric, struggle for a foothold in a usurped land.

They were the outposts and frontiers of Islamism. The Peninsula was the great battle-ground where the Gothic conquerors of the North and the Moslem conquerors of the East met and strove for mastery, and the fiery courage of the Arab was at length subdued by the obstinate and persevering valour of the Goth.

Never was the annihilation of a people more complete than that of the Morisco-Spaniards. Where are they? Ask the shores of Barbary and its desert places. The exiled remnant of their once powerful empire disappeared among the barbarians of Africa and ceased to be a nation. They have not even left a distinct name behind them, though for nearly eight centuries they were a distinct people. The home of their adoption and of their occupation for ages refuses to acknowledge them, except as invaders and usurpers. A few broken monuments are all that remain to bear witness to their power and dominion, as solitary rocks, left far in the interior, bear testimony to the extent of some vast inundation. Such is the Alhambra—a Moslem pile in the midst of a Christian land, an Oriental palace amidst the Gothic edifices of the West, an elegant memento of a brave, intelligent, and graceful people who conquered, ruled and passed away.

THE HOUSEHOLD

I T is time that I give some idea of my domestic arrangements
in this singular residence. The Royal Palace of the Alhambra is entrusted to the care of a good old maiden dame,
called Doña Antonia Molina, but who, according to Spanish
custom, goes by the more neighbourly appellation of *Tía Antonia* (Aunt Antonia). She maintains the Moorish halls and
gardens in order and shows them to strangers, in consideration
of which she is allowed all the perquisites received from visitors and all the produce of the gardens, excepting that she is
expected to pay an occasional tribute of fruits and flowers to
the Governor. Her residence is in a corner of the palace and
her family consists of a nephew and niece, the children of two
different brothers. The nephew, Manuel Molina, is a young
man of sterling worth and Spanish gravity. He has served in
the armies both in Spain and the West Indies, but is now studying medicine, in hopes of one day or other becoming physician to the fortress, a post worth at least a hundred and forty
dollars a year. As to the niece, she is a plump little black-eyed
Andalusian damsel named Dolores, but who from her bright
looks and cheerful disposition merits a merrier name. She is
the declared heiress of all her aunt's possessions, consisting of
certain ruinous tenements in the fortress, yielding a revenue of
about one hundred and fifty dollars. I had not been long in

the Alhambra, before I discovered that a quiet courtship was going on between the discreet Manuel and his bright-eyed cousin, and that nothing was wanting to enable them to join their hands and expectations, but that he should receive his doctor's diploma and purchase a dispensation from the Pope, on account of their consanguinity.

With the good dame Antonia I have made a treaty, according to which she furnishes me with board and lodging, while the merry-hearted little Dolores keeps my apartment in order, and officiates as handmaid at meal-times. I have also at my command a tall, stuttering yellow-haired lad named Pepe who works in the gardens, and would fain have acted as valet, but in this he was forestalled by Mateo Jiménez, «the son of the Alhambra». This alert and officious wight has managed somehow or other to stick by me ever since I first encountered him at the outer gate of the fortress and to weave himself into all my plans, until he has fairly appointed and installed himself my valet, cicerone, guide, guard and historiographic squire, and I have been obliged to improve the state of his wardrobe, that he may not disgrace his various functions, so that he has cast his old brown mantle as a snake does his skin, and now appears about the fortress with a smart Andalusian hat and jacket, to his infinite satisfaction and the great astonishment of his comrades. The chief fault of honest Mateo is an over-anxiety to be useful. Conscious of having foisted himself into my employ and that my simple and quiet habits render his situation a sinecure, he is at his wit's end to devise modes of making himself important to my welfare. I am in a manner the victim of his officiousness; I cannot put my foot over the threshold of the palace, to stroll about the fortress, but he is at my elbow to explain everything I see, and if I venture to ramble among the surrounding hills he insists upon attending me as a guard, though I vehemently suspect he would be more apt to trust to the length of his legs than the strengh of his arms in case of attack. After all, however, the poor fellow is at times an amusing companion; he is simple-minded and of infinite good humour with the loquacity and gossip of a village barber and knows all the small talk of the place and its environs, but what he chiefly values himself on, is his stock of local information, having the most marvellous stories to relate of every tower and vault and gateway of the fortress, in all of which he places the most implicit faith.

Most of these he has derived, according to his own account, from his grandfather, a little legendary tailor who lived to the age of nearly a hundred years, during which he made but two migrations beyond the precincts of the fortress. His shop, for the greater part of a century, was the resort of a knot of venerable gossips, where they would pass half the night talking about old times and the wonderful events and hidden secrets of the place. The whole living, moving, thinking, and acting of this historical little tailor had thus been bounded by the walls of the Alhambra; within them he had been born, within them he lived, breathed and had his being; within them he died and was buried. Fortunately for posterity, his traditionary lore died not with him. The authentic Mateo, when an urchin, used to be an attentive listener to the narratives of his grandfather and of the gossip group assembled round the shop-board, and is thus possessed of a stock of valuable knowledge concerning the Alhambra, not to be found in the books and well worthy the attention of every curious traveller.

Such are the personages that contribute to my domestic comforts in the Alhambra, and I question whether any of the potentates, Moslem or Christian, who have preceded me in the palace have been waited upon with greater fidelity or enjoyed a serener sway.

When I rise in the morning, Pepe, the stuttering lad from the gardens, brings me a tribute of fresh-culled flowers which are afterwards arranged in vases by the skilful hand of Dolores who takes a female pride in the decoration of my chamber. My meals are made wherever caprice dictates, sometimes in one of the Moorish halls, sometimes under the arcades of the Court of Lions, surrounded by flowers and fountains, and when I walk out, I am conducted by the assiduous Mateo to the most romantic retreats of the mountains and delicious haunts of the adjacent valleys, not one of which but is the scene of some wonderful tale.

Though fond of passing the greater part of my day alone, yet I occasionally repair in the evenings to the little domestic circle of Doña Antonia. This is generally held in an old Moorish chamber that serves for kitchen as well as hall, a rude fireplace having been made in one corner, the smoke from which has discoloured the walls and almost obliterated the ancient arabesques. A window with a balcony overhanging the valley of the Darro lets in the cool evening breeze, and here I take my frugal supper of fruit and milk, and mingle with the conversation of the family. There is a natural talent or mother wit, as it is called, about the Spaniards, which render them intellectual and agreeable companions, whatever may be their condition in life or however imperfect may have been their education; add to this, they are never vulgar; nature has endowed them with an inherent dignity of spirit. The good Tía Antonia is a woman of strong and intelligent though uncultivated mind, and the bright-eyed Dolores, though she has read but three or four books in the whole course of her life, has an engaging mixture of *naïveté* and good sense, and often surprises me by the pungency of her artless sallies. Sometimes the nephew entertains us by reading some old comedy of Calderón or Lope de Vega, to which he is evidently prompted by a desire to improve as well as amuse his cousin Dolores; though to his great mortification the little damsel generally falls asleep before the first act is completed. Sometimes Tía Antonia has a little levee of humble friends and dependents, the inhabitants of the adjacent hamlet, or the wives of the invalid soldiers. These look up to her with great deference as the custodian of the palace and pay their court to her by bringing the news of the place or the rumours that may have straggled up from Granada. In listening to these evening gossipings I have picked up many curious facts, illustrative of the manners of the people and the peculiarities of the neighbourhood. These are simple details of simple pleasures; it is the nature of the place alone that gives them interest and importance. I tread haunted ground and am surrounded by romantic associations. From earliest boyhood when on the banks of the Hudson I first pored over the pages of an old Spanish story about the wars of Granada, that city has ever been a subject of my waking dreams, and often have I trod in fancy the romantic halls of the Alhambra. Behold for once a day-dream realized; yet I can scarce credit my senses or believe that I do indeed inhabit the palace of Boabdil and look down from its balconies upon chivalric Granada. As I loiter through these Oriental chambers and hear the murmur of fountains and the song of the nightingale, as I inhale the odour of the rose and feel the influence of the balmy climate, I am almost tempted to fancy myself in the paradise of Mahomet and that the plump little Dolores is one of the bright-eyed houris, destined to administer to the happiness of true believers.

THE TRUANT

S INCE noting the foregoing pages, we have had a scene of
petty tribulation in the Alhambra which has thrown a cloud
over the sunny countenance of Dolores. This little damsel has
a female passion for pets of all kinds, and from the superabun-
dant kindness of her disposition one of the ruined courts of
the Alhambra is thronged with her favourites. A stately pea-
cock and his hen seem to hold regal sway here over pompous
turkeys, querulous guineafowls and a rabble rout of common
cocks and hens. The great delight of Dolores, however, has
for some time past been centred in a youthful pair of pigeons
who have lately entered into the holy state of wedlock and
who have even supplanted a tortoise-shell cat and kittens in
her affections.

As a tenement for them wherein to commence house-
keeping, she had fitted up a small chamber adjacent to the kitchen, the window of which looked into one of the quiet Moorish courts. Here they lived in happy ignorance of any world
beyond the court and its sunny roofs. Never had they aspired
to soar above the battlements or to mount to the summit of
the towers. Their virtuous union was at length crowned by
two spotless and milk-white eggs to the great joy of their che-
rishing little mistress. Nothing could be more praiseworthy
than the conduct of the young married folks on this interesting
occasion. They took turns to sit upon the nest until the eggs

61

were hatched and while their callow progeny required warmth and shelter; while one thus stayed at home, the other foraged abroad for food and brought home abundant supplies.

This scene of conjugal felicity has suddenly met with a reverse. Early this morning, as Dolores was feeding the male pigeon, she took a fancy to give him a peep at the great world. Opening a window therefore which looks down upon the valley of the Darro, she launched him at once beyond the walls of the Alhambra. For the first time in his life the astonished bird had to try the full vigour of his wings. He swept down into the valley and then rising upwards with a surge, soared almost to the clouds. Never before had he risen to such a height or experienced such delight in flying, and, like a young spendthrift just come to his estate, he seemed giddy with excess of liberty and with the boundless field of action suddenly opened to him. For the whole day he has been circling about in capricious flights, from tower to tower and tree to tree. Every attempt has been vain to lure him back by scattering grain upon the roofs; he seems to have lost all thought of home, of his tender helpmate and his callow young. To add to the anxiety of Dolores, he has been joined by two *palomas ladronas* or robber-pigeons whose instinct it is to entice wandering pigeons to their own dovecotes. The fugitive, like many other thoughtless youths on their first launching upon the world, seems quite fascinated with these knowing but graceless companions who have undertaken to show him life and introduce him to society. He has been soaring with them over all the roofs and steeples of Granada. A thunder-storm has passed over the city, but he has not sought his home; night has closed in and still he comes not. To deepen the pathos of the affair, the female pigeon, after remaining several hours on the nest, without being relieved, at length went forth to seek her recreant mate, but stayed away so long, that the young ones perished for want of the warmth and shelter of the parent bosom. At a late hour in the evening, word was brought to Dolores, that the truant bird had been seen upon the towers of the Generalife. Now it happens that the *administrador* of that ancient palace has likewise a dovecote, among the inmates of which are said to be two or three of these inveigling birds, the terror of all neighbouring pigeon-fanciers. Dolores immediately concluded that the two feathered sharpers who had been seen with her fugitive, were these bloods of the Generalife. A council of war was forthwith held in the chamber of Tía Antonia. The Generalife is a distinct jurisdiction from the Alhambra and of course some punctilio, if not jealousy, exists between their custodians. It was determined therefore to send Pepe, the stuttering lad of the gardens, as ambassador to the *administrador,* requesting that if such fugitive should be found in his dominions, he might be given up as a subject of the Alhambra. Pepe departed accordingly on his diplomatic expedition, through the moonlight groves and avenues, but returned in an hour with the afflicting intelligence, that no such bird was to be found in the dovecote of the Generalife. The *administrador,* however, pledged his sovereign word that if such a vagrant should appear there, even at midnight, he should instantly be arrested and sent back prisoner to his little black-eyed mistress.

Thus stands the melancholy affair, which has occasioned much distress throughout the palace and has sent the inconsolable Dolores to a sleepless pillow.

«Sorrow endureth for a night», says the proverb, «but joy cometh in the morning». The first object that met my eyes, on leaving my room this morning, was Dolores with the truant pigeon in her hands, and her eyes sparkling with joy. He had appeared at an early hour on the battlements, hovering shyly about from roof to roof, but at length entered the window, and surrendered himself prisoner. He gained little credit, however, by his return, for the ravenous manner in which he devoured the food set before him, showed that, like the prodigal son, he had been driven home by sheer famine. Dolores upbraided him for his faithless conduct, calling him all manner of vagrant names (though, womanlike, she fondled him at the same time to her bosom, and covered him with kisses). I observed, however, that she had taken care to clip his wings, to prevent all future soarings, a precaution which I mention for the benefit of all those who have truant lovers or wandering husbands. More than one valuable moral might be drawn from the story of Dolores and her pigeon.

THE AUTHOR'S CHAMBER

O N taking up my abode in the Alhambra, one end of a suite
of empty chambers of modern architecture, intended for
the residence of the Governor, was fitted up for my reception.
It was in front of the palace, looking forth upon the esplanade;
the further end communicated with a cluster of little chambers,
partly Moorish, partly modern, inhabited by Tía Antonia and
her family; these terminated in a large room which serves the
good old dame for parlour, kitchen and hall of audience. It had
boasted of some splendour in the time of the Moors, but a
fireplace had been built in one corner, the smoke from which
had discoloured the walls, nearly obliterated the ornaments,
and spread a sombre tint on the whole. From these gloomy
apartments, a narrow blind corridor and a dark winding staircase led down an angle of the tower of Comares, groping along
which and opening a small door at the bottom, you were suddenly dazzled by emerging into the brilliant antechamber of the
Hall of Ambassadors, with the fountain of the court of the
Alberca sparkling before you.

I was dissatisfied with being lodged in a modern and frontier
apartment of the palace and longed to ensconce myself in the
very heart of the building. As I was rambling one day about
the Moorish halls, I found in a remote gallery a door which I

65

had not before noticed, communicating apparently with an extensive apartment, locked up from the public. Here then was a mystery; here was the haunted wing of the castle. I procured the key, however, without difficulty; the door opened to a range of vacant chambers of European architecture, though built over a Moorish arcade, along the little garden of Lindara-xa. There were two lofty rooms, the ceilings of which were of deep panel-work of cedar, richly and skifully carved with fruits and flowers, intermingled with grotesque masks of faces, but broken in many places. The walls had evidently, in ancient times, been hung with damask, but were now naked, and scra-wled over with the insignificant names of aspiring travellers; the windows, which were dismantled and open to wind and weather, looked into the garden of Lindaraxa, and the orange and citron trees flung their branches into the chamber. Beyond these rooms were two saloons, less lofty, looking also into the garden. In the compartments of the panelled ceilings were baskets of fruit and garlands of flowers, painted by no mean hand and in tolerable preservation. The walls had also been painted in fresco in the Italian style, but the paintings were nearly obliterated; the windows were in the same shattered state as in the other chambers. This fanciful suite of rooms terminated in an open gallery with balustrades which ran at right angles along another side of the garden. The whole apart-ment had a delicacy and elegance in its decorations, and there was something so choice and sequestered in its situation along this retired little garden that it awakened an interest in its history. I found on inquiry that it was an apartment fitted up by Italian artists in the early part of the last century, at the time when Philip V. and the beautiful Elizabeth of Parma were expected at the Alhambra and was destined for the queen and the ladies of her train. One of the loftiest chambers had been her sleeping-room, and a narrow staircase leading from it, though now walled up, opened to the delightful belvedere, originally a *mirador* of the Moorish *sultanas,* but fitted up as a boudoir for the fair Elizabeth, and which still retains the name of the Tocador or Toilette of the Queen. The sleeping-room I have mentioned, commanded from one window a prospect of the Generalife and its embowered terraces; under another window played the alabaster fountain of the garden of Lindaraxa. That garden carried my thoughts still further back to the period of another reign of beauty, to the days of the Moorish *sultanas.*

«How beauteous is this garden!» says an Arabic inscription, «where the flowers of the earth vie with the stars of heaven! What can compare with the vase of yon alabaster fountain, filled with crystal water? Nothing but the moon in her fullness, shining in the midst of an unclouded sky!»

Centuries had elapsed, yet how much of this scene of apparently fragile beauty remained! The garden of Lindaraxa was still adorned with flowers, the fountain still presented its crystal mirror; it is true, the alabaster had lost its whiteness and the basin beneath, overrun with weeds, had become the nestling-place of the lizard, but there is something in the very decay that enhanced the interest of the scene, speaking, as it did, of that mutability which is the irrevocable lot of man and all his works. The desolation too of these chambers, once the abode of the proud and elegant Elizabeth, had a more touching charm for me than if I had beheld them in their pristine splendour, glittering with the pageantry of a court. I determined at once to take up my quarters in this apartment.

My determination excited great surprise in the family who could not imagine any rational inducement for the choice of so solitary, remote and forlorn an apartment. The good Tía Antonia considered it highly dangerous; the neighbourhood, she said, was infested by vagrants; thè caverns of the adjacent hills swarmed with gypsies; the palace was ruinous, and easy to be entered in many parts, and the rumour of a stranger quartered alone in one of the ruined apartments, out of the hearing of the rest of the inhabitants, might tempt unwelcome visitors in the night, specially as foreigners are always supposed to be well stocked with money. Dolores represented the frightful loneliness of the place, nothing but bats and owls flitting about; then there were a fox and a wild cat, that kept about the vaults and roamed about at night.

I was not to be diverted from my humour; so calling in the assistance of a carpenter and the ever-officious Mateo Jiménez, the doors and windows were soon placed in a state of tolerable security. With all these precautions, I must confess, the first night I passed in these quarters was inexpressibly dreary. I was escorted by the whole family to my chamber, and their taking leave of me and returning along the waste antechambers and echoing galleries, reminded me of those hobgoblin stories, where the hero is left to accomplish the adventure of an enchanted house.

Even the thoughts of the fair Elizabetta and the beauties of her court, who had once graced these chambers, now by a perversion of fancy added to the gloom. Here was the scene of their transient gaiety and loveliness; here the very traces of their elegance and enjoyment, but what and where were they? —Dust and ashes! Tenants of the tomb! Phantoms of the memory!

A vague and indescribable awe was creeping over me. I would fain have ascribed it to the thoughts of robbers awakened by the evening's conversation, but I felt that it was something more unreal and absurd. In a word, the long-buried impressions of the nursery were reviving and asserting their power over my imagination. Everything began to be affected by the working of my mind. The whispering of the wind among the citron-trees beneath my window had something sinister. I cast my eyes into the garden of Lindaraxa; the groves presented a gulf of shadows; the thickets, indistinct and ghastly shapes. I was glad to close the window, but my chamber itself became infected. A bat had found its way in and flitted about my head and athwart my solitary lamp; the grotesque faces carved in the cedar ceiling seemed to mope and mow at me.

Rousing myself and half smiling at this temporary weakness, I resolved to brave it and, taking lamp in hand, sallied forth to make a tour of the ancient palace. Notwithstanding every mental exertion, the task was a severe one. The rays of my lamp extended to but a limited distance around me. I walked as it were in a mere halo of light and all beyond was thick darkness. The vaulted corridors were lost in gloom; what unseen foe might not be lurking before or behind me! My own shadow playing about the walls, and the echoes of my own footsteps, disturbed me.

In this excited state, as I was traversing the great Hall of Ambassadors there were added real sounds to these conjectural fancies. Low moans and indistinct ejaculations, seemed to rise as it were beneath my feet. I paused and listened. They then appeared to resound from without the tower. Sometimes they resembled the howlings of an animal, at others they were stifled shrieks, mingled with articulate ravings. The thrilling effect of these sounds, in that still hour and singular place, destroyed all inclination to continue my lonely perambulation. I returned to my chamber with more alacrity than I had sallied forth and drew my breath more freely when once more within its walls and the door bolted behind me. When I awoke in the morning with the sun shining in at my window and lighting up every part of the building with his cheerful and truth-telling beams, I could scarcely recall the shadows and fancies conjured up by the gloom of the preceding night or believe that the scenes around me, so naked and apparent, could have been clothed with such imaginary horrors.

Still, the dismal howlings and ejaculations I had heard, were not ideal; but they were soon accounted for by my hand-maid Dolores, being the ravings of a poor maniac, a brother of her aunt, who was subject to violent paroxyms, during which he was confined in a vaulted room beneath the Hall of Ambassadors.

THE ALHAMBRA BY MOONLIGHT

I have given a picture of my apartment on my first taking possession of it; a few evenings have produced a thorough change in the scene and in my feelings. The moon which then was invisible has gradually gained upon the night and now rolls in full splendour above the towers, pouring a flood of tempered light into every court and hall. The garden beneath my windows is gently lighted up, the orange and citron-trees are tipped with silver, the fountain sparkles in the moonbeams and even the blush of the rose is faintly visible.

I have sat for hours at my window, inhaling the sweetness of the garden and musing on the chequered fortunes of those whose history is dimly shadowed out in the elegant memorials around. Sometimes I have issued forth at midnight, when everything was quiet, and have wandered over the whole building. Who can do justice to a moonlight night in such a climate and in such a place! The temperature of an Andalusian midnight in summer is perfectly ethereal. We seem lifted up into a purer atmosphere; there is a serenity of soul, a buoyancy of spirits, an elasticity of frame that render mere existence enjoyment. The effect of moonlight, too, on the Alhambra, has something like enchantment. Every rent and chasm of time, every mouldering tint and weather-stain disappears, the marble resumes its original whiteness, the long colonnades brighten in the moonbeams, the halls are illuminated with a softened radiance, until the whole edifice reminds one of the enchanted palace of an Arabian tale.

At such a time I have ascended to the little pavilion called the Queen's Toilette to enjoy its varied and extensive prospect. To the right, the snowy summits of the Sierra Nevada would gleam like silver clouds against the darker firmament, and all the outlines of the mountain would be softened, yet delicately defined. My delight, however, would be to lean over the parapet of the *tocador* and gaze down upon Granada, spread out like a map below me, all buried in deep repose and its white palaces and convents sleeping, as it were, in the moonshine.

Sometimes I would hear the faint sounds of castanets from some party of dancers lingering in the Alameda; at other times I have heard the dubious tones of a guitar and the notes of a single voice rising from some solitary street and have pictured to myself some youthful cavalier serenading his lady's window, a gallant custom of former days, but now sadly on the decline, except in the remote towns and villages of Spain. Such were the scenes that have detained me for many an hour loitering about the courts and balconies of the castle, enjoying that mixture of reverie and sensation which steal away existence in a southern climate, and it has been almost morning before I have retired to my bed and been lulled to sleep by the falling waters of the fountain of Lindaraxa.

INHABITANTS OF THE ALHAMBRA

I have often observed that the more proudly a mansion has been tenanted in the day of its prosperity, the humbler are its inhabitants in the day of its decline and that the palace of the king commonly ends in being the nestling-place of the beggar.

The Alhambra is in a rapid state of similar transition. Whenever a tower falls to decay, it is seized upon by some tatterdemalion family who become joint-tenants with the bats and owls of its gilded halls and hang their rags, those standards of poverty, out of its windows and loopholes.

I have amused myself with remarking some of the motley characters that have thus usurped the ancient abode of Royalty and who seem as if placed here to give a farcical termination to the drama of human pride. One of these even bears the mockery of a regal title. It is a little old woman named María Antonia Sabonea, but who goes by the appellation of *la Reina Coquina* or the Cockle-queen. She is small enough to be a fairy, and a fairy she may be for aught I can find out, for no one seems to know her origin. Her habitation is in a kind of closet under the outer staircase of the palace, and she sits in the cool stone corridor, plying her needle and singing from morning till night with a ready joke for every one that passes; for though one of the poorest, she is one of the merriest little women breathing. Her great merit is a gift for story-telling, having, I verily believe, as many stories at her command as the inex-

haustible Scheherezade of the Thousand and One Nights. Some
of these I have heard her relate in the evening *tertulias* of
Dame Antonia, at which she is occasionally an humble attendant.

That there must be some fairy gift about this mysterious
little old woman would appear from her extraordinary luck,
since, notwithstanding her being very little, very ugly and very
poor, she has had according to her own account five husbands
and a half reckoning as a half one, a young dragoon who died
during courtship. A rival personage to this little fairy queen is
a portly old fellow with a bottle nose, who goes about in a
rusty garb with a cocked hat of oil-skin and a red cockade. He
is one of the legitimate sons of the Alhambra and has lived
here all his life, filling various offices, such as deputy *alguacil,*
sexton of the parochial church, and marker of a fives court
established at the foot of one of the towers. He is as poor as
a rat, but as proud as he is ragged, boasting of his descent from
the illustrious house of Aguilar, from which sprang Gonzalvo
of Cordova, the Grand Captain. Nay, he actually bears the name
of Alonso de Aguilar, so renowned in the history of the conquest, though the graceless wags of the fortress have given
him the title of *El Padre Santo* or the Holy Father, the usual
appellation of the Pope, which I had though too sacred in
the eyes of true Catholics to be thus ludicrously applied. It is
a whimsical caprice of fortune to present in the grotesque person of this tatterdemalion a namesake and descendant of the
proud Alonso de Aguilar, the mirror of Andalusian chivalry,
leading an almost mendicant existence about this once haughty
fortress which his ancestor aided to reduce; yet such might
have been the lot of the descendants of Agamemnon and Achi-
lles, had they lingered about the ruins of Troy!

Of this motley community, I find the family of my gossiping squire, Mateo Jiménez, to form from their numbers at
least a very important part. His boast of being a son of the

Alhambra is not unfounded. His family has inhabited the fortress ever since the time of the Conquest, handing down an hereditary poverty from father to son, not one of them having ever been known to be worth a *maravedi*. His father by trade a riband-weaver and who succeeded the historical tailor as the head of the family is now near seventy years of age and lives in a hovel of reeds and plaster, built by his own hands just above the Iron Gate. The furniture consists of a crazy bed, a table and two or three chairs, a wooden chest, containing his clothes and the archives of his family, that is to say, a few papers concerning old law-suits which he cannot read; but the pride of his hovel is a blazon of the arms of the family, brilliantly coloured and suspended in a frame against the wall, clearly demonstrating, by its quarterings, the various noble houses with which this poverty-stricken brood claim affinity.

As to Mateo himself, he has done his utmost to perpetuate his line, having a wife and a numerous progeny who inhabit an almost dismantled hovel in the hamlet. How they manage to subsist, He only who sees into all mysteries can tell; the subsistence of a Spanish family of the kind, is always a riddle to me, yet they do subsist and what is more appear to enjoy their existence. The wife takes her holiday stroll in the Paseo of Granada with a child in her arms and half a dozen at her heels, and the eldest daughter, now verging into womanhood, dresses her hair with flowers and dances gaily to the castanets.

Here are two classes of people to whom life seems one long holiday, the very rich, and the very poor; one, because they need do nothing, the other, because they have nothing to do; but there are none who understand the art of doing nothing and living upon nothing better than the poor classes of Spain. Climate does one half and temperament the rest. Give a Spaniard the shade in summer and the sun in winter, a little bread, garlic, oil and *garbanzos,* an old brown cloak and a guitar, and let the world roll on as it pleases. Talk of poverty! With him it has no disgrace. It sits upon him with a grandiose style, like his ragged cloak. He is an *hidalgo* even when in rags.

The «sons of the Alhambra» are an eminent illustration of this practical philosophy. As the Moors imagined that the celestial paradise hung over this favoured spot, so I am inclined at times to fancy that a gleam of the golden age still lingers about the ragged community. They possess nothing, they do nothing, they care for nothing. Yet, though apparently idle all the week, they are as observant of all holidays and saints' days as the most laborious artisan. They attend all *fêtes* and dancings in Granada and its vicinity, light bonfires on the hills on St. John's eve and have lately danced away the moonlight nights on the harvest-home of a small field within the precincts of the fortress, which yielded a few bushels of wheat.

Before concluding these remarks, I must mention one of the amusements of the place, which has particularly struck me. I had repeatedly observed a long lean fellow perched on the top of one of the towers, manœuvring two or three fishing-rods, as though he was angling for the stars. I was for some time perplexed by the evolutions of this aërial fisherman and my perplexity increased on observing others employed in like manner on different parts of the battlements and bastions; it was not until I consulted Mateo Jiménez that I solved the mystery.

It seems that the pure and airy situation of this fortress has rendered it, like the castle of Macbeth, a prolific breeding-place for swallows and martlets who sport about its towers in myriads with the holiday glee of urchins just let loose from school. To entrap these birds in their giddy circlings, with hooks baited with flies, is one of the favourite amusements of the ragged «sons of the Alhambra», who, with the good-for-nothing ingenuity of arrant idlers, have thus invented the art of angling in the sky.

THE COURT OF LIONS

T HE peculiar charm of this old dreamy palace is its power of
calling up vague reveries and picturings of the past, and
thus clothing naked realities with the illusions of the memory
and the imagination. As I delight to walk in these «vain shadows», I am prone to seek those parts of the Alhambra which
are most favourable to this phantasmagoria of the mind, and
none are more so than the Court of Lions and its surrounding
halls. Here the hand of time has fallen the lightest and the traces of Moorish elegance and splendour exist in almost their
original brilliancy. Earthquakes have shaken the foundations of
this pile and rent its rudest towers, yet see, not one of those
slender columns has been displaced, not an arch of that light
and fragile colonnade has given way, and all the fairy fret-
work of these domes, apparently as unsubstantial as the crystal
fabrics of a morning's frost, yet exist after the lapse of centuries, almost as fresh as if from the hand of the Moslem artist.
I write in the midst of these mementoes of the past, in the
fresh hour of early morning, in the fated Hall of the Abencerrages. The blood-stained fountain, the legendary monument
of their massacre, is before me; the lofty jet almost casts its
dew upon my paper. How difficult to reconcile the ancient tale
of violence and blood with the gentle and peaceful scene around!
Everything here appears calculated to inspire kind and

happy feelings, for everything is delicate and beautiful. The very light falls tenderly from above through the lantern of a dome tinted and wrought as if by fairy hands. Through the ample and fretted arch of the portal I behold the Court of Lions with brilliant sunshine gleaming along its colonnades and sparkling in its fountains. The lively swallow dives into the Court and then surging upwards darts away twittering over the roofs; the busy bee toils humming among the flower-beds and painted butterflies hover from plant to plant and flutter up and sport with each other in the sunny air. It needs but a slight exertion of the fancy to picture some pensive beauty of the harem, loitering in these secluded haunts of Oriental luxury.

He, however, who would behold this scene under an aspect more in unison with its fortunes, let him come when the shadows of evening temper the brightness of the Court and throw a gloom into the surrounding halls. Then nothing can be more serenely melancholy or more in harmony with the tale of departed grandeur.

At such times I am apt to seek the Hall of Justice whose deep shadowy arcades extend across the upper end of the Court. Here was performed in presence of Ferdinand and Isabella and their triumphant Court the pompous ceremonial of high mass, on taking possesion of the Alhambra. The very cross is still to be seen upon the wall where the altar was erected, and where officiated the Grand Cardinal of Spain and others of the highest religious dignitaries of the land. I picture to myself the scene when this place was filled with the conquering host, that mixture of mitred prelate and shaven monk, steel-clad knight and silken courtier, when crosses and croziers and religious standards were mingled with proud armorial ensigns and the banners of the haughty chiefs of Spain, and flaunted in triumph through these Moslem halls. I picture to myself Columbus, the future discoverer of a world, taking his modest stand in a remote corner, the humble and neglected spectator of the pageant. I see in imagination the Catholic Sovereigns prostrating themselves before the altar and pouring forth thanks for their victory, while the vaults resounded with sacred minstrelsy and the deep-toned *Te Deum*.

The transient illusion is over—the pageant melts from the fancy—monarch, priest and warrior return into oblivion, with the poor Moslems over whom they exulted. The hall of their triumph is waste and desolate. The bat flits about its twilight vault and the owl hoots from the neighbouring tower of Comares.

On entering the Court of the Lions a few evenings since, I was startled at beholding a turbaned Moor quietly seated near the fountain. It seemed, for a moment, as if one of the superstitions of the place were realised and some ancient inhabitant of the Alhambra had broken the spell of centuries and become visible. He proved, however, to be a mere ordinary mortal, a native of Tetuan in Barbary, who had a shop in the Zacatín of Granada, where he sold rhubarb, trinkets and perfumes. As he spoke Spanish fluently, I was enabled to hold conversation with him, and found him shrewd and intelligent. He told me that he came up the hill occasionally in the Alhambra which reminded him of the old palaces in Barbary, which were built and adorned in similar style, though with less magnificence.

As we walked about the palace, he pointed out several of the Arabic inscriptions, as possessing much poetic beauty.

«Ah, *señor*», said he, «when the Moors held Granada they were a gayer people than they are now-a-days! They thought only of love, of music and poetry. They made stanzas upon every occasion and set them all to music. He who could make the best verses and she who had the most tuneful voice might be sure of favour and preferment. In those days, if anyone asked for bread, the reply was make me a couplet, and the poorest beggar, if he begged in rhyme, would often be rewarded with a piece of gold».

«And is the popular feeling for poetry», said I, «entirely lost among you?»

«By no means, *señor;* the people of Barbary, even those of the lower classes, still make couplets and good ones too, as in the olden time; but talent is not rewarded as it was then; the rich prefer the jingle of their gold to the sound of poetry or music.»

As he was talking, his eye caught one of the inscriptions that foretold perpetuity to the power and glory of the Moslem monarchs, the masters of this pile. He shook head and shrugged his shoulders, as he interpreted it. «Such might have been the case», said he, «the Moslems might still have been reigning in the Alhambra, had not Boabdil been a traitor and given up his capital to the Christian. The Spanish monarchs would never have been able to conquer it by open force».

I endeavoured to vindicate the memory of the unlucky Boabdil from this aspersion and to show that the dissensions which led to the downfall of the Moorish throne originated in the cruelty of his tiger-hearted father, but the Moor would admit of no palliation.

«Muley Hassan», said he, «might have been cruel, but he was brave, vigilant, and patriotic. Had he been properly seconded, Granada would still have been ours, but his son Boabdil thwarted his plans, crippled his power, sowed treason in his palace and dissension in his camp. May the curse of God light upon him for his treachery!» With these words the Moor left the Alhambra.

The indignation of my turbaned companion agrees with an anecdote related by a friend who in the course of a tour in Barbary, had an interview with the Pacha of Tetuán. The Moorish governor was particular in his inquires about the soil and especially concerning the favoured regions of Andalusia, the de-

lights of Granada and the remains of its royal palace. The replies awakened all those fond recollections, so deeply cherished by the Moors, of the power and splendour of their ancient empire in Spain. Turning to his Moslem attendants, the Pacha stroked his beard and broke forth in passionate lamentations that such a sceptre should have fallen from the sway of 'true believers. He consoled himself, however, with the persuasion that the power and prosperity of the Spanish nation were on the decline, that a time would come when the Moors would conquer their rightful domains and that the day was perhaps not far distant when Mahommedan worship would again be offered up in the Mosque of Cordova and a Mahommedan prince sit on his throne in the Alhambra.

Such is the general aspiration and belief among the Moors of Barbary, who consider Spain and especially Andalusia their rightful heritage, of which they have been despoiled by treachery and violence. These ideas are fostered and perpetuated by the descendants of the exiled Moors of Granada, scattered among the cities of Barbary. Several of these reside in Tetuan, preserving their ancient names, such as Páez and Medina, and refraining from intermarriage with any families who cannot claim the same high origin. Their vaunted lineage is regarded with a degree of popular deference rarely shown in Mahommedan communities to any hereditary distinction, except in the royal line.

These families, it is said, continue to sigh after the terrestrial paradise of their ancestors and to put up prayers in their mosques on Fridays, imploring Allah to hasten the time when Granada shall be restored to the faithful, an event to which they look forward as fondly and confidently as did the Christian crusaders to the recovery of the Holy Sepulchre. Nay, it is added, that some of them retain the ancient maps and deeds of the estates and gardens of their ancestors at Granada and even the keys of the houses, holding them as evidences of their hereditary claims, to be produced at the anticipated day of restoration.

The Court of the Lions has also its share of supernatural legends. I have already mentioned the belief in the murmuring of voices and clanking of chains, made at night by the spirits of the murdered Abencerrages. Mateo Jiménez, a few evenings since, at one of the gatherings in Dame Antonia's apartment related a fact which happened within the knowledge of his grandfather, the legendary tailor.

There was an invalid soldier, who had charge of the Alhambra to show it to strangers. As he was one evening about twilight passing through the Court of Lions, he heard footsteps in the Hall of the Abencerrages. Supposing some visitors to be lingering there, he advanced to attend upon them, when to his astonishment he beheld four Moors richly dressed with gilded cuirasses and scimitars and poniards glittering with precious stones. They were walking to and fro with solemn pace, but paused and beckoned to him. The old soldier, however, took to flight and could never afterwards be prevailed upon to enter the Alhambra. Thus it is that men sometimes turn their backs upon fortune, for it is the firm opinion of Mateo that the Moors intended to reveal the place where their treasures lay buried. A successor to the invalid soldier was more knowing; he came to the Alhambra poor, but at the end of a year went off to Malaga, bought houses, set up a carriage and still lives there one of the richest as well as oldest men of the place, all which, Mateo sagely surmises, was in consequence of his finding out the golden secret of these phantom Moors.

BOABDIL EL CHICO

M Y conversation with the man in the Court of Lions set me to musing on the singular fate of Boabdil. Never was surname applicable than that bestowed upon him by his subjects of «el Zogoybi» or «the Unlucky». His misfortunes began almost in his cradle. In his tender youth he was imprisoned and menaced with death by an inhuman father, and only escaped through a mother's stratagem; in after years his life was embittered and repeatedly endangered by the hostilities of an usurping uncle; his reign was distracted by external invasions and internal feuds; he was alternately the foe, the prisoner, the friend, and always the dupe of Ferdinand, until conquered and dethroned by the mingled craft and force of that perfidious monarch. An exile from his native land, he took refuge with one of the princes of Africa and fell obscurely in battle, fighting in the cause of a stranger. His misfortunes ceased not with his death. If Boabdil cherished a desire to leave an honourable name on the historic page, how cruelly has he been defrauded of his hopes! Who is there that has turned the least attention to the romantic history of the Moorish domination in Spain without kindling with indignation at the alleged atrocities of Boabdil? Who has not been touched with the woes of his lovely and gentle queen, subjected by him to a trial of life and death on a false charge of infidelity? Who has not been shocked by his alleged murder of his sister and her two children in a transport of passion? Who has not felt his blood boil at the inhuman massacre of the gallant Abencerrages, thirty-six of whom, it is affirmed, he ordered to be beheaded in the Court of Lions? All these charges have been reiterated in various forms; they have passed into ballads, dramas and romances, until they have taken too thorough possession of the public mind to be eradicated. There is not a foreigner of education that visits the Alhambra but asks for the fountain where the Abencerrages were beheaded and gazes with horror at the grated gallery where the Queen is said to have been confined; not a peasant of the Vega or the Sierra but sings the story in rude couplets to the accompaniment of his guitar while his hearers learn to execrate the very name of Boabdil.

Never, however, was name more foully and unjustly slandered. I have examined all the authentic chronicles and letters written by Spanish authors, contemporary with Boabdil, some of whom were in the confidence of the Catholic Sovereigns and actually present in the camp throughout the war. I have examined all the Arabian authorities I could get acces to, through the medium of translation, and can find nothing to justify these dark and hateful accusations. The whole of these tales may be traced to a work commonly called *The Civil Wars of Granada,* containing a pretended history of the feuds of the Zegries and Abencerrages, during the last struggle of the Moorish empire. This work appeared originally in Spanish, and professed to be translated from the Arabic by one Ginés Pérez de Hita, an inhabitant of Murcia. It has since passed into various languages and Florian has taken from it much of the fable of his Gonsalvo of Cordova; it has since in a great measure usurped the authority of real history, and is currently believed by the people and especially the peasantry of Granada. The whole of it, however, is a mass of fiction, mingled with a few disfigured truths which give it an air of veracity. It bears internal evidence of its falsity; the manners and customs of the Moors being extravagantly misrepresented in it and scenes depicted, totally incompatible with their habits and their faith, and which never could have been recorded by a Mahommedan writer.

I confess there seems to me something almost criminal in the wilful perversions of this work; great latitude is undoubtedly to be allowed to romantic fiction, but there are limits which it must not pass, and the names of the distinguished dead which belong to history are no more to be calumniated than those of the illustrious living. One would have thought, too, that the unfortunate Boabdil had suffered enough for his justifiable hostility to the Spaniards by being stripped of his kingdom, without having his name thus wantonly traduced and rendered a by-word and a theme of infamy in his native land, and in the very mansion of his fathers!

It is not intended hereby to affirm that the transactions imputed to Boabdil are totally without historic foundation, but as far as they can be traced, they appear to have been the acts of his father, Aben Hassan, who is represented by both Christian and Arabian chroniclers as being of a cruel and ferocious nature. It was he who put to death the cavaliers of the illustrious line of the Abencerrages, upon suspicion of their being engaged in a conspiracy to dispossess him of his throne.

The story of the accusation of the Queen of Boabdil and of her confinement in one of the towers may also be traced to an incident in the life of his tiger-hearted father. Aben Hassan in his advanced age married a beautiful Christian captive of noble descent, who took the Moorish appellation of Zorayda, by whom he had two sons. She was of an ambitious spirit and envious that her children should succeed to the crown. For this purpose she worked upon the suspicious temper of the King, inflaming him with jealousies of his children by other wives and concubines, whom she accused of plotting against his throne and life. Some of them were slain by the ferocious father. Ayxa *la Horra,* the virtuous mother of Boabdil, who had once been his cherished favourite, became likewise the object of his suspicion. He confined her and her son in the tower of Comares and would have sacrificed Boabdil to his fury, but that this tender mother lowered him from the tower in the night by means of the scarfs of herself and her attendants, and thus enabled him to escape to Guadix.

Such is the only shadow of a foundation that I can find for the story of the accused and captive Queen, and in this it appears that Boabdil was the persecuted, instead of the persecutor.

Throughout the whole of his brief, turbulent and disastrous reign, Boabdil gives evidence of a mild and amiable character. He in the first instance won the hearts of the people by his affable and gracious manners; he was always peaceable and never inflicted any severity of punishment upon those who occasionally rebelled against him. He was personally brave, but he wanted moral courage, and in times of difficulty and perplexity was wavering and irresolute. This feebleness of spirit hastened his downfall, while it deprived him of that heroic grace which would have given a grandeur and dignity to his fate and rendered him worthy of closing the splendid drama of the Moslem domination in Spain.

MEMENTOS OF BOABDIL

WHILE my mind was still warm with the subject of the unfortunate Boabdil, I set forth to trace the mementos connected with his story, which yet exist in this scene of his sovereignty and his misfortunes. In the picture-gallery of the Palace of the Generalife hangs his portrait. The face is mild, handsome and somewhat melancholy, with a fair complexion and yellow hair; if it be a true representation of the man, he may have been wavering and uncertain, but there is nothing of cruelty or unkindness in his aspect.

I next visited the dungeon where he was confined in his youthful days, when his cruel father meditated his destruction. It is a vaulted room in the tower of Comares under the Hall of Ambassadors; a similar room, separated by a narrow passage, was the prison of his mother, the virtuous Ayxa *la Horra.* The walls are of prodigious thickness and the small windows secured by iron bars. A narrow stone gallery with a low parapet extends round three sides of the tower, just below the windows, but at a considerable height from the ground. From this gallery, it is presumed, the Queen lowered her son with the scarfs of herself and her female attendants, during the darkness of night to the hill-side, at the foot of which waited a domestic with a fleet steed to bear the prince to the mountains.

As I paced this gallery, my imagination pictured the anxious Queen leaning over the parapet and listening with the throbbings of a mother's heart to the last echoes of the horse's hoofs, as her son scoured along the narrow valley of the Darro.

My next search was for the gate by which Boabdil departed from the Alhambra, when about to surrender his capital. With the melancholy caprice of a broken spirit he requested of the Catholic monarchs that no one afterwards might be permitted to pass through this gate. His prayer, according to ancient chronicles, was complied with, through the sympathy of Isabella and the gate walled up. For some time I inquired in vain for such a portal; at length, my humble attendant, Mateo, learned among the old residents of the fortress that a ruinous gateway still existed by which, according to tradition, the King *Chico* had left the fortress, but which had never been open within the memory of the oldest inhabitant.

He conducted me to the spot. The gateway is in the centre of what was once an inmense tower, called *La Torre de los Siete Suelos* or the Tower of Seven Floors. It is a place famous in the superstitious stories of the neighbourhood, for being the scene of strange apparitions and Moorish enchantments.

This once redoubtable tower is now a mere wreck, having been blown up with gunpowder by the French, when they abandoned the fortress. Great masses of the wall lie scattered about, buried in the luxuriant herbage or overshadowed by vines and fig-trees. The arch of the gateway, though rent by the shock still remains, but the last wish of poor Boabdil has again, though unintentionally, been fulfilled, for the portal has been closed up by loose stones gathered from the ruins and remains impassable.

Following up the route of the Moslem monarch, as it remains on record, I crossed on horseback the hill of Los Mártires, keeping along the garden of the convent of the same name, and thence down a rugged ravine, beset by thickets of aloes and Indian figs and lined by caves and hovels swarming with gypsies. It was the road taken by Boabdil to avoid passing through the city. The descent was so steep and broken that I was obliged to dismount and lead my horse.

Emerging from the ravine, and passing by the *Puerta de los Molinos* (the Gate of the Mills), I issued forth upon the public promenade called the Prado and pursuing the course of the Xenil arrived at a small Moorish mosque, now converted into the chapel or hermitage of San Sebastián. A tablet on the wall relates that on this spot Boabdil surrendered the keys of Granada to the Castilian sovereigns. From thence I rode slowly across the Vega to a village where the family and household of the unhappy King awaited him, for he had sent them forward on the preceding night from the Alhambra that his mother and wife might not participate in his personal humiliation or be exposed to the gaze of the conquerors. Following on in the route of the melancholy band of royal exiles, I arrived at the foot of a chain of barren and dreary heights, forming the skirt of the Alpuxarra mountains. From the summit of one of these the unfortunate Boabdil took his last look at Granada; it bears a name expressive of his sorrows: *La Cuesta de las Lágrimas* (the Hill of Tears). Beyond it, a sandy road winds across a rugged cheerless waste, doubly dismal to the unhappy monarch, as it led to exile.

I spurred my horse to the summit of a rock where Boabdil uttered his last sorrowful exclamation, as he turned his eyes from taking their farewell gaze; it is still denominated *El último Suspiro del Moro* (the Last Sigh of the Moor). Who can wonder at his anguish at being expelled from such a kingdom and such an abode? With the Alhambra he seemed to be yielding up all the honours of his line and all the glories and delights of life.

It was here, too, that his affliction was embittered by the reproach of his mother, Ayxa, who had so often assisted him in times of peril and had vainly sought to instil into him her own resolute spirit. «You do well», said she «to weep as a woman over what you could not defend as a man»—a speech that savours more of the pride of the princess than the tenderness of the mother.

When this anecdote was related to Charles V. by Bishop Guevara, the emperor joined in the expression of scorn at the weakness of the wavering Boabdil. «Had I been he or he been I», said the haughty potentate, «I would rather have made this Alhambra my sepulchre, than have lived without a kingdom in the Alpuxarra».

How easy it is for those in power and prosperity to preach heroism to the vanquished! How little can they understand that life itself may rise in value with the unfortunate, when nought but life remains!

THE BALCONY

I N the Hall of Ambassadors, at the central window there is a
balcony, of which I have already made mention; it projects
like a cage from the face of the tower, high in mid-air above
the tops of the trees that grow on the steep hill-side. It serves
me as a kind of observatory, where I often take my seat to
consider not merely the heaven above, but the earth beneath.
Besides the magnificent prospect which it commands of mountain, valley and *vega,* there is a busy little scene of human life
laid open to inspection immediately below. At the foot of the
hills is an *alameda* or public walk which, though not so fashionable as the more modern and splendid *paseo* of the Xenil,
still boasts a varied and picturesque concourse. Hither resort
the small gentry of the suburbs, together with priests and
friars, who walk for appetite and digestion, *majos* and *majas,*
the beaux and belles of the lower classes in their Andalusian
dresses, swaggering *contrabandistas* and sometimes half-muf-
fled and mysterious loungers of the higher ranks on some secret assignation.

It is a moving and motley picture of Spanish life and
character, which I delight to study, and as the naturalist has
his microscope to aid him in his investigations, so I have a
small pocket-telescope which brings the countenances of the
motley groups so close as almost, at times, to make me think I

can divine their conversation by the play and expression of their features. I am thus in a manner an invisible observer and, without quitting my solitude, can throw myself in an instant into the midst of society—a rare advantage to one of somewhat shy and quiet habits and who, like myself, is fond of observing the drama of life, without becoming an actor in the scene.

There is a considerable suburb lying below the Alhambra, filling the narrow gorge of the valley and extending up the opposite hill of the Albaicín. Many of the houses are built in the Moorish style round *patios* or courts, cooled by fountains and open to the sky, and as the inhabitants pass much of their time in these courts and on the terraced roofs during the summer season, it follows that many a glance at their domestic life may be obtained by an aërial spectator like myself who can look down on them from the clouds.

I enjoy in some degree the advantage of the student in the famous old Spanish story [1], who beheld all Madrid unroofed for his inspection, and my gossiping squire, Mateo Jiménez, officiates occasionally as my Asmodeus to give me anecdotes of the different mansions and their inhabitants.

I prefer, however, to form conjectural histories for myself and thus can sit for hours weaving from casual incidents and indications that pass under my eye the whole tissue of schemes, intrigues and occupations of certain of the busy mortals below. There is scarce a pretty face or a striking figure that I daily see, about which I have not thus gradually framed a dramatic story, though some of my characters will occasionally

---

[1] *i. e. El Diablo Cojuelo* (The Devil who limped) by Luis Vélez de Guevara, a sixteenth century writer. According to the story, a certain student named Don Cleofás Pérez Zambullo freed the imp Asmodeus from the bottle in which he was imprisoned; Asmodeus, out of gratitude, took him on a tour over the rooftops of Madrid, having removed the roofs beforehand. The result, naturally, is a subtle satire on the manners of the age. *(Ed. note.)*

act in direct opposition to the part assigned them and disconcert my whole drama. A few days since, as I was reconnoitring with my glass the streets of the Albaicín, I beheld the procession of a novice about to take the veil and remarked several circumstances that excited the strongest sympathy in the fate of the youthful being thus about to be consigned to a living tomb. I ascertained to my satisfaction that she was beautiful and by the paleness of her cheek that she was a victim rather than a votary. She was arrayed in bridal garments and decked with a chaplet of white flowers, but her heart evidently revolted at this mockery of a spiritual union and yearned after its earthly loves. A tall stern-looking man walked near her in the procession; it was evidently the tyrannical father who, from some bigoted or sordid motive had compelled this sacrifice. Amidst the crowd was a dark handsome youth in Andalusian garb, who seemed to fix on her an eye of agony. It was doubtless the secret lover from whom she was for ever to be separated. My indignation rose as I noted the malignant expression painted on the countenances of the attendant monks and friars. The procession arrived at the chapel of the convent; the sun gleamed for the last time upon the chaplet of the poor novice, as she crossed the fatal threshold and disappeared within the building. The throng poured in with cowl and cross and minstrelsy; the lover paused for a moment at the door. I could divine the tumult of his feelings, but he mastered them and entered. There was a long interval—I pictured to myself the scene passing within; the poor novice despoiled of her transient finery, clothed in the conventual garb, her bridal chaplet taken from her brow, her beautiful head shorn of its long silken tresses—I heard her murmur the irrevocable vow. I saw her extended on her bier, the death-pall spread over her; the funeral service was performed; I heard the deep tones of the organ and the plaintive requiem chanted by the nuns; the father looked on with a hard unfeeling countenance. The lover—but no, my imagination refused to paint the lover—there the picture remained a blank.

After a time the throng again poured forth and dispersed various ways to enjoy the light of the sun and mingle with the stirring scenes of life; the victim, however, remained behind. Almost the last that came forth were the father and the lover; they were in earnest conversation. The latter was vehement in his gesticulations; I expected some violent termination to my drama, but an angle of a building interfered and closed the scene. My eye has since frequently been turned to that convent with painful interest. I remarked late at night a light burning in a remote window of one of its towers. «There», said I, «the unhappy nun sits weeping in her cell, while perhaps her lover paces the street below in unavailing anguish.»

The officious Mateo interrupted my meditations, and destroyed in an instant the cobweb tissue of my fancy. With his usual zeal he had gathered facts concerning the scene that put my fictions all to flight. The heroine of my romance was neither young nor handsome; she had no lover; she had entered the convent of her own free will as a respectable asylum, and was one of the most cheerful residents within its walls.

It was some little while before I could forgive the wrong done me by the nun in being thus happy in her cell, in contradiction to all the rules of romance; I diverted my spleen, however, by watching for a day or two the pretty coquetries of a dark-eyed brunette who from the covert of a balcony shrouded with flowering shrubs and a silken awning was carrying on a mysterious correspondence with a handsome, dark well-whiskered cavalier who was frequently in the street beneath her window. Sometimes I saw him at an early hour stealing forth wrapped to the eyes in a mantle. Sometimes he loitered at a corner in various disguises apparently waiting for a private signal to slip into the house. Then there was the tinkling of a guitar at night and a lantern shifted from place to place in the balcony. I imagined another intrigue like that of Almaviva [1], but was again disconcerted in all my suppositions by being informed that the supposed lover was the husband of the lady and a noted *contrabandista,* and that all his mysterious signs and movements had doubtless some smuggling scheme in view.

I occasionally amused myself with noting from this balcony the gradual changes that came over the scenes below according to the different stages of the day.

Scarce has the grey dawn streaked the sky and the earliest cock crowed from the cottages of the hill-side, when the suburbs give signs of reviving animation, for the fresh hours of dawning are precious in the summer season in a sultry climate. All are anxious to get the start of the sun in the business of the day. The muleteer drives forth his loaded train for the journey, the traveller slings his carbine behind his saddle and mounts his steed at the gate of the hostel, the brown peasant urges his loitering beasts, laden with panniers of sunny fruit and fresh dewy vegetables, for already the thrifty housewives are hastening to the market.

The sun is up and sparkles along the valley, tipping the transparent foliage of the groves. The matin bells resound melodiously through the pure bright air, announcing the hour of devotion. The muleteer halts his burthened animals before the chapel, thrusts his staff through his belt behind and enters with hat in hand, smoothing his coal-black hair, to hear a mass and put up a prayer for a prosperous wayfaring across the *sierra.* And now steals forth on fairy foot the gentle *señora* in trim *basquiña,* with restless fan in hand and dark eye flashing from beneath the gracefully folded *mantilla;* she seeks some well-frequented church to offer up her morning orisons, but

---

[1] The author recalls us the plot of *Le barbier de Seville,* by Beaumarchais, the eighteenth century French writer, popularised in the nineteenth century through the opera of Rossini. *(Ed. note.)*

the nicely adjusted dress, the dainty shoe and cobweb stocking, the raven tresses, exquisitely braided, the fresh plucked rose that gleams among them like a gem show that earth divides with Heaven the empire of her thoughts. Keep an eye upon her, careful mother, or virgin aunt or vigilant *dueña,* whichever you be, that walk behind!

As the morning advances, the din of labour augments on every side; the streets are thronged with man and steed and beast of burden, and there is a hum and murmur, like the surges of the ocean. As the sun ascends to his meridian, the hum and bustle gradually decline; at the height of noon there is a pause. The panting city sinks into lassitude and for several hours there is a general repose. The windows are closed, the curtains drawn, the inhabitants retire into the coolest recesses of their mansions, the fullfed monk snores in his dormitory, the brawny porter lies stretched on the pavement beside his burden, the peasant and the labourer sleep beneath the trees of the Alameda, lulled by the sultry chirping of the locust. The streets are deserted, except by the water-carrier who refreshes the ear by proclaiming the merits of his sparkling beverage «colder than the mountain snow».

As the sun declines, there is again a gradual reviving, and when the vesper bell rings out his sinking knell, all nature seems to rejoice that the tyrant of the day has fallen. Now begins the bustle of enjoyment, when the citizens pour forth to breathe the evening air and revel away the brief twilight in the walks and gardens of the Darro and the Xenil.

As night closes, the capricious scene assumes new features. Light after light gradually twinkles forth, here a taper from a balconied window, there a votive lamp before the image of a saint. Thus by degrees the city emerges from the pervading gloom, and sparkles with scattered lights, like the starry firmament. Now break forth from court and garden and street and lane the tinkling of innumerable guitars and the clicking

of castanets; blending, at this lofty height in a faint but general concert. «Enjoy the moment», is the creed of the gay and amorous Andalusian, and at no time does he practise it more zealously than in the balmy night of summer, wooing his mistress with the dance, the love ditty and the passionate serenade.

I was one evening seated in the balcony, enjoying the light breeze that came rustling along the side of the hill among the tree-tops, when my humble historiographer Mateo who was at my elbow pointed out a spacious house in an obscure street of the Albaicín, about which he related, as nearly as I can recollect, the following anecdote.

THE ADVENTURE OF THE MASON

THERE was once upon a time a poor mason or bricklayer in Granada, who kept all the Saints' days and holidays and Saint Monday into the bargain, and yet with all his devotion he grew poorer and poorer and could scarcely earn bread for his numerous family. One night he was roused from his first sleep by a knocking at his door. He opened it, and beheld before him a tall, meagre, cadaverous looking priest.

«'Hark ye, honest friend!' said the stranger, 'I have observed that you are a good Christian and one to be trusted; will you undertake a job this very night?'

«'With all my heart, *señor padre,* on condition that I am paid accordingly.'

«'That you shall be, but you must suffer yourself to be blindfolded.'

«To this the mason made no objection. So, being hoodwinked, he was led by the priest through various rough lanes and winding passages, until they stopped before the portal of a house. The priest then applied a key, turned a creaking lock and opened what sounded like a ponderous door. They entered, the door was closed and bolted, and the mason was conducted through an echoing corridor and a spacious hall to an interior part of the building. Here the bandage was removed from his eyes and he found himself in a *patio* or court, dimly lighted by a single lamp. In the centre was the dry basin of an old

Moorish fountain, under which the priest requested him to form a small vault, bricks and mortar being at hand for the purpose. He accordingly worked all night, but without finishing the job. Just before daybreak, the priest put a piece of gold into his hand and having again blindfolded him, conducted him back to his dwelling.

«'Are you willing' said he, 'to return and complete your work?'

«'Gladly, *señor Padre,* provided I am so well paid.'

«'Well, then, to-morrow at midnight I will call again.'

«He did so, and the vault was completed.

«'Now', said the priest, 'you must help me to bring forth the bodies that are to be buried in this vault.'

«The poor mason's hair rose on his head at these words: he followed the priest with trembling steps into a retired chamber of the mansion, expecting to behold some ghastly spectacle of death, but was relieved on perceiving three or four portly jars standing in one corner. They were evidently full of money and it was with great labour that he and the priest carried them forth and consigned them to their tomb. The vault was then closed, the pavement replaced, and all traces of the work obliterated. The mason was again hoodwinked and led forth by a route different from that by which he had come. After they had wandered for a long time through a perplexed maze of lanes and alleys, they halted. The priest then put two pieces of gold into his hand: 'Wait here', said he, 'until you hear the cathedral bell toll for matins. If you presume to uncover your eyes before that time, evil will befall you'. So saying, he departed. The mason waited faithfully, amusing himself by weighing the gold pieces in his hand and clinking them against each other. The moment the cathedral bell rang its matin peal, he uncovered his eyes and found himself on the banks of the Xenil, whence he made the best of his way home and revelled with his family for a whole fortnight on the profits of his two nights work, after which he was as poor as ever.

«He continued to work a little and pray a good deal and keep saints' days and holidays, from year to year, while his family grew up as gaunt and ragged as a crew of gypsies. As he was seated one evening at the door of his hovel, he was accosted by a rich old curmudgeon who was noted for owning many houses and being a griping landlord. The man of money eyed him for a moment from beneath a pair of anxious shagged eyebrows.

«'I am told, friend, that you are very poor.'

«'There is no denying the fact, *señor,* it speaks for itself.'

«'I presume then, that you will be glad of a job, and will work cheap.'

«'As cheap, my master, as any mason in Granada.'

«'That's what I want. I have an old house fallen into decay, that costs me more money than it is worth to keep it in repair, for nobody will live in it, so I must contrive to patch it up and keep it together at as small expense as possible.'

«The mason was accordingly conducted to a large deserted house that seemed going to ruin. Passing through several empty halls and chambers, he entered an inner court, where his eye was caught by an old Moorish fountain. He paused for a moment, for a dreaming recollection of the place came over him.

«'Pray', said he, 'who occupied this house formerly?'

«'A pest upon him!' cried the landlord, 'it was an old miserly priest, who cared for nobody but himself. He was said to be immensely rich and, having no relations, it was thought he would leave all his treasures to the Church. He died suddenly and the priests and friars thronged to take possession of his wealth, but nothing could they find but a few ducats in a leathern purse. The worst luck has fallen on me, for since his death the old fellow continues to occupy my house without paying rent and there is no taking the law of a dead man. The people pretend to hear the clinking of gold all night in the chamber where the old priest slept, as if he were counting over his money, and sometimes a groaning and moaning about the court. Whether true or false, these stories have brought a bad name on my house and not a tenant will remain in it.'

«'Enough' said the mason sturdily: 'let me live in your house rent-free until some better tenant present and I will engage to put it in repair, and to quiet the troubled spirit that disturbs it. I am a good Christian and a poor man, and am not to be daunted by the Devil himself, even though he should come in the shape of a big bag of money!'

«The offer of the honest mason was gladly accepted; he moved with his family into the house, and fulfilled all his engagements. By little and little he restored it to its former state; the clinking of gold was no more heard at night in the chamber of the defunct priest, but began to be heard by day in the pocket of the living mason. In a word, he increased rapidly in wealth, to the admiration of all his neighbours and became one of the richest men in Granada. He gave large sums to the Church, by way, no doubt, of satisfying his conscience and never revealed the secret of the vault until on his death-bed to his son and heir.»

A RAMBLE AMONG THE HILLS

I use frequently to amuse myself towards the close of the day, when the heat has subsided, with taking long rambles about the neighbouring hills and the deep umbrageous valleys, accompanied by my historiographic squire, Mateo, to whose passion for gossiping I on such occasions give the most unbounded licence; and there is scarce a rock or ruin or broken fountain or lonely glen about which he has not some marvellous story or above all some golden legend, for never was poor devil so munificent in dispensing hidden treasures.

A few evenings since, we took a long stroll of the kind, in the course of which Mateo was more than usually communicative. It was towards sunset that we sallied forth from the Great Gate of Justice and, ascending an alley of trees, Mateo paused under a clump of fig and pomegranate trees at the foot of a huge ruined tower called the Tower of the Seven Floors (*de los Siete Suelos*). Here pointing to a low archway in the foundation of the tower, he informed me of a monstrous sprite or hobgoblin said to infest this tower ever since the time of the Moors and to guard the treasures of a Moslem King. Sometimes it issues forth in the dead of the night and scours the avenues of the Alhambra and the streets of Granada in the shape of a headless horse, pursued by six dogs with terrible yells and howlings.

«But have you ever met with it yourself, Mateo, in any of your rambles?», demanded I.

«No, *señor,* God be thanked! but my grandfather, the tailor, knew several persons that had seen it, for it went about much oftener in his time than at present, sometimes in one shape, sometimes in another. Everybody in Granada has heard of the *Belludo,* for the old women and the nurses frighten the children with it when they cry. Some say it is the spirit of a cruel Moorish King who killed his six sons and buried them in these vaults, and that they hunt him at nights in revenge.»

I forbear to dwell upon the marvellous details given by the simple-minded Mateo about this redoubtable phantom which has, in fact, been time out of mind a favourite theme of nursery tales and popular tradition in Granada and of which honourable mention is made by an ancient and learned historian and topographer of the place [1]. I would only observe that through this tower was the gateway by which the unfortunate Boabdil issued forth to surrender his capital.

Leaving this eventful pile, we continued our course, skirting the fruitful orchards of the Generalife, in which two or three nightingales were pouring forth a rich strain of melody. Behind these orchards we passed a number of Moorish tanks with a door cut into the rocky bosom of the hill, but closed up. These tanks, Mateo informed me, were favourite bathing-places of himself and his comrades in boyhood, until frightened away by a story of a hideous Moor who used to issue forth from the door in the rock to entrap unwary bathers.

Leaving these haunted tanks behind us, we pursued our ramble up a solitary mule-path that wound among the hills and soon found ourselves amidst wild and melancholy mountains, destitute of trees, and here and there tinted with scanty verdure. Everything within sight was severe and sterile, and it was scarcely possible to realise the idea that but a short distance

[1] *i. e.* the Padre Echevarría, who mentions this fable in his work *Paseos por Granada. (Ed. note.)*

behind us was the Generalife with its blooming orchards and terraced gardens and that we were in the vicinity of delicious Granada, that city of groves and fountains. But such is the nature of Spain—wild and stern the moment it escapes from cultivation. The desert and the garden are ever side by side.

The narrow defile up which we were passing is called, according to Mateo, *el Barranco de la Tinaja* or the Ravine of the Jar, because a jar full of Moorish gold was found here in old times. The brain of poor Mateo is continually running upon these golden legends.

«But what is the meaning of the cross I see yonder upon a heap of stones in that narrow part of the ravine?»

«Oh, that's nothing—a muleteer was murdered there some years since.»

«So then, Mateo, you have robbers and murderes even at the gates of the Alhambra?»

«Not at present, *señor,* that was formerly, when there used to be many loose fellows about the fortress, but they've all been weeded out. Not but that the gypsies who live in caves in the hill-sides just out of the fortress are many of them fit for anything, but we have had no murder about here for a long time past. The man who murdered the muleteer was hanged in the fortress.»

Our path continued up the *barranco* with a bold, rugged height to our left called the *Silla del Moro* or Chair of the Moor, from the tradition already alluded to that the unfortunate Boabdil fled thither during a popular insurrection and remained all day seated on the rocky summit looking mournfully down on his factious city.

We at length arrived on the highest part of the promontory above Granada, called the Mountain of the Sun. The evening was approaching; the setting sun just gilded the loftiest heights. Here and there, a solitary shepherd might be descried driving his flock down the declivities to be folded for the night, or a muleteer and his lagging animals, threading some mountain path, to arrive at the city gates before nightfall.

Presently the deep tones of the cathedral bell came swelling up the defiles, proclaiming the hour of *oración* or prayer. The note was responded to from the belfry of every church and from the sweet bells of the convents among the mountains. The shepherd paused on the fold of the hill, the muleteer in the midst of the road, each took off his hat and remained motionless for a time, murmuring his evening prayer. There is always something pleasingly solemn in this custom, by which at a melodious signal every human being throughout the land unites at the same moment in a tribute of thanks to God for the mercies of the day. It spreads a transient sanctity over the land; the sight of the sun sinking in all his glory adds not a little to the solemnity of the scene.

In the present instance the effect was heightened by the wild and lonely nature of the place. We were on the naked and broken summit of the haunted Mountain of the Sun, where ruined tanks and cisterns and the mouldering foundations of extensive buildings spoke of former populousness, but where all was now silent and desolate.

As we were wandering among these traces of old times, Mateo pointed out to me a circular pit that seemed to penetrate deep into the bosom of the mountain. It was evidently a deep well, dug by the indefatigable Moors, to obtain their favourite element in its greatest purity. Mateo, however, had a different story, and much more to his humour. This was, according to tradition, an entrance to the subterranean caverns of the mountain, in which Boabdil and his court lay bound in magic spell and from whence they sallied forth at night at allotted times to revisit their ancient abodes.

The deepening twilight which in this climate is of such short duration admonished us to leave this haunted ground. As we descended the mountain defiles, there was no longer herdsman or muleteer to be seen nor anything to be heard but our own footsteps and the lonely chirping of the cricket. The shadows of the valley grew deeper and deeper, until all was dark around us. The lofty summit of the Sierra Nevada alone retained a lingering gleam of daylight; its snowy peaks glaring against the dark blue firmament and seeming close to us from the extreme purity of the atmosphere.

«How near the Sierra looks this evening!», said Mateo, «it seems as if you could touch it with your hand, and yet it is many long leagues off.» While he was speaking, a star appeared over the snowy summit of the mountain, the only one yet visible in the heavens, and so pure, so large, so bright and beautiful, as to call forth ejaculations of delight from honest Mateo.

«¡ Qué estrella más hermosa! ¡Qué clara y limpia es! ¡No puede haber estrella más brillante!»

(What a beautiful star! How clear and lucid! No star could be more brilliant!)

I have often remarked this sensibility of the common people of Spain to the charms of natural objects. The lustre of a star, the beauty or fragrance of a flower, the crystal purity of a fountain will inspire them with a kind of poetical delight, and then what euphonious words their magnificent language affords, with which to give utterance to their transports!

«But what lights are those, Mateo, which I see twinkling along 'the Sierra Nevada, just below the snowy region and which might be taken for stars, only that they are ruddy and against the dark side of the mountain?»

«Those, señor, are fires, made by the men who gather snow and ice for the supply of Granada. They go up every afternoon with mules and asses, and take turns, some to rest and warm themselves by the fires, while others fill the panniers with ice. They then set off down the mountain, so as to reach the gates of Granada before sunrise. That Sierra Nevada, señor,

107

is a lump of ice in the middle of Andalusia to keep it all cool in summer.»

It was now completely dark; we were passing through the *barranco* where stood the cross of the murdered muleteer, when I beheld a number of lights moving at a distance and apparently advancing up the ravine. On nearer approach, they proved to be torches, borne by a train of uncouth figures arrayed in black; it would have been a procession dreary enough at any time, but was peculiarly so in this wild and solitary place.

Mateo drew near and told me in a low voice that it was a funeral train bearing a corpse to the burying ground among the hills.

As the procession passed by, the lugubrious light of the torches falling on the rugged features and funeral-weeds of the attendants had the most fantastic effect, but was perfectly ghastly, as it revealed the countenance of the corpse which, according to the Spanish custom, was borne uncovered on an open bier. I remained for some time gazing after the dreary train, as it wound up the dark defiles of the mountain. It put me in mind of the old story of a procession of demons bearing the body of a sinner up the crater of Stromboli.

«Ah! *señor*», cried Mateo, «I could tell you a story of a procession once seen among these mountains, but then you'd laugh at me and say it was one of the legacies of my grandfather, the tailor.»

«By no means, Mateo. There is nothing I realish more than a marvellous tale.»

«Well, *señor,* it is about one of those very men we have been talking of, who gather snow on the Sierra Nevada [1].

«You must know, that a great many years since, in my

---

[1] The *Camino de los Neveros* still exists. *Neveros* were porters who collected and transported ice and snow for consumption in the city. *(Ed. note.)*

grandfather's time, there was an old fellow, *Tío Nicolás* (Uncle Nicholas) by name who had filled the panniers of his mule with snow and ice, and was returning down the mountain. Being very drowsy he mounted upon the mule, and soon falling asleep, went with his head nodding and bobbing about from side to side while his sure-footed old mule stepped along the edge of precipices and down steep and broken *barrancos,* just as safe and steady as if it had been on plain ground. At length, *Tío Nicolás* awoke, and gazed about him and rubbed his eyes—and, in good truth, he had reason. The moon shone almost as bright as day and he saw the city below him, as plain as your hand, and shining with its white buildings, like a silver platter in the moonshine, but, Lord! *señor,* it was nothing like the city he had left a few hours before! Instead of the cathedral, with its great dome and turrets and the churches with their spires, and the convents with their pinnacles, all surmounted with the blessed cross, he saw nothing but Moorish mosques and minarets and cupolas, all topped off with glittering crescents, such as you see on the Barbary flags. Well, *señor,* as you may suppose, *Tío Nicolás* was mightily puzzled at all this, but while he was gazing down upon the city, a great army came marching up the mountain, windig along the ravines, sometimes in the moonshine, sometimes in the shades. As it drew nigh, he saw that there were horse and foot, all in Moorish armour. *Tío Nicolás* tried to scramble out of their way, but his old mule stood stock still and refused to budge, trembling, at the same time, like a leaf—for dumb beasts, *señor,* are just as much frightened at such things as human beings. Well, *señor,* the hobgoblin army came marching by; there were men that seemed to blow trumpets, and others to beat drums and strike cymbals, yet never a sound did they make; they all moved on without the least noise, just as I have seen painted armies move across the stage in the theatre of Granada and all looked as pale as death. At last, in the rear of the army, between two black Moorish horsemen, rode the Grand Inquisitor of Granada, on a mule as white as snow. *Tío Nicolás* wondered to see him in such company, for the Inquisitor was famous for his hatred of Moors and indeed of all kinds of infidels, Jews and heretics, and used to hunt them out with fire and scourge. However, *Tío Nicolás* felt himself safe, now that there was a priest of such sanctity at hand. So making the sign of the cross, he called out for his benediction, when, *¡hombre!* he received a blow that sent him and his old mule over the edge of a steep bank, down which they rolled, head over-heels, to the bottom! *Tío Nicolás* did not come to his senses until long after sunrise, when he found himself at the bottom of a deep ravine, his mule grazing beside him, and his panniers of snow completely melted. He crawled back to Granada sorely bruised and battered, but was glad to find the city looking as usual, with Christian churches and crosses. When he told the story of his night's adventure, every one laughed at him; some said he had dreamed it all, as he dozed on his mule; others thought it all a fabrication of his own— but what was strange, *señor,* and made people afterwards think more seriously of the matter, was that the Grand Inquisitor died within the year. I have often heard my grandfather, the tailor, say that there was more meant, by that hobgoblin army bearing off the resemblance of the priest than folks dared to surmise.»

«Then you would insinuate, friend Mateo, that there is a kind of Moorish limbo or purgatory in the bowels of these mountains, to which the *padre* Inquisitor was borne off?»

«God forbid, *señor!* I know nothing of the matter—I only relate what I heard from my grandfather.»

By the time Mateo had finished the tale which I have more succinctly related and which was interlarded with many comments, and spun out with minute details, we reached the gate of the Alhambra.

LOCAL TRADITIONS

THE common people of Spain have an Oriental passion for story-telling and are fond of the marvellous. They will gather round the doors of their cottages in summer evenings or in the great cavernous chimney corners of the *ventas* in the winter and listen with insatiable delight to miraculous legends of saints, perilous adventures of travellers and daring exploits of robbers and *contrabandistas*. The wild and solitary character of the country, the imperfect diffusion of knowledge, the scarceness of general topics of conversation and the romantic adventurous life that every one leads in a land where traveling is yet in its primitive state, all contribute to cherish this love of oral narration and to produce a strong infusion of the extravagant and incredible. There is no theme, however, more prevalent and popular than that of treasures buried by the Moors; it pervades the whole country. In traversing the wild *sierras,* the scenes of ancient fray and exploit, you cannot see a Moorish *atalaya* or watch-tower, perched among the cliffs or beetling above its rock-built village, but your muleteer, on being closely questioned, will suspend the smoking of his *cigarrillo* to tell some tale of Moslem gold buried beneath its foundations; nor is there a ruined *alcázar* in a city but has its golden tradition, handed down from generation to generation among the poor people of the neighbourhood.

These, like most popular fictions, have sprung from some scanty ground-work of fact. During the wars between Moor and Christian, which distracted this country for centuries, towns and castles were liable frequently and suddenly to change owners, and the inhabitants during sieges and assaults were fain to bury their money and jewels in the earth or hide them in vaults and wells, as is often done at the present day in the despotic and belligerent countries of the East. At the time of the expulsion of the Moors also many of them concealed their most precious effects, hoping that their exile would be but temporary and that they would be enabled to return and retrieve their treasures at some future day. It is certain that from time to time hoards of gold and silver coin have been accidentally dug up, after a lapse of centuries from among the ruins of Moorish fortresses and habitations, and it requires but a few facts of the kind to give birth to a thousand fictions.

The stories thus originating have generally something of the Arabic and the Gothic which seems to me to characterize everything in Spain, and especially in its southern provinces. The hidden wealth is always laid under magic and secured by charm and talisman. Sometimes it is guarded by uncouth monsters or fiery dragons, sometimes by enchanted Moors who sit by it in armour with drawn swords, but motionless as statues, maintaining a sleepless watch for ages.

The Alhambra, of course, from the peculiar circumstances of its history, is a strong-hold for popular fictions of the kind, and various relics dug up from time to time have contributed to strengthen them. At one time an earthen vessel was found containing Moorish coins and the skeleton of a cock which according to the opinion of certain shrewd inspectors must have been buried alive. At another time a vessel was dug up containing a great scarabaeus or beetle of baked clay, covered with Arabic inscriptions, which was pronounced a prodigious amulet of occult virtues. In this way the wits of the ragged

brood who inhabit the Alhambra have been set wool gathering, until there is not a hall or tower or vault of the old fortress that has not been made the scene of some marvellous tradition. Having, I trust, in the preceding papers made the reader in some degree familiar with the localities of the Alhambra, I shall now launch out more largely into the wonderful legends connected with it and which I have diligently wrought into shape and form from various legendary scraps and hints picked up in the course of my perambulations; in the same manner that an antiquary works out a regular historical document from a few scattered letters of an almost defaced inscription.

If anything in these legends should shock the faith of the over-scrupulous reader, he must remember the nature of the place and make due allowances. He must not expect here the same laws of probability that govern common-place scenes and every-day life; he must remember that he treads the halls of an enchanted palace and all is «haunted ground».

THE HOUSE OF THE WEATHERCOCK

O N the brow of the lofty hill of the Albaicín, the highest
part of the city of Granada, stand the remains of what was
once a royal palace, founded shortly after the conquest of Spain
by the Arabs. It is now converted into a manufactory and has
fallen into such obscurity that it cost me much trouble to
find it, notwithstanding that I had the assistance of the sagacious and all-knowing Mateo Jiménez. This edifice still bears
the name by which it has been known for centuries, namely,
La Casa del Gallo de Viento, i. e. The House of the Weathercock. It was so called from a bronze figure of a warrior on horseback, armed with shield and spear, erected on one of its
turrets, and turning with every wind; bearing an Arabic motto,
which, translated into Spanish, was as follows:

> *Dice el sabio Aben Habuz*
> *Que así se defiende el andaluz.*
>
> In this way, says Aben Habuz the Wise,
> The Andalusian his foe defies.

This Aben Habuz, according to Moorish chronicles, was a
captain in the invading army of Taric and was left by him as
alcaide of Granada. He is supposed to have intended this warlike effigy as a perpetual memorial to the Moslem inhabitants

that, surrounded as they were by foes, their safety depended upon being always on their guard, and ready for the field.

Traditions, however, give a different account of this Aben Habuz and his palace, and affirm that his bronze horseman was originally a talisman of great virtue, though in after ages it lost its magic properties and degenerated into a mere weathercock.

The following are the traditions alluded to.

LEGEND

OF

THE ARABIAN ASTROLOGER

IN old times many hundred years ago there was a Moorish King named Aben Habuz who reigned over the kingdom of Granada. He was a retired conqueror, that is to say, one who, having in his more youthful days led a life of constant foray and depredation, now that he was grown feeble and superannuated, «languished for repose» and desired nothing more than to live at peace with all the world, to husband his laurels and to enjoy in quiet the possessions he had wrested from his neighbours.

It so happened, however, that this most reasonable and pacific old monarch had young rivals to deal with, princes full of his early passion for fame and fighting, and who were disposed to call him to account for the scores he had run up with their fathers. Certain distant districts of his own territories, also, which during the days of his vigour he had treated with a high hand, were prone, now that he languished for repose, to rise in rebellion and threaten to invest him in his capital. Thus he had foes on every side, and as Granada is girt in by wild and craggy mountains which hide the approach of an enemy, the unfortunate Aben Habuz was kept in a constant state of vigilance and alarm, not knowing in what quarter hostilities might break out.

It was in vain that he built watch-towers on the mountains and stationed guards at every pass, with orders to make fires by night and smoke by day on the approach of an enemy. His alert foes, baffling every precaution, would break out of some unthought of defile, ravage his lands beneath his very nose and then make off with prisoners and booty to the mountains. Was ever peaceable and retired conqueror in a more uncomfortable predicament?

While Aben Habuz was harassed by these perplexities and molestations, an ancient Arabian physician arrived at his court. His grey beard descended to his girdle, and he had every mark of extreme age, yet he had travelled almost the whole way from Egypt on foot, with no other aid than a staff, marked with hieroglyphics. His fame had preceded him. His name was Ibrahim Ebn Abu Ajub; he was said to have lived ever since the days of Mahomet and to be the son of Abu Ajub, the last of the companions of the Prophet. He had, when a child, followed the conquering army of Amru into Egypt, where he had remained many years studying the dark sciences and particularly magic among the Egyptian priests.

It was, moreover, said that he had found out the secret of prolonging life, by means of which he had arrived to the great age of upwards of two centuries, though, as he did not discover the secret until well stricken in years, he could only perpetuate his grey hairs and wrinkles.

This wonderful old man was honourably entertained by the King who, like most superannuated monarchs, began to take physicians into favour. He would have assigned him an apartment in his palace, but the astrologer preferred a cave in the side of the hill which rises above the city of Granada, being the same on which the Alhambra has since been built. He caused the cave to be enlarged so as to form a spacious and lofty hall with a circular hole at the top, through which, as through a well, he could see the heavens and behold the stars even at mid-day. The walls of his hall were covered with Egyptian hieroglyphics, with cabalistic symbols and with the figures of the stars in their signs. This hall he furnished with many implements, fabricated under his directions by cunning artificers of Granada, but the occult properties of which were known only to himself.

In a little while the sage Ibrahim became the bosom counsellor of the King who applied to him for advice in every emergency. Aben Habuz was once inveighing against the injustice of this neighbours, and bewailing the restless vigilance he had to observe to guard himself against their invasion. When he had finished, the Astrologer remained silent for a moment and then replied. «Know, O King, that when I was in Egypt, I beheld a great marvel devised by a pagan priestess of old. On a mountain above the city of Borsa and overlooking the great valley of the Nile was a figure of a ram and above it a figure of a cock, both of molten brass, and turning upon a pivot. Whenever the country was threatened with invasion, the ram would turn in the direction of the enemy and the cock would crow; upon this the inhabitants of the city knew of the danger and of the quarter from which it was approaching, and could take timely means to guard against it.»

«God is great!» exclaimed the pacific Aben Habuz, «what a treasure would be such a ram to keep an eye upon these mountains around me and then such a cock to crow in time of danger! *Allah Akbar!* how securely I might sleep in my palace with such sentinels on the top!»

The astrologer waited until the ecstasies of the King had subsided and then proceeded:

«After the victorious Amru (may he rest in peace!) had finished his conquest of Egypt, I remained among the ancient priests of the land, studying the rites and ceremonies of their idolatrous faith, and seeking to make myself master of the hidden knowledge for which they are renowned. I was one day seated on the banks of the Nile, conversing with an ancient priest, when he pointed to the mighty pyramids which rose like mountains out of the neighbouring desert. 'All that we can teach thee', said he, 'is nothing to the knowledge locked up in those mighty piles. In the centre of the central pyramid is a sepulchral chamber, in which is enclosed the mummy of the high priest who aided in rearing that stupendous pile, and with him is buried a wondrous book of knowledge containing all the secrets of magic and art. This book was given to Adam after his fall and was handed down from generation to generation to king Solomon the Wise, and by its aid he built the Temple of Jerusalem. How it came into the possession of the builder of the pyramids is known to Him alone who knows all things'.

«When I heard these words of the Egyptian priest, my heart burned to get possession of that book. I could command the services of many of the soldiers of our conquering army and of a number of the native Egyptians, with these I set to work and pierced the solid mass of the pyramid, until after great toil I came upon one of its interior and hidden passages. Following this up and threading a fearful labyrinth, I penetrated into the very heart of the pyramid, even to the sepulchral chamber where the mummy of the high-priest had lain for ages. I broke through the outer cases of the mummy, unfolded its many wrappers and bandages, and at length, found the precious volume on its bosom. I seized it with a trembling hand and groped my way out of the pyramid, leaving the mummy in its dark and silent sepulchre, there to await the final day of resurrection and judgment.»

«Son of Abu Ajub», exclaimed Aben Habuz, «thou hast been a great traveller and seen marvellous things; but of what avail to me is the secret of the pyramid and the volume of knowledge of the wise Solomon?»

«This it is, O King! By the study of that book I am instructed in all magic arts, and can command the assistance of genii to accomplish my plans. The mystery of the Talisman of Borsa is therefore familiar to me, and such a talisman can I make, nay, one of greater virtues.»

«O wise son of Abu Ajub», cried Aben Habuz, «better were such a talisman than all the watch-towers on the hills, and sentinels upon the borders. Give me such a safeguard, and the riches of my treasury are at thy command.»

The astrologer immediately set to work to gratify the wishes of the monarch. He caused a great tower to be erected upon the top of the royal palace which stood on the brow of the Albaicín. The tower was built of stones brought from Egypt and taken, it is said, from one of the pyramids. In the upper part of the tower was a circular hall with windows looking toward every point of the compass, and before each window was a table, on which was arranged as on a chessboard a mimic army of horse and foot, with the effigy of the potentate that ruled in that direction, all carved of wood. To each of these tables there was a small lance, no bigger than a bodkin, on which were engraved certain Chaldaic characters. This hall was kept constantly closed by a gate of brass with a great lock of steel, the key of which was in possession of the King.

On the top of the tower was a bronze figure of a Moorish horseman, fixed on a pivot, with a shield on one arm and his lance elevated perpendicularly. The face of this horseman was towards the city, as if keeping guard over it, but if any foe were at hand, the figure would turn in that direction and would level the lance as if for action.

When this talisman was finished, Aben Habuz was all impatient to try its virtues and longed as ardently for an invasion, as he had ever sighed after repose. His desire was soon gratified. Tidings were brought, early one morning, by the sentinel appointed to watch the tower, that the face of the bronze horseman was turned towards the mountains of Elvira, and that his lance pointed directly against the Pass of Lope.

«Let the drums and trumpets sound to arms, and all Granada be put on the alert», said Aben Habuz.

«O King», said the astrologer, «let not your city be disquieted nor your warriors called to arms; we need no aid of force to deliver you from your enemies. Dismiss your attendants and let us proceed alone to the secret hall of the tower.»

The ancient Aben Habuz mounted the staircase of the tower, leaning on the arm of the still more ancient Ibrahim Ebn Abu Ajub. They unlocked the brazen door and entered. The window that looked towards the Pass of Lope was open. «In this direction», said the Astrologer, «lies the danger. Approach, O King, and behold the mystery of the table».

King Aben Habuz approached the seeming chess-board, on which were arranged the small wooden effigies, when to his surprise he perceived that they were all in motion. The horses pranced and curveted, the warriors brandished their weapons, and there was a faint sound of drums and trumpets and the clang of arms and neighing of steeds, but all no louder nor more distinct than the hum of the bee or the summer-fly in the drowsy ear of him who lies at noontide in the shade.

«Behold, O King», said the astrologer, «a proof that thy enemies are even now in the field. They must be advancing through yonder mountains by the Pass of Lope. Would you produce a panic and confusion amongst them, and cause them to retreat without loss of life, strike these effigies with the butt-end of this magic lance, but would you cause bloody feud and carnage among them, strike with the point.»

A livid streak passed across the countenance of the pacific Aben Habuz; he seized the mimic lance with trembling eagerness and tottered towards the table, his grey beard wagging with chuckling exultation: «Son of Abu Ajub», exclaimed he, «I think we will have a little blood!»

So saying, he thrust the magic lance into some of the pygmy effigies and belaboured others with the butt-end, upon which the former fell as dead upon the board and the rest turning upon each other began pell-mell a chance-medley fight.

It was with difficulty the astrologer could stay the hand of the most pacific of monarchs and prevent him from absolutely exterminating his foes; at length he prevailed upon him to leave the tower and to send out scouts to the mountains by the Pass of Lope.

They returned with the intelligence that a Christian army had advanced through the heart of the Sierra, almost within sight of Granada, where a dissension had broken out among them; they had turned their weapons against each other and after much slaughter had retreated over the border.

Aben Habuz was transported with joy on thus proving the efficacy of the talisman. «At length», said he, «I shall lead a life of tranquillity and have all my enemies in my power. O wise son of Abu Ajub, what can I bestow on thee in reward for such a blessing?»

«The wants of an old man and a philosopher, O King, are few and simple; grant me but the means of fitting up my cave as a suitable hermitage and I am content.»

«How noble is the moderation of the truly wise!» exclaimed Aben Habuz, secretly pleased at the cheapness of the recompense. He summoned his treasurer, and bade him dispense whatever sums might be required by Ibrahim to complete and furnish his hermitage.

The astrologer now gave orders to have various chambers hewn out of the solid rocks, so as to form ranges of apartments connected with his astrological hall; these he caused to be furnished with luxurious ottomans and divans, and the walls to be hung with the richest silks of Damascus. «I am an old man», said he, «and can no longer rest my bones on stone couches, and these damp walls require covering».

He had baths too constructed and provided with all kinds of perfumes and aromatic oils. «For a bath», said he, «is necessary to counteract the rigidity of age and to restore freshness and suppleness to the frame withered by study».

He caused the apartments to be hung with innumerable silver and crystal lamps which he filled with a fragrant oil, prepared according to a receipt discovered by him in the tombs of Egypt. This oil was perpetual in its nature and diffused a soft radiance like the tempered light of day. «The light of the sun», said he «is too garish and violent for the eyes of an old man and the light of the lamp is more congenial to the studies of a philosopher».

The treasurer of King Aben Habuz groaned at the sums daily demanded to fit up this hermitage, and he carried his complaints to the King. The royal word, however, was given; Aben Habuz shrugged his shoulders. «We must have patience», said he, «this old man has taken his idea of a philosophic retreat from the interior of the pyramids and of the vast ruins of Egypt; but all things have an end, and so will the furnishing of his cavern».

The King was in the right; the hermitage was at length complete and formed a sumptuous subterranean palace. «I am now content», said Ibrahim Ebn Abu Ajub to the treasurer, «I will shut myself up in my cell and devote my time to study. I desire nothing more, nothing, except a trifling solace to amuse me at the intervals of mental labour».

«O wise Ibrahim, ask what thou wilt, I am bound to furnish all that is necessary for thy solitude.»

«I would fain have, then, a few dancing women», said the philosopher.

«Dancing women!» echoed the treasurer with surprise.

«Dancing women», replied the sage gravely, «a few will

suffice, for I am an old man and a philosopher of simple habits and easily satisfied. Let them, however, be young and fair to look upon, for the sight of youth and beauty is refreshing to old age».

While the philosophic Ibrahim Ebn Abu Ajub, passed his time thus sagely in his hermitage, the pacific Aben Habuz carried on furious campaigns in effigy in his tower. It was a glorious thing for an old man like himself of quiet habits to have war made easy and to be enabled to amuse himself in his chamber by brushing away whole armies like so many swarms of flies.

For a time he rioted in the indulgence of his humours and even taunted and insulted his neighbours to induce them to make incursions, but by degrees they grew wary from repeated disasters, until no one ventured to invade his territories. For many months the bronze horseman remained on the peace establishment with his lance elevated in the air and the worthy old monarch began to repine at the want of his accustomed sport and to grow peevish at his monotonous tranquillity.

At length one day, the talismanic horseman veered suddenly round and lowering his lance made a dead point towards the mountains of Guadix. Aben Habuz hastened to his tower, but the magic table in that direction remained quiet; not a single warrior was in motion. Perplexed at the circumstance, he sent forth a troop of horse to scour the mountains and reconnoitre. They returned after three days' absence.

«We have searched every mountain pass», said they, «but not a helm or spear was stirring. All that we have found in the course of our foray was a Christian damsel of surpassing beauty, sleeping at noontide beside a fountain, whom we have brought away captive».

«A damsel of surpassing beauty!» exclaimed Aben Habuz, his eyes gleaming with animation, «let her be conducted into my presence».

The beautiful damsel was accordingly conducted into his presence. She was arrayed with all the luxury of ornament that had prevailed among the Gothic Spaniards at the time of the Arabian conquest. Pearls of dazzling whiteness were entwined with her raven tresses and jewels sparkled on her forehead, rivalling the lustre of her eyes. Around her neck was a golden chain, to which was suspended a silver lyre which hung by her side.

The flashes of her dark refulgent eye were like sparks of fire on the withered, yet combustible, heart of Aben Habuz; the swimming voluptuousness of her gait made his senses reel. «Fairest of women» cried he, with rapture, «who and what art thou?»

«The daughter of one of the Gothic princes, who but lately ruled over this land. The armies of my father have been destroyed as if by magic among these mountains; he has been driven into exile, and his daughter is a captive.»

«Beware, O King!» whispered Ibrahim Ebn Abu Ajub, «this may be one of those northern sorceresses of whom we have heard, who assume the most seductive forms to beguile the unwary. Methinks I read witchcraft in her eye, and sorcery in every movement. Doubtless this is the enemy pointed out by the talisman».

«Son of Abu Ajub», replied the King, «thou art a wise man, I grant, a conjurer for aught I know, but thou art little versed in the ways of woman. In that knowledge will I yield to no man, no, not to the wise Solomon himself notwithstanding the number of his wives and concubines. As to this damsel, I see no harm in her; she is fair to look upon and finds favour in my eyes».

«Hearken, O King!» replied the astrologer. «I have given thee many victories by means of my talisman, but have never shared any of the spoil. Give me then this stray captive to solace me in my solitude with her silver lyre. If she be indeed a sorceress, I have counter spells that set her charms at defiance.»

«What! more women!» cried Aben Habuz. «Hast thou not already dancing-women enough to solace thee?»

«Dancing-women have I, it is true, but no singing-women. I would fain have a little minstrelsy, to refresh my mind when weary with the toils of study.»

«A truce with thy hermit cravings», said the King impatiently. «This damsel have I marked for my own. I see much comfort in her, even such comfort as David, the father of Solomon the Wise, found in the society of Abishag the Shunammite.»

Further solicitations and remonstrances of the astrologer only provoked a more peremptory reply from the monarch and they parted in high displeasure.

The sage shut himself up in his hermitage to brood over his disappointment; ere he departed, however, he gave the King one more warning to beware of his dangerous captive. But where is the old man in love that will listen to counsel? Aben Habuz resigned himself to the full sway of his passion. His only study was how to render himself amiable in the eyes of the Gothic beauty. He had not youth to recommend him, it is true, but then he had riches, and when a lover is old, he is generally generous. The Zacatín of Granada was ransacked for the most precious merchandise of the East; silks, jewels, precious gems, exquisite perfumes, all that Asia and Africa yielded of rich and rare, were lavished upon the princess. All kinds of spectacles and festivities were devised for her entertainment; minstrelsy, dancing, tournaments, bull-fights. Granada for a time was a scene of perpetual pageants. The Gothic princess regarded all this splendour with the air of one accustomed to magnificence. She received everything as an homage due to her rank or rather to her beauty, for beauty is more lofty in its exactions even than rank. Nay, she seemed to take a secret pleasure in exciting the monarch to expenses that made his treasury shrink and then treating his extravagant generosity as a mere matter of course. With all his assiduity and munificence, also, the venerable lover could not flatter himself that he had made any impression on her heart. She never frowned on him, it is true, but then she never smiled. Whenever he began to plead his passion, she struck her silver lyre. There was a mystic charm in the sound. In an instant the monarch began to nod; a drowsiness stole over him and he gradually sank into a sleep, from which he awoke wonderfully refreshed, but perfectly cooled for the time of his passion. This was very baffling to his suit, but then these slumbers were accompanied by agreeable dreams that completely enthralled the senses of the drowsy lover; so he continued to dream on, while all Granada scoffed at his infatuation and groaned at the treasures lavished for a song.

At length a danger burst on the head of Aben Habuz, against which his talisman yielded him no warning. An insurrection broke out in his very capital; his palace was surrounded by an armed rabble who menaced his life and the life of his Christian paramour. A spark of his ancient warlike spirit was awakened in the breast of the monarch. At the head of a handful of his guards he sallied forth, put the rebels to flight and crushed the insurrection in the bud.

When quiet was again restored, he sought the astrologer who still remained shut up in his hermitage, chewing the bitter cud of resentment.

Aben Habuz approached him with a conciliatory tone. «O wise son of Abu Ajub», said he, «well didst thou predict dangers to me from this captive beauty; tell me then thou who art so quick at foreseeing peril what I should do to avert it.»

«Put from thee the infidel damsel who is the cause.»

«Sooner would I part with my kingdom», cried Aben Habuz.

128

Patio
de
Leon

«Thou art in danger of losing both», replied the astrologer.

«Be not harsh and angry, O most profound of philosophers; consider the double distress of a monarch and a lover, and devise some means of protecting me from the evils by which I am menaced. I care not for grandeur, I care not for power. I languish only for repose; would that I had some quiet retreat where I might take refuge from the world and all its cares and pomps and troubles, and devote the remainder of my days to tranquillity and love!»

The astrologer regarded him for a moment from under his bushy eyebrows.

«And what wouldst thou give, if I could provide thee such a retreat?»

«Thou shouldst name thy own reward; and whatever it might be, if within the scope of my power, as my soul liveth, it should be thine.»

«Thou hast heard, O King, of the garden of Irem, one of the prodigies of Arabia the happy?»

«I have heard of that garden; it is recorded in the Koran, even in the chapter entitled 'The Dawn of Day'. I have, moreover, heard marvellous things related of it by pilgrims who had been to Mecca, but I considered them wild fables, such as travellers are wont to tell who have visited remote countries.»

«Discredit not, O King, the tales of travellers», rejoined the astrologer gravely, «for they contain precious rarities of knowledge brought from the ends of the earth. As to the palace and garden of Irem, what is generally told of them is true; I have seen them with mine own eyes. Listen to my adventure, for it has a bearing upon the object of your request.

«In my younger days, when a mere Arab of the desert, I tended my father's camels. In traversing the Desert of Aden, one of them strayed from the rest and was lost. I searched after it for several days, but in vain, until wearied and faint

I laid myself down one noontide and slept under a palm-tree by the side of a scanty well. When I awoke, I found myself at the gate of a city. I entered and beheld noble streets and squares and market-places, but all were silent and without an inhabitant. I wandered on until I came to a sumptuous palace with a garden, adorned with fountains and fish-ponds and groves and flowers and orchards laden with delicious fruit, but still no one was to be seen. Upon which, appalled at this loneliness, I hastened to depart and after issuing forth at the gate of the city, I turned to look upon the place, but it was no longer to be seen, nothing but the silent desert extended before my eyes.

«In the neighbourhood I met with an aged dervish, learned in the traditions and secrets of the land, and related to him what had befallen me. 'This' said he, 'is the far-famed garden of Irem, one of the wonders of the desert. It only appears at times to some wanderer like thyself, gladdening him with the sight of towers and palaces and garden walls overhung with richly-laden fruit trees, and then vanishes, leaving nothing but a lonely desert. And this is the story of it. In old times, when this country was inhabited by the Addites, King Sheddad, the son of Ad, the great grandson of Noah, founded here a splendid city. When it was finished and he saw its grandeur, his heart was puffed up with pride and arrogance, and he determined to build a royal palace with gardens that should rival all that was related in the Koran of the celestial paradise. But the curse of heaven fell upon him for his presumption. He and his subjects were swept from the earth, and his splendid city and palace and gardens were laid under a perpetual spell that hides them from the human sight, excepting that they are seen at intervals, by way of keeping his sin in perpetual remembrance.

«This story, O King, and the wonders I had seen, ever dwelt in my mind, and in after years, when I had been in

Egypt and was possessed of the book of knowledge of Solomon the Wise, I determined to return and revisit the garden of Irem. I did so and found it revealed to my instructed sight. I took possession of the palace of Sheddad and passed several days in his mock paradise. The genii who watch over the place were obedient to my magic power and revealed to me the spells by which the whole garden had been, as it were, conjured into existence, and by which it was rendered invisible. Such a palace and garden, O King, can I make for thee, even here, on the mountain above thy city. Do I not know all the secret spells? And am I not in possession of the book of knowledge of Solomon the Wise?»

«O wise son of Abu Ajub!» exclaimed Aben Habuz, trembling with eagerness, «thou art a traveller indeed, and hast seen and learned marvellous things! Contrive me such a paradise and ask any reward, even to the half of my kingdom».

«Alas!» replied the other, «thou knowest I am an old man and a philosopher and easily satisfied; all the reward I ask is the first beast of burden with its load that shall enter the magic portal of the palace».

The monarch gladly agreed to so moderate a stipulation and the astrologer began his work. On the summit of the hill, immediately above his subterranean hermitage, he caused a great gateway or barbican to be erected, opening through the centre of a strong tower.

There was an outer vestibule or porch with a lofty arch and within it a portal secured by massive gates. On the keystone of the portal the astrologer with his own hand wrought the figure of a huge key and on the keystone of the outer arch of the vestibule, which was loftier than that of the portal, he carved a gigantic hand. These were potent talismans, over which he repeated many sentences in an unknown tongue.

When this gateway was finished, he shut himself up for two days in his astrological hall, engaged in secret incantations;

on the third he ascended the hill and passed the whole day on its summit. At a late hour of the night he came down and presented himself before Aben Habuz. «At length, O King», said he, «my labour is accomplished. On the summit of the hill stands one of the most delectable palaces that ever the head of man devised or the heart of man desired. It contains sumptuous halls and galleries, delicious gardens, cool fountains and fragrant baths; in a word, the whole mountain is converted into a paradise. Like the garden of Irem, it is protected by a mighty charm which hides it from the view and search of mortals, excepting such as possess the secret of its talismans».

«Enough!» cried Aben Habuz, joyfully, «to-morrow morning with the first light we will ascend and take possession.» The happy monarch slept but little that night. Scarcely had the rays of the sun begun to play about the snowy summit of the Sierra Nevada, when he mounted his steed and, accompanied only by a few chosen attendants, ascended a steep and narrow road leading up the hill. Beside him on a white palfrey rode the Gothic princess, her whole dress sparkling with jewels, while round her neck was suspended her silver lyre. The astrologer walked on the other side of the King, assisting his steps with his hieroglyphic staff for he never mounted steed of any kind.

Aben Habuz looked to see the towers of the palace brightening above him and the embowered terraces of its gardens stretching along the heights, but as yet nothing of the kind was to be descried. «That is the mystery and safeguard of the place», said the astrologer, «nothing can be discerned until you have passed the spell-bound gateway and been put in possession of the place».

As they approached the gateway, the astrologer paused and pointed out to the King the mystic hand and key carved upon the portal and the arch. «These», said he, «are the talismans which guard the entrance to this paradise. Until yonder hand shall reach down and seize that key, neither mortal power nor magic artifice can prevail against the lord of this mountain».

While Aben Habuz was gazing with open mouth and silent wonder at these mystic talismans, the palfrey of the princess proceeded and bore her in at the portal to the very centre of the barbican.

«Behold», cried the astrologer, «my promised reward, the first animal with its burden that should enter the magic gateway».

Aben Habuz smiled at what he considered a pleasantry of the ancient man, but when he found him to be in earnest, his grey beard trembled with indignation.

«Son of Abu Ajub», said he sternly, «what equivocation is this? Thou knowest the meaning of my promise: the first beast of burden with its load that should enter this portal. Take the strongest mule in my stables, load it with the most precious things of my treasury and it is thine, but dare not to raise thy thoughts to her who is the delight of my heart».

«What need I of wealth?» cried the astrologer scornfully, «have I not the book of knowledge of Solomon the Wise, and through it the command of the secret treasures of the earth? The princess is mine by right; thy royal word is pledged. I claim her as my own».

The princess looked down haughtily from her palfrey and a light smile of scorn curled her rosy lip at this dispute between two grey-beards for the possession of youth and beauty. The wrath of the monarch got the better of his discretion. «Base son of the desert», cried he, «thou mayest be master of many arts, but know me for thy master and presume not to juggle with thy King».

«My master!» echoed the astrologer, «my King! The monarch of a mole-hill to claim sway over him who possesses the talismans of Solomon! Farewell, Aben Habuz; reign over thy petty kingdom and revel in thy paradise of fools; for me, I will laugh at thee in my philosophic retirement».

So saying, he seized the bridle of the palfrey, smote the earth with his staff and sank with the Gothic princess through the centre of the barbican. The earth closed over them and no trace remained of the opening by which they had descended.

Aben Habuz was struck dumb for a time with astonishment. Recovering himself, he ordered a thousand workmen to dig with pickaxe and spade into the ground where the astrologer had disappeared. They digged and digged, but in vain; the flinty bosom of the hill resisted their implements or, if they did penetrate a little way, the earth filled in again as fast as they threw it out. Aben Habuz sought the mouth of the cavern at the foot of the hill, leading to the subterranean palace of the astrologer, but it was nowhere to be found. Where once had been an entrance, was now a solid surface of primeval rock. With the disappearance of Ibrahim Ebn Abu Ajub, ceased the benefit of his talismans. The bronze horseman remained fixed with his face turned towards the hill and his spear pointed to the spot where the astrologer had descended as if there still lurked the deadliest foe of Aben Habuz.

From time to time the sound of music and the tones of a female voice could be faintly heard from the bosom of the hill, and a peasant one day brought word to the King, that in the preceding night he had found a fissure in the rock, by which he had crept in, until he looked down into a subterranean hall, in which sat the astrologer on a magnificent divan slumbering and nodding to the silver lyre of the princess, which seemed to hold a magic sway over his senses.

Aben Habuz sought the fissure in the rock, but it was again closed. He renewed the attempt to unearth his rival, but all in vain. The spell of the hand and key was too potent to be counteracted by human power. As to the summit of the mountain, the site of the promised palace and garden, it remained a naked waste; either the boasted elysium was hidden from sight by enchantment or was a mere fable of the astrologer. The world charitably supposed the latter, and some used to call the place «The King's Folly», while others named it «The Fool's Paradise».

To add to the chagrin of Aben Habuz, the neighbours whom he had defied and taunted and cut up at his leisure while master of the talismanic horseman, finding him no longer protected by magic spell, made inroads into his territories from all sides and the remainder of the life of the most pacific of monarchs was a tissue of turmoils.

At length Aben Habuz died and was buried. Ages have since rolled away. The Alhambra has been built on the eventful mountain and in some measure realises the fabled delights of the garden of Irem. The spell-bound gateway still exists entire, protected no doubt by the mystic hand and key, and now forms the Gate of Justice, the grand entrance to the fortress. Under that gateway, it is said, the old astrologer remains in his subterranean hall, nodding on his divan, lulled by the silver lyre of the princess.

The old invalid sentinels who mount guard at the gate hear the strains occasionally in the summer nights and, yielding to their soporific power, doze quietly at their posts. Nay, so drowsy an influence pervades the place, that even those who watch by day may generally be seen nodding on the stone benches of the barbican or sleeping under the neighbouring trees, so that in fact it is the drowsiest military post in all Christendom. All this, say the ancient legends, will endure from age to age. The princess will remain captive to the astrologer and the astrologer bound up in magic slumber by the princess, until the last day, unless the mystic hand shall grasp the fated key and dispel the whole charm of this enchanted mountain.

THE TOWER OF LAS INFANTAS

I N an evening's stroll up a narrow glen, overshadowed by
fig-trees, pomegranates and myrtles, which divides the
lands of the fortress from those of the Generalife, I was struck
with the romantic appearance of a Moorish tower in the outer
wall of the Alhambra, that rose high above the tree-tops and
caught the ruddy rays of the setting sun. A solitary window
at a great height commanded a view of the glen and, as I was
regarding it, a young female looked out with her head adorned with flowers. She was evidently superior to the usual class
of people that inhabit the old towers of the fortress, and this
sudden and picturesque glimpse of her reminded me of the
descriptions of captive beauties in fairy tales. These fanciful
associations of my mind were increased on being informed by
my attendant Mateo that this was the Tower of the Princesses
(*La Torre de las Infantas*), so called from having been,
according to tradition, the residence of the daughters of the
Moorish kings. I have since visited the tower. It is not generally shown to strangers, though well worthy of attention, for
the interior is equal for beauty of architecture and delicacy of
ornament to any part of the palace. The elegance of the central
hall with its marble fountain, its lofty arches and richly fretted dome, the arabesques and stucco-work of the small but
well-proportioned chamber, though injured by time and ne-

glect, all accord with the story of its being anciently the abode of royal beauty.

The little old fairy queen who lives under the staircase of the Alhambra and frequents the evening *tertulias* of Dame Antonia tells some fanciful traditions about three Moorish princesses who were once shut up in this tower by their father, a tyrant king of Granada, and were only permitted to ride out at night about the hills, when no one was permitted to come in their way under pain of death. They still, according to her account, may be seen occasionally when the moon is at the full, riding in lonely places along the mountain side on palfreys richly caparisoned and sparkling with jewels, but they vanish on being spoken to.

But before I relate anything further respecting these princesses, the reader may be anxious to know something about the fair inhabitant of the tower with her head dressed with flowers, who looked out from the lofty window. She proved to be the newly-married spouse of the worthy adjutant of invalids, who, though well stricken in years, has had the courage to take to his bosom a young and buxom Andalusian damsel. May the good old cavalier be happy in his choice and find the Tower of the Princesses a more secure residence for female beauty than it seems to have proved in the time of the Moslem, if we may believe the following legend.

LEGEND

OF

THE THREE BEAUTIFUL PRINCESSES

I N old times there reigned a Moorish king in Granada whose name was Mohamed, to which his subjects added the appellation of *El Hayzari* or «The Left-handed». Some say he was so called on account of his being really more expert with his sinister than his dexter hand; others because he was prone to take everything by the wrong end or in other words to mar wherever he meddled. Certain it is either through misfortune or mismanagement, he was continually in trouble; thrice was he driven from his throne and on one occasion barely escaped to Africa with his life in the disguise of a fisherman. Still he was as brave as he was blundering and, though left-handed, wielded his scimitar to such purpose that he each time reestablished himself upon his throne by dint of hard fighting. Instead, however, of learning wisdom from adversity, he hardened his neck and stiffened his left arm in wilfulness. The evils of a public nature which he thus brought upon himself and his kingdom may be learned by those who will delve into the Arabian annals of Granada; the present legend deals but with his domestic policy.

As this Mohamed was one day riding forth with a train

of his courtiers by the foot of the mountain of Elvira, he met a band of horsemen returning from a foray into the land of the Christians. They were conducting a long string of mules laden with spoil and many captives of both sexes, among whom the monarch was struck with the appearance of a beautiful damsel, richly attired, who sat weeping on a low palfrey and heeded not the consoling words of a *dueña* who rode beside her.

The monarch was struck with her beauty and, on inquiring of the captain of the troop, found that she was the daughter of the *alcaide* of a frontier fortress that had been surprised and sacked in the course of the foray. Mohamed claimed her as his royal share of the booty and had her conveyed to his harem in the Alhambra. There everything was devised to soothe her melancholy and the monarch, more and more enamoured, sought to make her his queen. The Spanish maid at first repulsed his addresses—he was an infidel; he was the open foe of her country; what was worse, he was stricken in years!

The monarch, finding his assiduities of no avail, determined to enlist in his favour the *dueña* who had been captured with the lady. She was an Andalusian by birth, whose Christian name is forgotten, being mentioned in Moorish legends by no other appellation than that of the discreet Kadiga, and discreet in truth she was, as her whole history makes evident. No sooner had the Moorish king held a little private conversation with her than she saw at once the cogency of his reasoning and undertook his cause with her young mistress.

«Go to, now!» cried, she «what is there in all this to weep and wail about? Is it not better to be mistress of this beautiful palace with all its gardens and fountains than to be shut up within your father's old frontier tower? As to this Mohamed being an infidel, what is that to the purpose? You marry him, not his religion; and if he is waxing a little old, the sooner will you be a widow and mistress of yourself. At

140

any rate, you are in his power, and must either be a queen or a slave. When in the hands of a robber, it is better to sell one's merchandise for a fair price than to have it taken by main force».

The arguments of the discreet Kadiga prevailed. The Spanish lady dried her tears and became the spouse of Mohamed the Left-handed; she even conformed in appearance to the faith of her royal husband and her discreet *dueña* immediately became a zealous convert to the Moslem doctrines. It was then the latter received the Arabian name of Kadiga and was permitted to remain in the confidential employ of her mistress.

In due process of time the Moorish king was made the proud and happy father of three lovely daughters, all born at a birth; he could have wished they had been sons, but consoled himself with the idea that three daughters at a birth were pretty well for a man somewhat stricken in years and left-handed!

As usual with all Moslem monarchs, he summoned his astrologers on this happy event. They cast the nativities of the three princesses and shook their heads. «Daughters, O King» said they, «are always precarious property, but these will most need your watchfulness when they arrive at a marriageable age; at that time gather them under your wings, and trust them to no other guardianship».

Mohamed the Left-handed was acknowledged to be a wise king by his courtiers and was certainly so considered by himself. The prediction of the astrologers caused him but little disquiet, trusting to his ingenuity to guard his daughters and outwit the Fates.

The threefold birth was the last matrimonial trophy of the monarch; his queen bore him no more children and died within a few years, bequeathing her infant daughters to his love and to the fidelity of the discreet Kadiga.

Many years had yet to elapse before the princesses would

arrive at that period of danger—the marriageable age. «It is good, however, to be cautious in time», said the shrewd Monarch; so he determined to have them reared in the royal Castle of Salobreña. This was a sumptuous palace incrusted, as it were, in a powerful Moorish fortress, on the summit of a hill that overlooks the Mediterranean sea. It was a royal retreat, in which the Moslem monarchs shut up such of their relations as might endanger their safety, allowing them all kinds of luxuries and amusements, in the midst of which they passed their lives in voluptuous indolence.

Here the princesses remained, immured from the world, but surrounded by enjoyments and attended by female slaves who anticipated their wishes. They had delightful gardens for their recreation, filled with the rarest fruits and flowers, with aromatic groves and perfumed baths. On three sides the castle looked down upon a rich valley, enamelled with all kinds of culture and bounded by the lofty Alpuxarra Mountains; on the other side it overlooked the broad sunny sea.

In this delicious abode, in a propitious climate and under a cloudless sky, the three princesses grew up into wondrous beauty, but, though all reared alike, they gave early tokens of diversity of character. Their names were Zayda, Zorayda and Zorahayda, and such was their order of seniority, for there had been precisely three minutes between their births.

Zayda, the eldest, was of an intrepid spirit and took the lead of her sisters in everything, as she had done in entering first into the world. She was curious and inquisitive and fond of getting at the bottom of things.

Zorayda had a great feeling for beauty, which was the reason, no doubt, of the delighting to regard her own image in a mirror or a fountain, and of her fondness for flowers and jewels and other tasteful ornaments.

As to Zorahayda, the youngest, she was soft and timid and extremely sensitive, with a vast deal of disposable tenderness, as was evident from her number of pet-flowers and pet-birds and pet-animals, all of which she cherished with the fondest care. Her amusements, too, were of a gentle nature and mixed up with musing and reverie. She would sit for hours in a balcony, gazing on the sparkling stars of a summer's night or on the sea when lit up by the moon, and at such times the song of a fisherman, faintly heard from the beach or the notes of a Moorish flute from some gliding bark, sufficed to elevate her feelings into ecstasy. The least uproar of the elements, however, filled her with dismay, and a clap of thunder was enough to throw her into a swoon.

Years rolled on smoothly and serenely; the discreet Kadiga, to whom the princesses were confided, was faithful to her trust and attended them with unremitting care.

The Castle of Salobreña, as has been said, was built upon a hill on the sea-coast. One of the exterior walls straggled down the profile of the hill, until it reached a jutting rock overhanging the sea with a narrow sandy beach at its foot, laved by the rippling billows. A small watch-tower on this rock had been fitted up as a pavilion with latticed windows to admit the sea-breeze. Here the princesses used to pass the sultry hours of mid-day.

The curious Zayda was one day seated at one of the windows of the pavilion, as her sisters reclining on ottomans were taking the *siesta* or noontide slumber. Her attention had been attracted to a galley which came coasting along with measured strokes of the oar. As it drew near, she observed that it was filled with armed men. The galley anchored at the foot of the tower; a number of Moorish soldiers landed on the narrow beach, conducting several Christian prisoners. The curious Zayda awakened her sisters and all three peeped cautiously through the close jalousies of the lattice which screened them from sight. Among the prisoners were three Spanish cavaliers, richly dressed. They were in the flower of youth and of noble presence, and the lofty manner in which they carried themselves, though loaded with chains and surrounded with enemies, bespoke the grandeur of their souls. The princesses gazed with intense and breathless interest. Cooped up as they had been in this castle among female attendants, seeing nothing of the male sex but black slaves or the rude fishermen of the sea-coast, it is not to be wondered at that the appearance of three gallant cavaliers in the pride of youth and manly beauty should produce some commotion in their bosoms.

«Did ever nobler being tread the earth than that cavalier in crimson?» cried Zayda, the eldest of the sisters. «See how proudly he bears himself, as though all around him were his slaves!»

«But notice that one in green!» exclaimed Zorayda. «What grace! what elegance! what spirit!»

The gentle Zorahayda said nothing, but she secretly gave preference to the cavalier in blue.

The princesses remained gazing until the prisoners were out of sight; then heaving long-drawn sighs, they turned round looked at each other for a moment and sat down, musing and pensive on their ottomans.

The discreet Kadiga found them in this situation; they related to her what they had seen, and even the withered heart of the *dueña* was warmed. «Poor youths!» exclaimed she, «I'll warrant their captivity makes many a fair and highborn lady's heart ache in their native land. Ah! my children, you have little idea of the life these cavaliers lead in their own country. Such prankling at tournaments! Such devotion to the ladies! Such courting and serenading!»

The curiosity of Zayda was fully aroused; she was insatiable in her inquiries and drew from the *dueña* the most animated pictures of the scenes of her youthful days and native land. The beautiful Zorayda bridled up and slyly regarded herself in a mirror, when the theme turned upon the charms of

the Spanish ladies; while Zorahayda suppressed a struggling sigh at the mention of moonlight serenades.

Every day the curious Zayda renewed her inquiries and every day the sage *dueña* repeated her stories, which were listened to with profound interest, though with frequent sighs, by her gentle auditors. The discreet old woman at length awakened to the mischief she might be doing. She had been accustomed to think of the princesses only as children, but they had imperceptibly ripened beneath her eye and now bloomed before her three lovely damsels of the marriageable age. 'It is time, thought the *dueña,* to give notice to the king'.

Mohamed the Left-handed was seated one morning on a divan in one of the cool halls of the Alhambra, when a slave arrived from the fortress of Salobreña with a message from the sage Kadiga, congratulating him on the anniversary of his daughters' birth-day. The slave at the same time presented a delicate little basket decorated with flowers within which on a couch of vine and fig-leaves lay a peach, an apricot and a nectarine with their bloom and down and dewy sweetness upon them, and all in the early stage of tempting ripeness. The monarch was versed in the Oriental language of fruit and flowers, and readily divined the meaning of this emblematical offering.

«So», said he, «the critical period pointed out by the astrologers is arrived; my daughters are at a marriageable age. What is to be done? They are shut up from the eyes of men; they are under the eyes of the discreet Kadiga—all very good—but still they are not under my own eye, as was prescribed by the astrologers; I must gather them under my wing and trust to no other guardianship».

So saying, he ordered that a tower of the Alhambra should be prepared for their reception, and departed at the head of his guards for the fortress of Salobreña to conduct them home in person.

About three years had elapsed since Mohamed had beheld his daughters and he could scarcely credit his eyes at the wonderful change which that small space of time had made in their appearance. During the interval they had passed that wondrous boundary line in female life which separates the crude, uniformed and thoughtless girl from the blooming, blushing, meditative woman. It is like passing from the flat, bleak, uninteresting plain of La Mancha, to the voluptuous valleys and swelling hills of Andalusia.

Zayda was tall and finely formed with a lofty demeanour and a penetrating eye. She entered with a stately and decided step, and made a profound reverence to Mohamed, treating him more as her sovereign than her father. Zorayda was of the middle height with an alluring look and swimming gait, and a sparkling beauty heightened by the assistance of the toilette. She approached her father with a smile, kissed his hand and saluted him with several stanzas from a popular Arabian poet with which the monarch was delighted. Zorahayda was shy and timid, smaller than her sisters and with a beauty of that tender beseeching kind which looks for fondness and protection. She was little fitted to command like her elder sister or to dazzle like the second, but was rather formed to creep to the bosom of manly affection, to nestle within it and be content. She drew near her father with a timid and almost faltering step, and would have taken his hand to kiss, but on looking up into his face and seeing it beaming with a paternal smile, the tenderness of her nature broke forth and she threw herself upon his neck.

Mohamed the Left-handed surveyed his blooming daughters with mingled pride and perplexity, for while he exulted in their charms, he bethought himself of the prediction of the astrologers. «Three daughters! three daughters!» muttered he repeatedly to himself, «and all of a marriageable age! Here's tempting Hesperian fruit, that requires a dragon watch!»

He prepared for his return to Granada by sending heralds before him, commanding every one to keep out of the road by which he was to pass, and that all doors and windows should be closed at the approach of the princesses. This done, he set forth, escorted by a troop of black horsemen of hideous aspect and clad in shining armour.

The princesses rode beside the king closely veiled on beautiful white palfreys with velvet caparisons embroidered with gold and sweeping the ground; the bits and stirrups were of gold, and the silken bridles adorned with pearls and precious stones. The palfreys were covered with little silver bells that made the most musical tinkling as they ambled gently along. Woe to the unlucky wight, however, who lingered in the way when he heard the tinkling of these bells!—the guards were ordered to cut him down without mercy.

The cavalcade was drawing near to Granada, when it overtook, on the banks of the river Xenil, a small body of Moorish soldiers with a convoy of prisoners. It was too late for the soldiers to get out of the way, so they threw themselves on their faces on the earth, ordering their captives to do the like. Among the prisoners were the three identical cavaliers whom the princesses had seen from the pavilion. They either did not understand or were too haughty to obey the order and remained standing and gazing upon the cavalcade as it approached.

The ire of the monarch was kindled at this flagrant defiance of his orders. Drawing his scimitar and pressing forward, he was about to deal a left-handed blow that would have been fatal to at least one of the gazers, when the princesses crowded round him and implored mercy for the prisoners; even the timid Zorayda forgot her shyness and became eloquent on their behalf. Mohamed paused with uplifted scimitar, when the captain of the guard threw himself at his feet. «Let not your highness», said he, «do a deed that may cause great scandal throughout the kingdom. These are three brave and noble Spanish knights who have been taken in battle, fighting like lions; they are of high birth and may bring great ransoms». —«Enough!»» said the king; «I will spare their lives, but punish their audacity—let them be taken to the Vermilion Towers and put to hard labour».

Mohamed was making one of his usual left-handed blunders. In the tumult and agitation of this blustering scene, the veils of the three princesses had been thrown back and the radiance of their beauty revealed, and in prolonging the parley, the king had given that beauty time to have its full effect. In those days people fell in love much more suddenly than at present, as all ancient stories make manifest; it is not a matter of wonder, therefore, that the hearts of the three cavaliers were completely captured, especially as gratitude was added to their admiration; it is a little singular, however, though no less certain, that each of them was enraptured with a several beauty. As to the princesses, they were more than ever struck with the noble demeanour of the captives and cherished in their breasts all that they had heard of their valour and noble lineage.

The cavalcade resumed its march; the three princesses rode pensively along on their tinkling palfreys, now and then stealing a glance behind in search of the Christian captives, and the latter were conducted to their allotted prison in the Vermilion Towers.

The residence provided for the princesses was one of the most dainty that fancy could devise. It was in a tower somewhat apart from the main palace of the Alhambra, though connected with it by the main wall that encircled the whole summit of the hill. On one side it looked into the interior of the fortress, and had at its foot a small garden filled with the rarest flowers. On the other side it overlooked a deep embowered ravine that separated the grounds of the Alhambra from those of the Generalife. The interior of the tower was divided into small fairy apartments, beautifully ornamented in the light Arabian style, surrounding a lofty hall, the vaulted roof of which rose almost to the summit of the tower. The walls and ceiling of the hall were adorned with arabesques and fret-work, sparkling with gold and with brilliant pencilling. In the centre of the marble pavement was an alabaster fountain, set round with aromatic shrubs and flowers, and throwing up a jet of water that cooled the whole edifice and had a lulling sound. Round the hall were suspended cages of gold and silver wire, containing singing-birds of the finest plumage or sweetest note.

The princesses had been represented as always cheerful when in the Castle of Salobreña; the king had expected to see them enraptured with the Alhambra. To his surprise, however, they began to pine and grow melancholy and dissatisfied with everything around them. The flowers yielded them no fragance, the song of the nightingale disturbed their night's rest, and they were out of all patience with the alabaster fountain with its eternal dropdrop and splash-splash from morning till night and from night till morning.

The king who was somewhat of a testy, tyrannical disposition took this at first in high dudgeon, but he reflected that his daughters had arrived at an age when the female mind expands and its desires augment. «They are no longer children», said he to himself «they are women grown, and require suitable objects to interest them». He put in requisition, therefore, all the dress-makers and the jewellers and the artificers in gold and silver throughout the Zacatín of Granada, and the princesses were overwhelmed with robes of silk and of tissue and of brocade, cashmere shawls and necklaces of pearls and diamonds, rings and bracelets and anklets and all manner of precious things.

All, however, was of no avail; the princesses continued pale and languid in the midst of their finery, and looked like three blighted rose-buds, drooping from one stalk. The king was at his wits' end. He had in general a laudable confidence in his own judgment, and never took advice. «The whims and caprices of three marriageable damsels, however, are sufficient», said he, «to puzzle the shrewdest head». So for once in his life he called in the aid of counsel.

The person to whom he applied was the experienced *dueña*.

«Kadiga», said the king, «I know you to be one of the most discreet women in the whole world, as well as one of the most trustworthy; for these reasons I have always continued you about the persons of my daughters. Fathers cannot be too wary in whom they repose such confidence; I now wish you to find out the secret malady that is preying upon the princesses and to devise some means of restoring them to health and cheerfulness».

Kadiga promised implicit obedience. In fact she knew more of the malady of the princesses than they did themselves. Shutting herself up with them, however, she endeavoured to insinuate herself into their confidence.

«My dear children, what is the reason you are so dismal and downcast in so beautiful a place where you have everything that heart can wish?»

The princesses looked vacantly round the apartment and sighed.

«What more then would you have? Shall I get you the wonderful parrot that talks all languages and is the delight of Granada?»

«Odious!» exclaimed the princess Zayda. «A horrid, screaming bird that chatters words without ideas; one must be without brains to tolerate such a pest.»

«Shall I send for a monkey from the rock of Gibraltar to divert you with his antics?»

«A monkey, faugh!» cried Zorayda; «the detestable mimic of man. I hate the nauseous animal».

«What say you to the famous black singer Casem, from the royal harem in Morocco? They say he has a voice as fine as a woman's.»

«I am terrified at the sight of these black slaves», said the delicate Zorahayda, «besides, I have lost all relish for music.»

«Ah! my child, you would not say so», replied the old woman slyly, «had you heard the music I heard last evening from the three Spanish cavaliers, whom we met on our journey. But, bless me, children! what is the matter that you blush so and are in such a flutter?»

«Nothing, nothing, good mother; pray proceed.»

«Well, as I was passing by the Vermilion Towers last evening, I saw the three cavaliers resting after their day's labour. One was playing on the guitar, so gracefully, and the others sang by turns, and they did it in such style that the very guards seemed like statues or men enchanted. Allah forgive me! I could not help being moved at hearing the songs of my native country. And then to see three such noble and handsome youths in chains and slavery!»

Here the kind-hearted old woman could not restrain her tears.

«Perhaps, mother, you could manage to procure us a sight of these cavaliers», said Zayda.

«I think», said Zorayda, «a little music would be quite reviving».

The timid Zorahayda said nothing, but threw her arms round the neck of Kadiga.

«Mercy on me!» exclaimed the discreet old woman, «what are you talking of, my children? Your father would be the death of us all if he heard of such a thing. To be sure, these cavaliers are evidently well-bred and high-minded youths, but what of that? They are the enemies of our faith and you must not even think of them but with abhorrence».

There is an admirable intrepidity in the female will, particularly when about the marriageable age, which is not to be deterred by dangers and prohibitions. The princesses hung round their old *dueña* and coaxed and entreated and declared that a refusal would break their hearts.

What could she do?—She was certainly the most discreet old woman in the whole world and one of the most faithful servants to the king, but was she to see three beautiful princesses break their hearts for the mere tinkling of a guitar? Besides, though she had been so long among the Moors and changed her faith in imitation of her mistress, like a trusty follower, yet she was a Spaniard born and had the lingerings of Christianity in her heart. So she set about to contrive how the wish of the princesses might be gratified.

The Christian captives, confined in the Vermilion Towers, were under the charge of a big-whiskered broad-shouldered *renegado,* called Hussein Baba, who was reputed to have a most itching palm. She went to him privately and, slipping a broad piece of gold into his hand, «Hussein Baba», said she, «my mistresses, the three princesses who are shut up in the tower and in sad want of amusement have heard of the musical talents of the three Spanish cavaliers and are desirous of hearing a specimen of their skill. I am sure you are too kind-hearted to refuse them so innocent a gratification».

«What! and to have my head set grinning over the gate of my own tower! for that would be the reward, if the king should discover it.»

«No danger of anything of the kind; the affair may be managed so that the whim of the princesses may be gratified and their father be never the wiser. You know the deep ravine outside of the walls, that passes immediately below the tower. Put the three Christians to work there, and at the intervals of their labour let them play and sing, as if for their own recreation. In this way the princesses will be able to hear them from the windows of the tower and you may be sure of their paying well for your compliance.»

As the good old woman concluded her harangue, she kindly pressed the rough hand of the *renegado* and left within it another piece of gold.

Her eloquence was irresistible. The very next day the three cavaliers were put to work in the ravine. During the noontide heat when their fellow-labourers were sleeping in the shade and the guard nodding drowsily at his post, they seated themselves among the herbage at the foot of the tower and sang a Spanish roundelay to the accompaniment of the guitar.

The glen was deep, the tower was high, but their voices rose distinctly in the stillness of the summer noon. The princesses listened from their balcony; they had been taught the Spanish language by their *dueña* and were moved by the tenderness of the song. The discreet Kadiga, on the contrary, was terribly shocked. «Allah preserve us!» cried she, «they are singing a love ditty, addressed to yourselves. Did ever mortal hear of such audacity? I will run to the slave-master and have them soundly bastinadoed».

«What! bastinado such gallant cavaliers and for singing so charmingly!» The three beautiful princesses were filled with horror at the idea. With all her virtuous indignation the good old woman was of a placable nature and easily appeased. Besides, the music seemed to have a beneficial effect upon her young mistresses. A rosy bloom had already come to their cheeks and their eyes began to sparkle. She made no further objection therefore to the amorous ditty of the cavaliers.

When it was finished the princesses remained silent for a time; at length Zorayda took up a lute and with a sweet, though faint and trembling voice, warbled a little Arabian air, the burden of which was, «The rose is concelaed among her leaves, but she listens with delight to the song of the nightingale».

From this time forward the cavaliers worked almost daily in the ravine. The considerate Hussein Baba became more and more indulgent, and daily more prone to sleep at his post. For some time a vague intercourse was kept up by popular songs and romances which in some measure responded to each other and breathed the feelings of the parties. By degrees the princesses showed themselves at the balcony, when they could do so without being perceived by the guards. They conversed with the cavaliers also by means of flowers, with the symbolical language of which they were mutually acquainted; the difficulties of their intercourse added to its charms and strengthened the passion they had so singularly conceived, for love delights to struggle with difficulties and thrives the most hardily on the scantiest soil.

The change effected in the looks and spirits of the princesses by this secret intercourse surprised and gratified the lefthanded king, but no one was more elated than the discreet Kadiga who considered it all owing to her able management.

At length there was an interruption in this telegraphic correspondence; for several days the cavaliers ceased to make their appearance in the glen. The three beautiful princesses looked out from the tower in vain. In vain they stretched their swanlike necks from the balcony. In vain they sang like captive nightingales in their cage. Nothing was to be seen of their Christian lovers; not a note responded from the groves. The discreet Kadiga sallied forth in quest of intelligence and soon returned with a face full of trouble. «Ah, my children!» cried she, «I saw what all this would come to, but you would have your way; you may now hang up your lutes on the willows. The Spanish cavaliers are now ransomed by their families; they are down in Granada and preparing to return to their native country».

The three beautiful princesses were in despair at the tidings. The fair Zayda was indignant at the slight put upon them in thus being deserted without a parting word. Zorayda wrung her hands and cried and looked in the glass and wiped away her tears and cried afresh. The gentle Zorahayda leaned over the balcony and wept in silence, and her tears fell drop by drop among the flowers of the bank where the faithless cavaliers had so often been seated.

The discreet Kadiga did all in her power to soothe their sorrow. «Take comfort, my children», said she, «this is nothing when you are used to it. This is the way of the world. Ah! when you are as old as I am, you will know how to value these men. I'll warrant these cavaliers have their loves among the Spanish beauties of Cordova and Seville, and will soon be serenading under their balconies and thinking no more of the Moorish beauties in the Alhambra. Take comfort therefore, my children, and drive them from your hearts».

The comforting words of the discreet Kadiga only redoubled the distress of the three princesses and for two days they continued inconsolable. On the morning of the third, the good old woman entered their apartment, all ruffling with indignation.

«Who would have believed such insolence in mortal man!» exclaimed she, as soon as she could find words to express herself, «but I am rightly served for having connived at this deception of your worthy father. Never talk more to me of your Spanish cavaliers».

«Why, what has happened, good Kadiga?» exclaimed the princesses, in breathless anxiety.

«What has happened! Treason has happened! or, what is almost as bad, treason has been proposed, and to me, the most faithful of subjects, the trustiest of *dueñas!* Yes, my children, the Spanish cavaliers have dared to tamper with me, that I should persuade you to fly with them to Cordova and become their wives!»

Here the excellent old woman covered her face with her hands and gave way to a violent burst of grief and indignation. The three beautiful princesses turned pale and red, pale and red, and trembled and looked down and cast shy looks at each other, but said nothing. Meantime the old woman sat rocking backward and forward in violent agitation, and now and then breaking out into exclamations. «That ever I should live to be so insulted!—I, the most faithful of servants!»

At length the eldest princess who had most spirit and always took the lead approached her and laying her hand upon her shoulder, «Well, mother», said she, «supposing we were willing to fly with these Christian cavaliers, is such a thing possible?»

The good old woman paused suddenly in her grief, and looking up, «Possible!» echoed she, «to be sure, it is possible. Have not the cavaliers already bribed Hussein Baba, the *renegado* captain of the guard, and arranged the whole plan? But, then, to think of deceiving your father, your father who has placed such confidence in me!» Here the worthy woman gave way to a fresh burst of grief and began again to rock backward and forward, and to wring her hands.

«But our father never placed any confidence in us», said the eldest princess, «but has trusted to bolts and bars, and treated us as captives».

«Why, that is true enough», replied the old woman, again pausing in her grief; «he has indeed treated you most unreasonably, keeping you shut up here to waste your bloom in a moping old tower, like roses to wither in a flower-jar. But, then, to fly from your native land!»

«And is not the land we fly to the native land of our mother where we shall live in freedom? And shall we not each have a youthful husband, in exchange for a severe old father?»

«Why, that again is all very true, and your father, I must confess, is rather tyrannical. But, what, then», relapsing into her grief, «would you leave me behind to bear the brunt of his vengeance?»

«By no means, my good Kadiga; cannot you fly with us?»

«Very true, my child, and, to tell the truth, when I talked the matter over with Hussein Baba, he promised to take care of me, if I would accompany you in your flight. But, then, bethink you, my children, are you willing to renounce the faith of your father?»

«The Christian faith was the original faith of our mother», said the eldest princess, «I am ready to embrace it, and so, I am sure, are my sisters».

«Right again!» exclaimed the old woman, brightening up, «it was the original faith of your mother, and bitterly did she lament on her death-bed that she had renounced it. I promised her then to take care of your souls, and I rejoice to see that they are now in a fair way to be saved. Yes, my children, I too was born a Christian and have remained a Christian in my heart, and am resolved to return to the faith. I have talked on the subject with Hussein Baba who is a Spaniard by birth and comes from a place not far from my native town. He is equally anxious to see his own country and to be reconciled to the Church, and the cavaliers have promised that, if we are disposed to become man and wife, on returning to our native land, they will provide for us handsomely».

In a word, it appeared that this extremely discreet and provident old woman had consulted with the cavaliers and the *renegado,* and had concerted the whole plan of escape. The eldest princess immediately assented to it, and her example, as usual, determined the conduct of her sisters. It is true the youngest hesitated, for she was gentle and timid of soul, and there was a struggle in her bosom between filial feeling and youthful passion; the latter, however, as usual, gained the victory, and with silent tears and stifled sighs she prepared herself for flight.

The rugged hill on which the Alhambra is built, was in old times perforated with subterranean passages, cut through the rock, and leading from the fortress to various parts of the city and to distant sally-ports on the banks of the Darro and the Xenil. They had been constructed at different times by the Moorish Kings, as means of escape from sudden insurrections or of secretly issuing forth on private enterprises. Many of them are now entirely lost, while others remain, partly choked up with rubbish and partly walled up, monuments of the jealous precautions and warlike stratagems of the Moorish government. By one these passages, Hussein Baba had undertaken to conduct the princesses to a sally-port beyond the walls of the city, where the cavaliers were to be ready with fleet steeds to bear the whole party over the borders.

The appointed night arrived; the tower of the princesses had been locked up as usual and the Alhambra was buried in deep sleep. Towards midnight the discreet Kadiga listened from the balcony of a window that looked into the garden. Hussein Baba, the *renegado,* was already below and gave the appointed signal. The *dueña* fastened the end of a ladder of ropes to the balcony, lowered it into the garden and descended. The two eldest princesses followed her with beating hearts; but when it came to the turn of the youngest princess, Zorahayda, she hesitated and trembled. Several times she ventured a delicate little foot upon the ladder and as often drew it back, while her poor little heart fluttered more and more the longer she delayed. She cast a wistful look back into the silken chamber; she had lived in it, to be sure, like a bird in a cage, but within it she was secure. Who could tell what dangers might beset her, should she flutter forth into the wide world! Now she bethought her of her gallant Christian lover and her little foot was instantly upon the ladder, and anon she thought of her father, and shrank back. But fruitless is the attempt to describe the conflict in the bosom of one so young and tender and loving, but so timid and so ignorant of the world.

In vain her sisters implored, the *dueña* scolded and the renegado blasphemed beneath the balcony; the gentle little Moorish maid stood doubting and wavering on the verge of elopement, tempted by the sweetness of the sin, but terrified at its perils.

Every moment increased the danger of discovery. A distant tramp was heard. «The patrols are walking the rounds», cried the *renegado;* «if we linger, we perish. Princess, descend instantly or we leave you».

Zorahayda was for a moment in fearful agitation; then loosening the ladder of ropes with desperate resolution she flung it from the balcony.

«It is decided!» cried she; «flight is now out of my power! Allah guide and bless ye, my dear sisters!»

The two eldest princesses were shocked at the thoughts of leaving her behind and would fain have lingered, but the patrol was advancing; the *renegado* was furious and they were hurried away to the subterraneous passage. They groped their way through a fearful labyrinth, cut through the heart of the mountain, and succeeded in reaching undiscovered an iron gate that opened outside of the walls. The Spanish cavaliers were waiting to receive them, disguised as Moorish soldiers of the guard, commanded by the *renegado*.

The lover of Zorahayda was frantic when he learned that she had refused to leave the tower, but there was no time to waste in lamentations. The two princesses were placed behind their lovers, the discreet Kadiga mounted behind the *renegado,* and all set off at a round pace in the direction of the Pass of Lope which leads through the mountains towards Cordova.

They had not proceeded far when they heard the noise of drums and trumpets from the battlements of the Alhambra.

«Our flight is discovered», said the *renegado*.

«We have fleet steeds, the night is dark and we may distance all pursuit», replied the cavaliers.

They put spurs to their horses and scoured across the Vega. They attained to the foot of the mountain of Elvira which stretches like a promontory into the plain. The *renegado* paused and listened.

«As yet», said he, «there is no one on our traces, we shall make good our escape to the mountains». While he spoke, a pale fire sprang up in a light blaze on the top of the watch-tower of the Alhambra.

«Confusion!» cried the *renegado*, «that fire will put all the guards of the passes on the alert. Away! away! Spur like mad; there is no time to be lost!»

Away they dashed. The clattering of their horses' hoofs echoed from rock to rock, as they swept along the road that skirts the rocky mountain of Elvira. As they galloped on, they beheld that the pale fire of the Alhambra was answered in every direction; light after light blazed on the *atalayas* or watch-towers of the mountains.

«Forward! forward!» cried the *renegado* with many an oath, «to the bridge, to the bridge, before the alarm has reached there!»

They doubled the promontory of the mountains and arrived in sight of the famous Puente de Pinos that crosses a rushing stream often dyed with Christian and Moslem blood. To their confusion, the tower on the bridge blazed with lights and glittered with armed men. The *renegado* pulled up his steed, rose in his stirrups and looked about him for a moment; then beckoning to the cavaliers, he struck off from the road, skirted the river for some distance and dashed into its waters. The cavaliers called upon the princesses to cling to them and did the same. They were borne for some distance down the rapid current; the surges roared round them, but the beautiful prin-

160

cesses clung to their Christian knights and never uttered a complaint. The cavaliers attained the opposite bank in safety, and were conducted by the *renegado* by rude and unfrequented paths and wild *barrancos* through the heart of the mountains, so as to avoid all the regular passes. In a word, they succeeded in reaching the ancient city of Cordova where their restoration to their country and friends was celebrated with great rejoicing, for they were of the noblest families. The beautiful princesses were forthwith received into the bosom of the Church and after being in all due form made regular Christians, were rendered happy wives.

In our hurry to make good the escape of the princesses across the river and up the mountains, we forgot to mention the fate of the discreet Kadiga. She had clung like a cat to Hussein Baba in the scamper across the Vega, screaming at every bound and drawing many an oath from the whiskered *renegado;* but when he prepared to plunge his steed into the river, her terror knew no bounds. «Grasp me not so tightly», cried Hussein Baba, «hold on by my belt and fear nothing». She held firmly with both hands by the leathern belt that girded the broad-backed *renegado,* but when he halted with the cavaliers to take breath on the mountain summit, the *dueña* was no longer to be seen.

«What has become of Kadiga?» cried the princesses in alarm.

«Allah alone knows!» replied the *renegado*, «my belt came loose when in the midst of the river and Kadiga was swept with it down the stream. The will of Allah be done! But it was an embroidered belt and of great price».

There was no time to waste in idle regrets, yet bitterly did the princesses bewail the loss of their discreet counsellor. That excellent old woman, however, did not lose more than half of her nine lives in the stream. A fisherman who was drawing his nets some distance down the stream brought her to land and was not a little astonished at his miraculous draught. What further became of the discreet Kadiga, the legend does not mention; certain it is that she evinced her discretion in never venturing within the reach of Mohamed the Lefthanded.

Almost as little is known of the conduct of that sagacious monarch when he discovered the escape of his daughters and the deceit practised upon him by the most faithful of servants. It was the only instance in which he had called in the aid of counsel and he was never afterwards known to be guilty of a similar weakness. He took good care, however, to guard his remaining daughter who had no disposition to elope. It is thought indeed that she secretly repented having remained behind. Now and then she was seen leaning on the battlements of the tower and looking mournfully towards the mountains in the direction of Cordova, and sometimes the notes of her lute were heard accompanying plaintive ditties, in which she was said to lament the loss of her sisters and her lover, and to bewail her solitary life. She died young and, according to popular rumour, was buried in a vault beneath the tower, and her untimely fate has given rise to more than one traditionary fable.

VISITORS TO THE ALHAMBRA

I T is now nearly three months since I took up my abode in the Alhambra, during which time the progress of the season has wrought many changes. When I first arrived everything was in the freshness of May; the foliage of the trees was still tender and transparent; the pomegranate had not yet shed its brilliant crimson blossoms; the orchards of the Xenil and the Darro were in full bloom; the rocks were hung with wild flowers, and Granada seemed completely surrounded by a wilderness of roses, among which innumerable nightingales sang, not merely in the night, but all day long.

The advance of summer has withered the rose and silenced the nightingale, and the distant country begins to look parched and sunburnt; though a perennial verdure reigns immediately round the city and in the deep narrow valleys at the foot of the snow-capped mountains.

The Alhambra possesses retreats graduated to the heat of the weather, among which the most peculiar is the almost subterranean apartment of the baths. This still retains its ancient Oriental character, though stamped with the touching traces of decline. At the entrance, opening into a small court formerly adorned with flowers, is a hall, moderate in size, but light and graceful in architecture. It is overlooked by a small gallery supported by marble pillars and Morisco arches. An alabaster fountain in the centre of the pavement still throws up a jet of water to cool the place. On each side are deep alcoves with raised platforms, where the bathers after their ablutions reclined on luxurious cushions, soothed to voluptuous repose by the fragrance of the perfumed air and the notes of soft music from the gallery. Beyond this hall are the interior chambers, still more private and retired, where no light is admitted but through small apertures in the vaulted ceilings. Here was the *sanctum sanctorum* of female privacy, where the beauties of the harem indulged in the luxury of the baths. A soft mysterious light reigns through the place; the broken baths are still there and traces of ancient elegance. The prevailing silence and obscurity have made this a favourite resort of bats who nestle during the day in the dark nooks and corners, and on being disturbed, flit mysteriously about the twilight chambers, heightening in an indescribable degree their air of desertion and decay.

In this cool and elegant, though dilapidated retreat which has the freshness and seclusion of a grotto, I have of late passed the sultry hours of the day, emerging towards sunset and bathing or rather swimming at night in the great reservoir of the main court. In this way I have been enabled in a measure to counteract the relaxing and enervating influence of the climate.

My dream of absolute sovereignty, however, is at an end. I was roused from it lately by the report of fire-arms, which reverberated among the towers, as if the castle had been taken by surprise. On sallying forth, I found an old cavalier, with a number of domestics in possession of the Hall of Ambassadors. He was an ancient count who had come up from his palace in Granada to pass a short time in the Alhambra for the benefit of purer air and who, being a veteran and inveterate sportsman, was endeavouring to get an appetite for his breakfast by shooting at swallows from the balconies. It was a harmless amusement, for though by the alertness of his attendants in loading his pieces he was enabled to keep up a brisk fire, I could not accuse him of the death of a single swallow. Nay, the birds themselves seemed to enjoy the sport and to deride his want of skill, skimming in circles close to the balconies and twittering as they darted by.

The arrival of this old gentleman has in some manner changed the aspect of affairs, but has likewise afforded matter for agreeable speculation. We have tacitly shared the empire between us, like the last kings of Granada, excepting that we maintain a most amicable alliance. He reigns absolute over the Court of the Lions and its adjacent halls, while I maintain peaceful possession of the regions of the baths and the little garden of Lindaraxa. We take our meals together under the arcades of the court, where the fountains cool the air and bubbling rills run along the channels of the marble pavement.

In the evening, a domestic circle gathers about the worthy old cavalier. The countess comes up from the city with a favourite daughter about sixteen years of age. Then there are the official dependents of the count, his chaplain, lawyer, his secretary, his steward and other officers and agents of his extensive possessions. Thus he holds a kind of domestic court, where every person seeks to contribute to his amusement without sacrificing his own pleasure or self-respect. In fact, whatever may be said of Spanish pride, it certainly does not enter into social or domestic life. Among no people are the relations between kindred more cordial or between superior and dependent more frank and genial; in these respects there still remains in the provincial life of Spain much of the vaunted simplicity of the olden time.

The most interesting member of this family group, however, is the daughter of the count, the charming though almost infantine little Carmen. Her form has not yet attained its maturity, but has already the exquisite symmetry and pliant grace so prevalent in this country. Her blue eyes, fair complexion and light hair are unusual in Andalusia, and give a mildness and gentleness to her demeanour in contrast to the usual fire of Spanish beauty, but in perfect unison with the guileless and confiding innocence of her manners. She has, however, all the innate aptness and versatility of her fascinating country-women, and sings, dances and plays the guitar and other instruments to admiration.

A few days after taking up his residence in the Alhambra, the count gave a domestic *fête* on his saint's day, assembling round him the members of his family and household, while several old servants came from his distant possessions to pay their reverence to him and partake of the good cheer. This patriarchal spirit which characterized the Spanish nobility in the days of their opulence has declined with their fortunes, but some who, like the count, still retain their ancient family possessions, keep up a little of the ancient system and have their estates overrun and almost eaten up by generations of idle retainers. According to this magnificent old Spanish system, in which the national pride and generosity bore equal parts, a superannuated servant was never turned off, but became a charge for the rest of his days; nay, his children and his children's children and often their relatives to the right and left, became gradually entailed upon the family. Hence the huge palaces of the Spanish nobility, which have such an air of empty ostentation from the greatness of their size compared with the mediocrity and scantiness of their furniture, were absolutely required in the golden days of Spain by the patriarchal habits of their possessors. They were little better than vast barracks for the hereditary generations of hangers-on that battened at the expense of a Spanish noble. The worthy old count who has estates in various parts of the kingdom assures me that some of them barely feed the hordes of dependents nestled upon them, who consider themselves entitled to be maintained upon the place rent-free, because their forefathers have been so for generations.

The domestic *fête* of the count broke in upon the usual still life of the Alhambra; music and laughter resounded through its late silent halls; there were groups of the guests amusing themselves about the galleries and gardens, and officious servants from town hurrying through the courts, bearing viands to the ancient kitchen which was again alive with the tread of cooks and scullions, and blazed with unwonted fires.

The feast, for a Spanish set dinner is literally a feast, was laid in the beautiful Morisco hall called «*La Sala de las Dos Hermanas*» (the Saloon of the Two Sisters). The table groaned with abundance and a joyous conviviality prevailed round the board, for though the Spaniards are generally an abstemious people, they are complete revellers at a banquet. For my own part, there was something peculiarly interesting in thus sitting at a feast in the royal halls of the Alhambra, given by the representative of one of its most renowned conquerors, for the venerable count, though unwarlike himself, is the lineal descendant and representative of the «Great Captain», the illustrious Gonsalvo of Cordova, whose sword he guards in the archives of his palace at Granada.

The banquet ended, the company adjourned to the Hall of Ambassadors. Here every one contributed to the general amusement by exerting some peculiar talent—singing, improvising, telling wonderful tales or dancing to that all-pervading talisman of Spanish pleasure, the guitar.

The life and charm of the whole assemblage, however, was the gifted little Carmen. She took her part in two or three scenes from Spanish comedies, exhibiting a charming dramatic talent; she gave imitations of the popular Italian singers with singular and whimsical felicity, and a rare quality of voice; she imitated the dialects, dances and ballads of the gypsies and the neighbouring peasantry, but did everything with a facility, a neatness, a grace and an all-pervading prettiness, that were perfectly fascinating.

The great charm of her performances, however, was their being free from all pretension or ambition of display. She seemed unconscious of the extent of her own talents; and in fact is accustomed only to exert them casually, like a child, for the amusement of the domestic circle. Her observation and tact must be remarkably quick, for her life is passed in the bosom of her family, and she can only have had casual and transient glances at the various characters and traits, brought out *impromptu* in moments of domestic hilarity like the one in question. It is pleasing to see the fondness and admiration with which every one of the household regards her: she is never spoken of, even by the domestics, by any other appellation than that of *La Niña,* «the child», an appellation which, thus applied, has something peculiarly kind and endearing in the Spanish language.

Never shall I think of the Alhambra without remembering the lovely little Carmen, sporting in happy and innocent girlhood in its marble halls, dancing to the sound of the Moorish castanets or mingling the silver warbling of her voice with the music of the fountains.

On this festive occasion several curious and amusing legends and traditions were told, many of which have escaped my memory, but out of those that most struck me, I will endeavour to shape forth some entertainment for the reader.

LEGEND OF PRINCE AHMED AL KAMEL

OR

THE PILGRIM OF LOVE

THERE was once a Moorish king of Granada, who had but one son whom he named Ahmed, to which his courtiers added the surname of *al Kamel* or the Perfect from the indubitable signs of superexcellence which they perceived in him in his very infancy. The astrologers countenanced them in their foresight, predicting everything in his favour that could make a perfect prince and a prosperous sovereign. One cloud only rested upon his destiny, and even that was of a roseate hue. He would be of an amorous temperament and run great perils from the tender passion. If, however, he could be kept from the allurements of love until of mature age, these dangers would be averted and his life thereafter be one uninterrupted course of felicity.

To prevent all danger of the kind, the king wisely determined to rear the prince in a seclusion where he should never see a female face nor hear even the name of love. For this purpose he built a beautiful palace on the brow of the hill above the Alhambra in the midst of delightful gardens, but surrounded by lofty walls, being, in fact, the palace known at the present day by the name of the Generalife. In this palace the youthful prince was shut up and entrusted to the guardianship and instruction of Eben Bonabben, one of the wisest and dryest of Arabian sages, who had passed the greatest part of his life in Egypt, studying hieroglyphics and making researches among the tombs and pyramids and who saw more charms in an Egyptian mummy than in the most tempting of living beauties. The sage was ordered to instruct the prince in all kinds of knowledge but one. He was to be kept utterly ignorant of love. «Use every precaution for the purpose you may think proper», said the king, «but remember, O Eben Bonabben, if my son learns aught of that forbidden knowledge while under your care, your head shall answer for it». A withered smile came over the dry visage of the wise Bonabben at tne menace. «Let your majesty's heart be as easy about your son, as mine is about my head. Am I a man likely to give lessons in the idle passion?»

Under the vigilant care of the philosopher, the prince grew up in the seclusion of the palace and its gardens. He had black slaves to attend upon him—hideous mutes who knew nothing of love or, if they did, had not words to communicate it. His mental endowments were the peculiar care of Eben Bonabben who sought to initiate him into the abstruse lore of Egypt, but in this the prince made little progress, and it was soon evident that he had no turn for philosophy.

He was, however, amazingly ductile for a youthful prince, ready to follow any advice and always guided by the last counsellor. He suppressed his yawns and listened patiently to the long and learned discourses of Eben Bonabben, from which he imbibed a smattering of various kinds of knowledge, and thus happily attained his twentieth year, a miracle of princely wisdom—but totally ignorant of love.

About this time, however, a change came over the conduct of the prince. He completely abandoned his studies and took to strolling about the gardens and musing by the side of the fountains. He had been taught a little music among his various accomplishments; it now engrossed a great part of his time and a turn for poetry became apparent. The sage Eben Bonabben took the alarm and endeavoured to work these idle humours out of him by a severe course of algebra, but the prince turned from it with distaste. «I cannot endure algebra», said he, «it is an abomination to me. I want something that speaks more to the heart.»

The sage Eben Bonabben shook his dry head at the words. «Here is an end to philosophy», thought he. «The prince has discovered he has a heart!» He now kept anxious watch upon his pupil and saw that the latent tenderness of his nature was in activity and only wanted an object. He wandered about the gardens of the Generalife in an intoxication of feelings of which he knew not the cause. Sometimes he would sit plunged in a delicious reverie; then he would seize his lute and draw from it the most touching notes, and then throw it aside and break forth into sighs and ejaculations.

By degrees this loving disposition began to extend to inanimate objects; he had his favourite flowers which he cherished with tender assiduity; then he became attached to various trees, and there was one in particular of a graceful form and drooping foliage, on which he lavished his amorous devotion, carving his name on its bark, hanging garlands on its branches and singing couplets in its praise to the accompaniment of his lute.

The sage Eben Bonabben was alarmed at this excited state of his pupil. He saw him on the very brink of forbidden knowledge—the least hint might reveal to him the fatal secret. Trembling for the safety of the prince and the security of his own head, he hastened to draw him from the seductions of the garden and shut him up in the highest tower of the Generalife. It contained beautiful apartments and commanded an almost boundless prospect, but was elevated far above that atmosphere of sweets and those witching bowers so dangerous to the feelings of the too susceptible Ahmed.

What was to be done, however, to reconcile him to this restraint and to beguile the tedious hours? He had exhausted almost all kinds of agreeable knowledge, and algebra was not to be mentioned. Fortunately Eben Bonabben had been instructed, when in Egypt, in the language of birds by a Jewish rabbin who had received it in lineal transmission from Solomon the Wise who had been taught it by the Queen of Sheba. At the very mention of such a study, the eyes of the prince sparkled with animation, and he applied himself to it with such avidity that he soon became as great an adept as his master.

The tower of the Generalife was no longer a solitude; he had companions at hand with whom he could converse. The first acquaintance he formed was with a hawk who built his nest in a crevice of the lofty battlements, from whence he soared far and wide in quest of prey. The prince, however, found little to like or esteem im him. He was a mere pirate of the air, swaggering and boastful, whose talk was all about rapine and courage and desperate exploits.

His next acquaintance was an owl, a mighty wise-looking bird, with a huge head and staring eyes, who sat blinking and goggling all day in a hole in the wall, but roamed forth at night. He had great pretensions to wisdom, talked something of astrology and the moon, and hinted at the dark sciences, but he was grievously given to metaphysics, and the prince found his prosings even more ponderous than those of the sage Eben Bonabben.

Then there was a bat that hung all day by his heels in the dark corner of a vault, but sallied out in a slipshod style at twilight. He, however, had but twilight ideas on all subjects, derided things of which he had taken but an imperfect view and seemed to take delight in nothing.

Besides these there was a swallow, with whom the prince was at first much taken. He was a smart talker, but restless, bustling and for ever on the wing; seldom remaining long enough for any continued conversation. He turned out in the end to be a mere smatterer who did but skim over the surface of things, pretending to know everything, but knowing nothing thoroughly.

These were the only feathered associates with whom the prince had any opportunity of exercising his newly acquired language; the tower was too high for any other birds to frequent it. He soon grew weary of his new acquaintances, whose conversation spoke so little to the head and nothing to the heart; and gradually relapsed into his loneliness. A winter passed away, spring opened with all its bloom and verdure and breathing sweetness and the happy time arrived for birds to pair and build their nests. Suddenly, as it were, a universal burst of song and melody broke forth from the groves and gardens of the Generalife, and reached the prince in the solitude of his tower. From every side he heard the same universal theme—love—love—love—chanted forth and responded to in every variety of note and tone. The prince listened in silence and perplexity. «What can be this love», thought he, «of which the world seems so full and of which I know nothing?» He applied for information to his friend the hawk. The ruffian bird answered in a tone of scorn: «You must apply», said he, «to the vulgar peaceable birds of earth, who are made for the prey of us princes of the air. My trade is war and fighting my delight. In a word, I am a warrior and know nothing of this thing called love».

The prince turned from him with disgust and sought the owl in his retreat. «This is a bird», said he, «of peaceful habits, and may be able to solve my question». So he asked the owl to tell him what was this love about which all the birds in the groves below were singing.

Upon this, the owl put on a look of offended dignity. «My nights», said he, «are taken up in study and research, and my days in ruminating in my cell upon all that I have learnt. As to these singing birds of whom you talk, I never listen to them—I despise them and their themes. Allah be praised, I cannot sing; I am a philosopher and know nothing of this thing called love».

The prince now repaired to the vault, where his friend the bat was hanging by the heels and propounded the same question. The bat wrinkled up his nose into a most snappish expression. «Why do you disturb me in my morning's nap with such an idle question?» said he peevishly. «I only fly by twilight, when all birds are asleep, and never trouble myself with their concerns. I am neither bird nor beast, and I thank heaven for it. I have found out the villany of the whole of them and hate them one and all. In a word, I am a misanthrope, and know nothing of this thing called love.»

As a last resort, the prince now sought the swallow and stopped him just as he was circling about the summit of the tower. The swallow, as usual, was in a prodigious hurry and had scarce time to make a reply. «Upon my word», said he, «I have so much public business to attend to and so many pursuits to follow that I have had no time to think on the subject. I have every day a thousand visits to pay, a thousand affairs of importance to examine into, that leave me not a moment of leisure for these little sing song matters. In a word, I am a citizen of the world. I know nothing of this thing called love». So saying, the swallow dived into the valley and was out of sight in a moment.

The prince remained disappointed and perplexed, but with curiosity still more piqued by the difficulty of gratifying it. While in this mood, his ancient guardian entered the tower. The prince advanced eagerly to meet him. «O sage Eben Bonabben», cried he, «thou hast revealed to me much of the wisdom of the earth, but there is one thing of which I remain in utter ignorance and would fain be informed».

«My prince has but to make the inquiry and everything within the limited range of his servant's intellect is at his command».

«Tell me then, O most profound of sages, what is the nature of this thing called love?»

The sage Eben Bonabben was struck as with a thunderbolt. He trembled and turned pale, and felt as if head sat but loosely on his shoulders.

«What could suggest such a question to my prince, where could he have learnt so idle a word?»

The prince led him to the window of the tower. «Listen, O Eben Bonabben», said he. The sage listened. The nightingale sat in a thicket below the tower, singing to his paramour the rose; from every blossomed spray and tufted grove arose a strain of melody, and love—love—love—was still the unvarying strain.

«*Allah Akbar!* God is great!» exclaimed the wise Bonabben. «Who shall pretend to keep this secret from the heart of man, when even the birds of the air conspire to betray it?»

Then turning to Ahmed, «O my prince», cried he, «shut thine ears to these seductive strains. Close thy mind against this dangerous knowledge. Know that this love is the cause of half the ills of wretched mortality. It is this which produces bitterness and strife between brethren and friends, which causes treacherous murder and desolating war. Care and sorrow, weary days and sleepless nights are its attendants. It withers the bloom and blights the joys of youth and brings on the ills and griefs of premature old age. Allah preserve thee, my prince, in total ignorance of this thing called love!»

The sage Eben Bonabben hastily retired, leaving the prince plunged in still deeper perplexity. It was in vain he attempted to dismiss the subject from his mind; it still continued upper-

175

most in his thoughts, and teased and exhausted him with vain conjectures.

«Surely» said he to himself, as he listened to the tuneful strains of the birds, «there is no sorrow in those notes; everything seems tenderness and joy. If love be a cause of such wretchedness and strife, why are not these birds drooping in solitude or tearing each other in pieces, instead of fluttering cheerfully about the groves or sporting with each other among flowers?»

He lay one morning on his couch meditating on this inexplicable matter. The window of his chamber was open to admit the soft morning breeze which came laden with the perfume of orange-blossoms from the valley of the Darro. The voice of the nightingale was faintly heard, still chanting the wonted theme. As the prince was listening and sighing, there was a sudden rushing noise in the air; a beautiful dove, pursued by a hawk, darted in at the window and fell panting on the floor, while the pursuer, balked of his prey, soared off to the mountains.

The prince took up the gasping bird, smoothed its feathers and nestled it in his bosom. When he had soothed it by his caresses, he put it in a golden cage and offered it with his own hands the whitest and finest of wheat and the purest of water. The bird, however, refused food and sat drooping and pining, and uttering piteous moans.

«What aileth thee?» said Ahmed. «Hast thou not everything thy heart can wish?»

«Alas, no!» replied the dove; «am I not separated from the partner of my heart, and that too in the happy spring-time, the very season of love!»

«Of love!» echoed Ahmed; «I pray thee, my pretty bird, canst thou then tell me what is love?»

«Too well can I, my prince. It is the torment of one, the felicity of two, the strife and enmity of three. It is a charm

176

which draws two beings together and unites them by delicious sympathies, making it happiness to be with each other, but misery to be apart. Is there no being to whom you are drawn by these ties of tender affection?»

«I like my old teacher Eben Bonabben better than any other being, but he is often tedious and I occasionally feel myself happier without his society.»

«That is not the sympathy I mean. I speak of love, the great mystery and principle of life, the intoxicating revel of youth, the sober delight of age. Look forth, my prince, and behold how at this blest season all nature is full of love. Every created being has its mate; the most insignificant bird sings to its paramour; the very beetle woos its lady-beetle in the dust, and yon butterflies which you see fluttering high above the tower and toying in the air are happy in each other's loves. Alas, my prince! hast thou spent so many of the precious days of youth without knowing anything of love? Is there no gentle being of another sex, no beautiful princess or lovely damsel who has ensnared your heart, and filled your bosom with a soft tumult of pleasing pains and tender wishes?»

«I begin to understand», said the prince, sighing, «such a tumult I have more than once experienced without knowing the cause—and where should I seek for an object, such as you describe, in this dismal solitude?»

A little further conversation ensued and the first amatory lesson of the prince was complete.

«Alas!» said he, «if love be indeed such a delight, and its interruption such a misery, Allah forbid that I should mar the joy of any of its votaries!» He opened the cage, took out the dove and, having fondly kissed it, carried it to the window. «Go, happy bird», said he, «rejoice with the partner of thy heart in the days of youth and spring-time. Why should I make thee a fellow-prisoner in this dreary tower where love can never enter?»

‎‎‎‎‎ ·The dove flapped its wings in rapture, gave one vault into the air and then swooped downward on whistling wings to the blooming bowers of the Darro.

The prince followed him Kith his eyes and then gave way to bitter repining. The singing of the birds which once delighted him, now added to his bitterness. Love! love! love! Alas, poor youth! he now understood the strain.

His eyes flashed fire when next he beheld the sage Bonabben. «Why hast thou kept me in this abject ignorance?» cried he. «Why has the great mystery and principle of life been withheld from me, in which I find the meanest insect is so learned? Behold all nature is in a revel of delight. Every created being rejoices with its mate. This, this is the love about which I have sought instruction. Why am I alone debarred its enjoyment? Why has so much of my youth been wasted without a knowledge of its raptures?»

The sage Bonabben saw that all further reserve was useless, for the prince had acquired the dangerous and forbidden knowledge. He revealed to him, therefore, the predictions of the astrologers and the precautions that had been taken in his education to avert the threatened evil. «And now, my prince», added he, «my life is in your hands. Let the king your father discover that you have learned the passion of love while under my guardianship and my head must answer for it».

The prince was as reasonable as most young men of his age and easily listened to the remonstrances of his tutor, since nothing pleaded against them. Besides, he really was attached to the sage Bonabben, and being as yet but theoretically acquainted with the passion of love, he consented to confine the knowledge of it to his own bosom, rather than endanger the head of the philosopher.

His discretion was doomed, however, to be put to still further proofs. A few mornings afterwards, as he was ruminating on the battlements of the tower, the dove which had been released by him came hovering in the air and alighted fearlessly upon his shoulder.

The prince fondled it to his heart. «Happy bird!» said he, «who can fly, as it were, with the wings of the morning to the uttermost parts of the earth. Where hast thou been since we parted?»

«In a far country, my prince, from whence I bring you tidings in reward for my liberty. In the wild compass of my flight which extends over plain and mountain, as I was soaring in the air, I beheld below me a delightful garden with all kinds of fruits and flowers. It was in a green meadow, on the banks of a wandering stream, and in the centre of the garden was a stately palace. I alighted in one of the bowers to repose after my weary flight. On the green bank below me was a youthful princess in the very sweetness and bloom of her years. She was surrounded by female attendants, young like herself, who decked her with garlands and coronets of flowers, but no flower of field or garden could compare with her for loveliness. Here, however, she bloomed in secret, for the garden was surrounded by high walls and no mortal man was permitted to enter. When I beheld this beauteous maid, thus young and innocent and unspotted by the world, I thought, here is the being formed by Heaven to inspire my prince with love».

The description was a spark of fire to the combustible heart of Ahmed; all the latent amorousness of his temperament had at once found an object and he conceived an immeasurable passion for the princess. He wrote a letter, couched in the most impassioned language, breathing his fervent devotion, but bewailing the unhappy thraldom of his person, which prevented him from seeking her out and throwing himself at her feet. He added couplets of the most tender and moving eloquence, for he was a poet by nature and inspired by love. He addressed his letter—«To the unknown beauty, from the captive Prince Ahmed»; then perfuming it with musk and roses, he gave it to the dove.

«Away, trustiest of messengers!» said he. «Fly over mountain and valley and river and plain; rest not in bower nor set foot on earth, until thou hast given this letter to the mistress of my heart.»

The dove soared high in air and, taking his course, darted away in one undeviating direction. The prince followed him with his eye until he was a mere speck on a cloud and gradually disappeared behind a mountain.

Day after day he watched for the return of the messenger of love, but he watched in vain. He began to accuse him of forgetfulness, when towards sunset one evening the faithful bird fluttered into his apartment and falling at his feet, expired. The arrow of some wanton archer had pierced his breast, yet he had struggled with the lingerings of life to execute his mission. As the prince bent with grief over this gentle martyr to fidelity, he beheld a chain of pearls round his neck, attached to which beneath his wing was a small enamelled picture. It represented a lovely princess in the very flower of her years. It was doubtless the unknown beauty of the garden, but who and where was she? How had she received his letter, and was this picture sent as a token of her approval of his passion? Unfortunately the death of the faithful dove left everything in mystery and doubt.

The prince gazed on the picture till his eyes swam with tears. He pressed it to his lips and to his heart; he sat for hours contemplating it, almost in an agony of tenderness. «Beautiful image!» said he, «alas, thou art but an image! Yet thy dewy eyes beam tenderly upon me; those rosy lips look as though they would speak encouragement. Vain fancies! Have they not looked the same on some more happy rival? But where in this wide world shall I hope to find the original?

Who knows what mountains, what realms may separate us, what adverse chances may intervene? Perhaps now, even now, lovers may be crowding around her, while I sit here a prisoner in a tower, wasting my time in adoration of a painted shadow».

The resolution of Prince Ahmed was taken. «I will fly from this palace», said he, «which has become an odious prison and, a pilgrim of love, will seek this unknown princess throughout the world». To escape from the tower in the day, when every one was awake might be a difficult matter but at night the palace was slightly guarded, for no one apprehended any attempt of the kind from the prince who had always been so passive in his captivity. How was he to guide himself, however, in his darkling flight, being ignorant of the country? He bethought him of the owl who was accustomed to roam at night and must know every by-lane and secret pass. Seeking him in his hermitage, he questioned him touching his knowledge of the land. Upon this the owl put on a mighty self-important look. «You must know, O prince», said he, «that we owls are of a very ancient and extensive family, though rather fallen to decay, and possess ruinous castles and palaces in all parts of Spain. There is scarcely a tower of the mountains or a fortress of the plains or an old citadel of a city, but has some brother, or uncle, or cousin quartered in it, and in going the rounds to visit this my numerous kindred, I have pried into every nook and corner and made myself acquainted with every secret of the land». The prince was overjoyed to find the owl so deeply versed in topography and now informed him in confidence of his tender passion and his intended elopement, urging him to be his companion and counsellor.

«Go to!» said the owl with a look of displeasure, «am I a bird to engage in a love-affair? I, whose whole time is devoted to meditation and the moon?»

«Be not offended, most solemn owl», replied the prince;

«abstract thyself for a time from meditation and the moon, and aid me in my flight, and thou shalt have whatever heart can wish».

«I have that already», said the owl, «a few mice are sufficient for my frugal table, and this hole in the wall is spacious enough for my studies; and what more does a philosopher like myself desire?»

«Bethink thee, most wise owl, that while moping in thy cell and gazing at the moon, all thy talents are lost to the world. I shall one day be a sovereign prince and may advance thee to some post of honour and dignity.»

The owl, though a philosopher and above the ordinary wants of life, was not above ambition, so he was finally prevailed on to elope with the prince and be his guide and mentor in his pilgrimage.

The plans of a lover are promptly executed. The prince collected all his jewels and concealed them about his person as travelling funds. That very night he lowered himself by his scarf from a balcony of the tower, clambered over the outer walls of the Generalife and, guided by the owl, made good his escape before morning to the mountains.

He now held a council with his mentor as to his future course.

«Might I advise», said the owl, «I would recommend you to repair to Seville. You must know, that many years since I was on a visit to an uncle, an owl of great dignity and power, who lived in a ruined wing of the Alcázar of that place. In my hoverings at night over the city, I frequently remarked a light burning in a lonely tower. At length I alighted on the battlements and found it to proceed from the lamp of an Arabian magician; he was surrounded by his magic books and on his shoulder was perched his familiar, an ancient raven who had come with him from Egypt. I am acquainted with that raven and owe to him a great part of the knowledge I possess. The magician is since dead, but the raven still inhabits the tower, for these birds are of wonderful long life. I would advise you, O prince, to seek that raven, for he is a soothsayer and a conjuror, and deals in the black art, for which all ravens, and especially those of Egypt, are renowned».

The prince was struck with the wisdom of this advice and accordingly bent his course towards Seville. He travelled only in the night to accommodate his companion, and lay by during the day in some dark cavern or mouldering watch-tower, for the owl knew every hiding hole of the kind and had a most antiquarian taste for ruins.

At length, one morning at daybreak they reached the city of Seville, where the owl who hated the glare and bustle of crowded streets halted without the gate and took up his quarters in a hollow tree.

The prince entered the gate and readily found the magic tower which rose above the houses of the city, as a palm-tree rises above the shrubs of the desert; it was in fact the same tower that is standing at the present day and known as the Giralda, the famous Moorish tower of Seville.

The prince ascended by a great winding staircase to the summit of the tower, where he found the cabalistic raven, an old, mysterious, grey-headed bird, ragged in feather, with a film over one eye that gave him the glare of a spectre. He was perched on one leg, with his head turned on one side, poring with his remaining eye on a diagram described on the pavement.

The prince approached him with the awe and reverence naturally inspired by his venerable appearance and supernatural wisdom. «Pardon me, most ancient and darkly wise raven», exclaimed he, «if for a moment I interrupt those studies which are the wonder of the world. You behold before you a votary of love, who would fain seek your counsel how to obtain the object of his passion».

«In other words», said the raven with a significant look, «you seek to try my skill in palmistry. Come, show me your hand and let me decipher the mysterious lines of fortune».

«Excuse me», said the prince, «I come not to pry into the decrees of fate, which are hidden by Allah from the eyes of mortals; I am a pilgrim of love and seek but to find a clue to the object of my pilgrimage».

«And can you be at any loss for an object in amorous Andalusia?» said the old raven, leering upon him with his single eye, «above all, can you be at a loss in wanton Seville, where black-eyed damsels dance the *zambra* under every orange grove?»

The prince blushed and was somewhat shocked at hearing an old bird with one claw in the grave talk thus loosely. «Believe me», said he gravely, «I am on none such light and vagrant errand as thou dost insinuate. The black-eyed damsels of Andalusia who dance among the orange groves of the Guadalquivir are as nought to me. I seek one unknown but immaculate beauty, the original of this picture, and I beseech thee, most potent raven, if it be within the scope of thy knowledge or the reach of thy art, inform me where she may be found».

The grey-headed raven was rebuked by the gravity of the prince.

«What know I», replied he drily, «of youth and beauty? My visits are to the old and withered, not the fresh and fair. The harbinger of fate am I who croak bodings of death from the chimney top, and flap my wings at the sick man's window. You must seek elsewhere for tidings of your unknown beauty».

«And where can I seek, if not among the sons of wisdom, versed in the book of destiny? A royal prince am I, fated by the stars, and sent on a mysterious enterprise, on which may hang the destiny of empires.»

When the raven heard that it was a matter of vast moment,

in which the stars took interest, he changed his tone and manner, and listened with profound attention to the story of the prince. When it was concluded, he replied, «Touching this princess, I can give thee no information of myself, for my flight is not among gardens or around ladies' bowers, but hie thee to Cordova, seek the palm-tree of the great Abderahman, which stands in the court of the principal mosque; at the foot of it thou wilt find a great traveller who has visited all countries and courts, and been a favorite with queens and princeses. He will give thee tildings of the object of thy search».

«Many thanks for this precious information», said the prince. «Farewell, most venerable conjuror».

«Farewell, pilgrim of love», said the raven drily and again fell to pondering on the diagram.

The prince sallied forth from Seville, sought his fellow-traveller, the owl, who was still dozing in the hollow tree and set off for Cordova.

He approached it along hanging gardens and orange and citron groves, overlooking the fair valley of the Guadalquivir. When he arrived at its gates the owl flew up to a dark hole in the wall, and the prince proceeded in quest of the palm-tree planted in days of yore by the Great Abderahman. It stood in the midst of the great court of the Mosque, towering from amidst orange and cypress trees. Dervishes and faquirs were seated in groups under the cloisters of the court, and many of the faithful were performing their ablutions at the fountains before entering the Mosque.

At the foot of the palm-tree was a crowd listening to the words of one who appeared to be talking with great volubility. «This», said the prince to himself, «must be the great traveller who is to give me tidings of the unknown princess». He mingled in the crowd, but was astonished to perceive that they were all listening to a parrot who with his bright green coat, pragmatical eye and consequential top-knot, had the air of a bird on excellent terms with himself.

«How is this», said the prince to one of the by-standers, «that so many grave persons can be delighted with the garrulity of a chattering bird?»

«You know not whom you speak of», said the other, «this parrot is a descendant of the famous parrot of Persia, renowned for his story-telling talent. He has all the learning of the East at the tip of his tongue and can quote poetry as fast as he can talk. He has visited various foreign courts, where he has been considered an oracle of erudition. He has been a universal favourite also with the fair sex who have an vast admiration for erudite parrots that can quote poetry».

«Enough», said the prince. «I will have some private talk with this distinguished traveller».

He sought a private interview and expounded the nature of his errand. He had scarcely mentioned it when the parrot burst into a fit of dry rickety laughter, that absolutely brought tears in his eyes. «Excuse my merriment», said he, «but the mere mention of love always sets me laughing».

The prince was shocked at this ill-timed merriment. «Is not love», said he, «the great mystery of nature, the secret principle of life, the universal bond of sympathy?»

«A fig's end!» cried the parrot, interrupting him, «prithee where hast thou learnt this sentimental jargon? Trust me, love is quite out of vogue; one never hears of it in the company of wits and people of refinement».

The prince sighed as he recalled the different language of his friend the dove. But this parrot, thought he, has lived about the court; he affects the wit and the fine gentleman; he knows nothing of the thing called love. Unwilling to provoke any more ridicule of the sentiment which filled his heart, he now directed his inquiries to the immediate purport of his visit.

«Tell me», said he, «most accomplished parrot, thou who hast everywhere been admitted to the most secret bowers of beauty, hast thou in the course of thy travels met with the original of this portrait?»

The parrot took the picture in his claw, turned his head from side to side and examined it curiously with either eye. «Upon my honour», said he, «a very pretty face, very pretty, but then one sees so many pretty women in one's travels that one can hardly—but hold—bless me! Now I look at it again —sure enough this is the Princess Aldegonda. How could I forget one that is so prodigious a favourite with me?»

«The Princess Aldegonda!» echoed the prince, «and where is she to be found?»

«Softly, softly», said the parrot, «easier to be found than gained. She is the only daughter of the Christian king who reigns at Toledo and is shut up from the world until her seventeenth birthday, on account of some prediction of those meddlesome fellows the astrologers. You'll not get a sight of her; no mortal man can see her. I was admitted to her presence to entertain her, and I assure you on the word of a parrot who has seen the world, I have conversed with much sillier princesses in my time».

«A word in confidence, my dear parrot», said the prince; «I am heir to a kingdom, and shall one day sit upon a throne. I see that you are a bird of parts and understand the world. Help me to gain possession of this princess, and I will advance you to some distinguished place about court».

«With all my heart», said the parrot: «but let it be a sinecure, if possible, for we wits have a great dislike of labour».

Arrangements were promptly made; the prince sallied forth from Cordova through the same gate by which he had entered, called the owl down from the hole in the wall, introduced him to his new travelling companion, as a brother savant, and away they set off on their journey.

They travelled much more slowly than accorded with the impatience of the prince, but the parrot was accustomed to high life and did not like to be disturbed early in the morning. The owl, on the other hand, was for sleeping at mid-day and lost a great deal of time by his long *siestas*. His antiquarian taste also was in the way, for he insisted on pausing and inspecting every ruin, and had long legendary tales to tell about every old tower and castle in the country. The prince had supposed that he and the parrot, being both birds of learning, would delight in each other's society, but never had he been more mistaken. They were eternally bickering. The one was a wit, the other a philosopher. The parrot quoted poetry, was critical on new readings and eloquent on small points of erudition; the owl treated all such knowledge as trifling and relished nothing but metaphysics. Then the parrot would sing songs and repeat *bons mots* and crack jokes upon his solemn neighbour and laugh outrageously at his own wit, all which proceedings the owl considered as a grievous invasion of his dignity, and would scowl and sulk and swell and be silent for a whole day together.

The prince heeded not the wranglings of his companions, being wrapped up in the dreams of his own fancy and the contemplation of the portrait of the beautiful princess. In this way they journeyed through the stern passes of the Sierra Morena, across the sunburnt plains of La Mancha and Castile, and along the banks of the «Golden Tagus», which winds its wizard mazes over one half of Spain and Portugal. At length they came in sight of a strong city with walls and towers, built on a rocky promontory, round the foot of which the Tagus circled with brawling violence.

«Behold», exclaimed the owl, «the ancient and renowned city of Toledo, a city famous for its antiquities. Behold those venerable domes and towers, hoary with time and clothed with legendary grandeur, in which so many of my ancestors have meditated».

«Pish!» cried the parrot, interrupting his solemn antiquarian rapture, «what have we to do with antiquities and legends and your ancestry? Behold what is more to the purpose—behold the abode of youth and beauty—behold at length, O prince, the abode of your long-sought princess».

The prince looked in the direction indicated by the parrot and beheld in a delightful green meadow on the banks of the Tagus a stately palace rising from amidst the bowers of a delicious garden. It was just such a place as had been described by the dove as the original of the picture. He gazed at it with a throbbing heart. «Perhaps at this moment», thought he, «the beautiful princess is sporting beneath those shady bowers, or pacing with delicate step those stately terraces or reposing beneath those lofty roofs!» As he looked more narrowly, he perceived that the walls of the garden were of great height, so as to defy access, while numbers of armed guards patrolled around them.

The prince turned to the parrot. «O most accomplished of birds», said he, «thou hast the gift of human speech. Hie thee to yon garden, seek the idol of my soul and tell her that Prince Ahmed, a pilgrim of love, and guided by the stars, has arrived in quest of her on the flowery banks of the Tagus».

The parrot, proud of his embassy, flew away to the garden, mounted above its lofty walls and after soaring for a time over the lawns and groves, alighted on the balcony of a pavilion that overhung the river. Here, looking in at the casement, he beheld the princess reclining on a couch with her eyes fixed on a paper while tears gently stole after each other down her pallid cheek.

Pluming his wings for a moment, adjusting his bright green coat and elevating his top-knot, the parrot perched himself beside her with a gallant air; then assuming a tenderness of tone, «Dry thy tears, most beautiful of princesses», said he, «I come to bring solace to thy heart».

The princess was startled on hearing a voice, but turning and seeing nothing but a little green-coated bird bobbing and bowing before her; «Alas! what solace canst thou yield», said she, «seeing thou art but a parrot?»

The parrot was nettled at the question. «I have consoled many beautiful ladies in my time», said he, «but let that pass. At present I come ambassador from a royal prince. Know that Ahmed, the prince of Granada, has arrived in quest of thee, and is encamped even now on the flowery banks of the Tagus».

The eyes of the beautiful princess sparkled at these words even brighter than the diamonds in her coronet. «O sweetest of parrots» cried she, «joyful indeed are thy tidings, for I was faint and weary and sick almost unto death with doubt of the constancy of Ahmed. Hie thee back and tell him that the words of his letter are engraven in my heart and his poetry has been the food of my soul. Tell him, however, that he must prepare to prove his love by force of arms; to-morrow is my seventeenth birthday, when the king my father holds a great tournament; several princes are to enter the lists and my hand is to be the prize of the victor».

The parrot again took wing and rustling through the groves, flew back to where the prince awaited his return. The rapture of Ahmed on finding the original of his adored portrait and finding her kind and true can only be conceived by those favoured mortals who have had the good fortune to realise day-dreams and turn a shadow into subtance. Still there was one thing that alloyed his transport—this impending tournament. In fact, the banks of the Tagus were already glittering with arms and resounding with trumpets of the various knights who with proud retinues were prancing on towards Toledo to attend the ceremonial. The same start that had controlled the destiny of the prince had governed that of the princess and until her seventeenth birthday she had been shut up from the world to guard her from the tender passion. The fame of her charms, however, had been enhanced rather than obscured by this seclusion. Several powerful princes had contended for her alliance, and her father who was a king of wondrous shrewdness, to avoid making enemies by showing partiality had referred them to the arbitrement of arms. Among the rival candidates were several renowned for strength and prowess. What a predicament for the unfortunate Ahmed, unprovided as he was with weapons, and unskilled in the exercises of chivalry! «Luckless prince that I am», said he, «to have been brought up in seclusion under the eye of a philosopher! Of what avail are algebra and philosophy in affairs of love? Alas, Eben Bonabben! why hast thou neglected to instruct me in the management of arms?» Upon this the owl broke silence, preluding his harangue with a pious ejaculation, for he was a devout Mussulman.

«*Allah Akbar!* God is great» exclaimed he; «in his hands are all secret things. He alone governs the destiny of princes! Know, O prince, that this land is full of mysteries, hidden from all but those who like myself can grope after knowledge in the dark. Know that in the neighbouring mountains there is a cave, and in that cave there is an iron table, and on that table there lies a suit of magic armour, and beside that table there stands a spell-bound steed which has been shut up there for many generations».

The prince stared with wonder, while the owl, blinking his huge round eyes and erecting his horns, proceeded.

«Many years since I accompanied my father to these parts on a tour of his estates, and we sojourned in that cave, and thus became I acquainted with the mystery. It is a tradition in our family which I have heard from my grandfather, when I was yet but a very little owlet, that this armour belonged to a Moorish magician who took refuge in this cavern when Toledo was captured by the Christians and died here, leaving his steed and weapons under a mystic spell, never to be used but by a Moslem and by him only from sunrise to mid-day. In that interval, whoever uses them will overthrow every opponent.»

«Enough; let us seek this cave!» exclaimed Ahmed.

Guided by his legendary mentor, the prince found the cavern which was in one of the wildest recesses of those rocky cliffs which rise around Toledo; none but the mousing eye of an owl or an antiquary could have discovered the entrance to it. A sepulchral lamp of everlasting oil shed a solemn light through the place. On an iron table in the centre of the cavern lay the magic armour; against it leaned the lance and beside it stood an Arabian steed, caparisoned for the field, but motionless as a statue. The armour was bright and unsullied as it had gleamed in days of old; the steed in as good condition as if just from the pasture, and when Ahmed laid his hand upon his neck, he pawed the ground and gave a loud neigh of joy that shook the walls of the cavern. Thus amply provided with «horse to ride and weapon to wear», the prince determined to defy the field in the impending tourney.

The eventful morning arrived. The lists for the combat were prepared in the *Vega* or plain, just below the cliff-built walls of Toledo, where stages and galeries were erected for the spectators, covered with rich tapestry and sheltered from the sun by silken awnings. All the beauties of the land were assembled in those galleries, while below pranced plumed knights with their pages and esquires, among whom figured conspicuously the princes who were to contend in the tourney. All the beauties of the land, however, were eclipsed when the princess Aldegonda appeared in the royal pavilion and for the first time broke forth upon the gaze of an admiring world. A murmur of wonder ran through the crowd at her trascen-

dent loveliness, and the princes who were candidates for her hand merely on the faith of her reported charms now felt tenfold ardour for the conflict.

The princess, however, had a troubled look. The colour came and went from her cheek and her eye wandered with a restless and unsatisfied expression over the plumed throng of knights. The trumpets were about sounding for the encounter, when the herald announced the arrival of a stranger knight, and Ahmed rode into the field. A steel helmet studded with gems rose above his turban; his cuirass was embossed with gold; his scimitar and dagger were of the workmanship of Fez and flamed with precious stones. A round shield was at his shoulder and in his hand he bore the lance of charmed virtue. The caparison of his Arabian steed was richly embroidered and swept the ground, and the proud animal pranced and snuffed the air and neighed with joy at once more beholding the array of arms. The lofty and graceful demeanour of the prince struck every eye, and when his appellation was announced, «The Pilgrim of Love», an universal flutter and agitation prevailed among the fair dames in the galleries.

When Ahmed presented himself at the lists, however, they were closed against him: none but princes, he was told, were admitted to the contest. He declared his name and rank. «Still worse!»—he was a Moslem and could not engage in a tourney where the hand of a Christian princess was the prize.

The rival princes surrounded him with haughty and menacing aspects; and one of insolent demeanour and herculean frame sneered at his light and youthful form and scoffed at his amorous appellation. The ire of the prince was roused. He defied his rival to the encounter. They took distance, wheeled and charged, and at the first touch of the magic lance, the brawny scoffer was tilted from his saddle. Here the prince would have paused, but alas! he had to deal with a demoniac horse and armour—once in action nothing could control them.

193

The Arabian steed charged into the thickest of the throng; the lance overturned everything that presented; the gentle prince was carried pell-mell about the field, strewing it with high and low, gentle and simple, and grieving at his own involuntary exploit. The king stormed and raged at this outrage on his subjects and his guests. He ordered out all his guards—they were unhorsed as fast as they came up. The king threw off his robes, grasped buckler and lance, and rode forth to awe the stranger with the presence of majesty itself. Alas! majesty fared no better than the vulgar—the steed and lance were no respecters of persons; to the dismay of Ahmed, he was borne full tilt against the king, and in a moment the royal heels were in the air and the crown was rolling in the dust.

At this moment the sun reached the meridian; the magic spell resumed its power. The Arabian steed scoured across the plain, leaped the barrier, plunged into the Tagus, swam its raging current, bore the prince breathless and amazed to the cavern, and resumed his station like a statue beside the iron table. The prince dismounted right gladly and replaced the armour to abide the further decrees of fate. Then seating himself in the cavern, he ruminated on the desperate state to which this demoniac steed and armour had reduced him. Never should he dare to show his face at Toledo after inflicting such disgrace upon its chivalry, and such an outrage on its king. What, too, would the princess think of so rude and riotous an achievement? Full of anxiety, he sent forth his winged messengers to gather tidings. The parrot resorted to all the public places and crowded resorts of the city, and soon returned with a world of gossip. All Toledo was in consternation. The princess had been borne off senseless to the palace; the tournament had ended in confusion; every one was talking of the sudden apparition, prodigious exploits and strange disappearance of the Moslem knight. Some pronounced him a Moorish magician; others thought him a demon who had assumed a human shape, while others related traditions of enchanted warriors hidden in the caves of the mountains and thought it might be one of these, who had made a sudden irruption from his den. All agreed that no mere ordinary mortal could have wrought such wonders or unhorsed such accomplished and stalwart Christian warriors.

The owl flew forth at night and hovered about the dusky city, perching on the roofs and chimneys. He then wheeled his flight up to the royal palace which stood on the rocky summit of Toledo and went prowling about its terraces and battlements, eaves-dropping at every cranny and glaring in with his big goggling eyes at every window where there was a light, so as to throw two or three maids of honour into fits. It was not until the grey dawn began to peer above the mountains that he returned from his mousing expedition and related to the prince what he had seen.

«As I was prying about one of the loftiest towers of the palace», said he, «I beheld through a casement a beautiful princess. She was reclining on a couch with attendants and physicians around her, but she would have none of their ministry and relief. When they retired, I beheld her draw forth a letter from her bosom and read and kiss it, and give way to loud lamentations, at which, philosopher as I am, I could not but be greatly moved».

The tender heart of Ahmed was distressed at these tidings. «Too true were thy words, O sage Eben Bonabben», cried he, «care and sorrow and sleepless nights are the lot of lovers. Allah preserve the princess from the blighting influence of this thing called love!»

Further intelligence from Toledo corroborated the report of the owl. The city was a prey to uneasiness and alarm. The princess was conveyed to the highest tower of the palace, every avenue to which was strongly guarded. In the meantime a devouring melancholy had seized upon her, of which no one could divine the cause. She refused food and turned a deaf ear to every consolation. The most skilful physicians had essayed their art in vain; it was thought some magic spell had been practised upon her, and the king made proclamation, declaring that whoever should effect her cure should receive the richest jewel in the royal treasury.

When the owl, who was dozing in a corner, heard of this proclamation, he rolled his large eyes and looked more mysterious than ever.

«*Allah Akbar!*» exclaimed he, «happy the man that shall effect that cure, should he but know what to choose from the royal treasury».

«What mean you, most reverend owl?», said Ahmed.

«Hearken, O prince, to what I shall relate. We owls, you must know, are a learned body and much given to dark and dusty research. During my late prowling at night about the domes and turrets of Toledo, I discovered a college of antiquarian owls who hold their meeting in a great vaulted tower where the royal treasury is deposited. Here they were discussing the forms and inscriptions and designs of ancient gems and jewels, and of golden and silver vessels, heaped up in the treasury, the fashion of every country and age, but mostly they were interested about certain relics and talismans that have remained in the treasury since the time of Roderick the Goth. Among these was a box of sandal-wood secured by bands of steel of Oriental workmanship and inscribed with mystic characters known only to the learned few. This box and its inscription had occupied the college for several sessions, and had caused much long and grave dispute. At the time of my visit a very ancient owl who had recently arrived from Egypt was seated on the lid of the box lecturing upon the inscription, and he proved from it that the coffer contained the silken carpet of the throne of Solomon the Wise, which doubtless had been brought to Toledo by the Jews who took refuge there after the downfall of Jerusalem.»

When the owl had concluded his antiquarian harangue, the prince remained for a time absorbed in thought. «I have heard», said he, «from the sage Eben Bonabben of the wonderful properties of that talisman which disappeared at the fall of Jerusalem and was supposed to be lost to mankind. Doubtless it remains a sealed mystery to the Christians of Toledo. If I can get possession of that carpet, my fortune is secure».

The next day the prince laid aside his rich attire, and arrayed himself in the simple garb of an Arab of the desert. He dyed his complexion to a tawny hue, and no one could have recognised in him the splendid warrior who had caused such admiration and dismay at the tournament. With staff in hand and scrip by his side and a small pastoral reed, he repaired to Toledo and, presenting himself at the gate of the royal palace, announced himself as a candidate for the reward offered for the cure of the princess. The guards would have driven him away with blows. «What can a vagrant Arab like thyself pretend to do», said they, «in a case where the most learned of the land have failed?» The king, however, overheard the tumult and ordered the Arab to be brought into his presence.

«Most potent king», said Ahmed, «you behold before you a Bedouin Arab, the greater part of whose life has been passed in the solitudes of the desert. These solitudes, it is well known, are the haunts of demons and evil spirits who beset us poor shepherds in our lonely watching, enter into and possess our flocks and herds, and somethimes render even the patient camel furious; against these our counter-charm is music and we have legendary airs handed down from generation to generation, that we chant and pipe to cast forth these evil spirits. I am of a gifted line and possess this power in its fullest force. If it be any evil influence of the kind that holds a spell over thy daughter, I pledge my head to free her from its sway».

The king who was a man of understanding and knew the wonderful secrets possessed by the Arabs was inspired with hope by the confident language of the prince. He conducted him immediately to the lofty tower, secured by several doors, in the summit of which was the chamber of the princess. The window opened upon a terrace with balustrades, commanding a view over Toledo and all the surrounding country. The windows were darkened, for the princess lay within, a prey to a devouring grief that refused all alleviation.

The prince seated himself on the terrace and performed several wild Arabian airs on his pastoral pipe, which he had learnt from his attendants in the Generalife at Granada. The princess continued insensible, and the doctors who were present shook their heads and smiled with incredulity and contempt. At length the prince laid aside the reed and to a simple melody chanted the amatory verses of the letter which had declared his passion.

The princess recognized the strain; a fluttering joy stole to her heart, she raised her head and listened, tears rushed to her eyes and streamed down her cheeks, her bosom rose and fell with a tumult of emotions. She would have asked for the minstrel to be brought into her presence but maiden coyness held her silent. The king read her wishes and at his command Ahmed was conducted into the chamber. The lovers were discreet; they but exchanged glances, yet those glances spoke volumes. Never was triumph of music more complete. The rose had returned to the soft cheek of the princess, the freshness to her lip and the dewy light to her languishing eyes.

All the physicians present stared at each other with astonishment. The king regarded the Arab minstrel with admiration mixed with awe. «Wonderful youth!» exclaimed he «thou shalt henceforth be the first physician of my court, and no other prescription will I take but thy melody. For the present receive thy reward, the most precious jewel in my treasury».

«O king», replied Ahmed, «I care not for silver or gold or precious stones. One relic hast thou in thy treasury, handed down from the Moslems who once owned Toledo—a box of sandal-wood containing a silken carpet. Give me that box and I am content».

All present were surprised at the moderation of the Arab, and still more when the box of sandal-wood was brought and the carpet drawn forth. It was of fine green silk, covered with Hebrew and Chaldaic characters. The court physicians looked at each other and shrugged their shoulders and smiled at the simplicity of this new practitioner who could be content with so paltry a fee.

«This carpet», said the prince, «once covered the throne of Solomon the Wise; it is worthy of being placed beneath the feet of beauty».

So saying, he spread it on the terrace beneath an ottoman that had been brought forth for the princess, then seating himself at her feet.

«Who», said he, «shall counteract what is written in the book of fate? Behold the prediction of the astrologers verified. Know, O king, that your daughter and I have long loved each other in secret. Behold in me the Pilgrim of Love!»

These words were scarcely from his lips when the carpet rose in the air, bearing off the prince and princess. The king and the physicians gazed after it with open mouths and straining eyes, until it became a little speck on the white bosom of a cloud and then disappeared in the blue vault of heaven

The king in a rage summoned his treasurer. «How is this», said he, «that thou hast suffered an infidel to get possession of such a talisman?»

«Alas, sire, we knew not its nature nor could we decipher the inscription of the box. If it be indeed the carpet of the throne of the wise Solomon, it is possessed of magic power and can transport its owner from place to place through the air».

The king assembled a mighty army and set off for Granada in pursuit of the fugitives. His march was long and toilsome. Encamping in the Vega, he sent a herald to demand restitution of his daughter. The king himself came forth with all his court to meet him. In the king he beheld the real minstrel, for Ahmed had succeeded to the throne on the death of his father and the beautiful Aldegonda was his sultana.

The Christian king was easily pacified when he found that his daughter was suffered to continue in her faith—not that he was particularly pious, but religion is always a point of pride and etiquette with princes. Instead of bloody battles, there was a succession of feasts and rejoicings after which the king returned well pleased to Toledo, and the youthful couple continued to reign as happily as wisely in the Alhambra.

It is proper to add, that the owl and the parrot had severally followed the prince by easy stages to Granada, the former travelling by night and stopping at the various hereditary possessions of his family, the latter figuring in gay circles of every town and city on his route.

Ahmed gratefully requited the services which they had rendered on his pilgrimage. He appointed the owl his prime minister, the parrot his master of ceremonies. It is needless to say that never was a realm more sagely administered or a court conducted with more exact punctilio.

LEGEND OF THE MOOR'S LEGACY

J UST within the fortress of the Alhambra in front of the royal palace is a broad open esplanade called the Place or
Square of the Cisterns (*la Plaza de los Aljibes*), so called from
being undermined by reservoirs of water, hidden from sight,
and which have existed from the time of the Moors. At one
corner of this esplanade is a Moorish well, cut through the
living rock to a great depth, the water of which is cold as ice
and clear as crystal. The wells made by the Moors are always
in repute, for it is well known what pains they took to penetrate to the purest and sweetest springs and fountains. The
one of which we now speak is famous throughout Granada
insomuch that the water-carriers, some bearing great water-
jars on their shoulders, others driving asses before them laden
with earthen vessels, are ascending and descending the steep
woody avenues of the Alhambra from early dawn until a late
hour of the night.

Fountains and wells, ever since the scriptural days, have
been noted gossiping places in hot climates, and, at the well
in question, there is a kind of perpetual club kept up during
the livelong day by the invalids, old women and other curious
do-nothing folk of the fortress who sit here on the stone benches under an awning spread over the well to shelter the
toll-gatherer from the sun and dawdle over the gossip of the

201

fortress and question every water-carrier that arrives about the news of the city and make long comments on everything they hear and see. Not an hour of the day but loitering housewives and idle maid-servants may be seen, lingering with pitcher on head or in hand, to hear the last of the endless tattle of these worthies.

Among the water-carriers who once resorted to this well, there was a sturdy, strong backed, bandy-legged little fellow, named Pedro Gil, but called Peregil for shortness. Being a water-carrier, he was a *gallego,* or native of Galicia, of course. Nature seems to have formed races of men, as she has of animals, for diferent kinds of drudgery. In France the shoe-blacks are all Savoyards, the porters of hotels all Swiss, and in the days of hoops and hairpowder in England, no man could give the regular swing to a sedan-chair but a bog-trotting Irishman. So in Spain, the carriers of water and bearers of burdens are all sturdy little natives of Galicia. No man says, «Get me a porter»—but, «Call a *gallego*».

To return from this digression, Peregil the *gallego* had begun business with merely a great earthen jar which he carried upon his shoulder; by degrees he rose in the world and was enabled to purchase an assistant of a corresponding class of animals—being a stout shaggy-haired donkey. On each side of this his long-eared aide-de-camp in a kind of pannier were slung his water-jars, covered with fig-leaves to protect them from the sun. There was not a more industrious water-carrier in all Granada, nor one more merry withal. The streets rang with his cheerful voice, as he trudged after his donkey, singing forth the usual summer note that resounds through the Spanish towns: «*¿Quién quiere agua, agua más fría que la nieve?*» «Who wants water, water colder than snow? Who wants water from the well of the Alhambra, cold as ice and clear as crystal?» When he served a customer with a sparkling glass, it was always with a pleasant word that caused a smile, and if, perchance, it was a comely dame or dimpling damsel, it was always with a sly leer and a compliment to her beauty that was irresistible. Thus Peregil, the *gallego*, was noted throughout all Granada for being one of the civilest, pleasantest and happiest of mortals. Yet it is not he who sings loudest and jokes most that has the lightest heart. Under all this air of merriment honest Peregil had his cares and troubles. He had a large family of ragged children to support, who were hungry and clamorous as a nest of young swallows and beset him with their outcries for food whenever he came home of an evening. He had a helpmate too, who was anything but a help to him. She had been a village beauty before marriage, noted for her skill at dancing the *bolero* and rattling the castanets, and she still retained her early propensities, spending the hard earnings of honest Peregil in frippery and laying the very donkey under requisition for junketing parties into the country on Sundays and saints' days and those innumerable holidays which are rather more numerous in Spain than the days of the week. With all this she was a little of a slattern, something more of a lie-abed, and above all a gossip of the first water, neglecting house, household and everything else, to loiter slipshod in the houses of her gossip neighbours.

He, however, who tempers the wind to the shorn lamb accommodates the yoke of matrimony to the submissive neck. Peregil bore all the heavy dispensations of wife and children with as meek a spirit as his donkey bore the water-jars and, however he might shake his ears in private, never ventured to question the household virtues of his slattern spouse.

He loved his children, too, even as an owl loves its owlets, seeing in them his own image multiplied and perpetuated, for they were a sturdy, long-backed, bandy-legged little brood. The great pleasure of honest Peregil was whenever he could afford himself a scanty holiday and had a handful of *maravedíes* to take the whole litter forth with him—some in his arms, some tugging at his skirts and some trudging at his heels —and to treat then to a gambol among the orchards of the Vega, while his wife was dancing with her holiday friends in the *angosturas* of the Darro.

It was a late hour one summer night and most of the water-carriers had desisted from their toils. The day had been uncommonly sultry; the night was one of those delicious moonlights which tempt the inhabitants of those southern climes to indemnify themselves for the heat and inaction of the day, by lingering in the open air and enjoying its tempered sweetness until after midnight. Customers for water were therefore still abroad. Peregil, like a considerate, painstaking little father, thought of his hungry children. «One more journey to the well, said he to himself, «to earn a Sunday's *puchero* for the little ones». So saying, he trudged manfully up the steep avenue of the Alhambra, singing as he went, and now and then bestowing a hearty thwack with a cudgel on the flanks of his donkey, either by way of cadence to the song or refreshment to the animal, for dry blows serve in lieu of provender in Spain for all beasts of burden.

When he arrived at the well, he found it deserted by every one except a solitary stranger in Moorish garb, seated on the stone bench in the moonlight. Peregil paused at first and regarded him with surprise, not unmixed with awe, but the Moor feebly beckoned him to approach. «I am faint and ill», said he, «aid me to return to the city and I will pay the double what thou couldst gain by thy jars of water».

The honest heart of the little water-carrier was touched with compassion at the appeal of the stranger. «God forbid», said he, «that I should ask fee or reward for doing a common act of humanity». He accordingly helped the Moor on his donkey and set off slowly for Granada, the poor Moslem being so weak that it was necessary to hold him on the animal to keep him from falling to the earth.

When they entered the city, the water-carrier demanded whither he should conduct him. «Alas!» said the Moor faintly, «I have neither home nor habitation, I am a stranger in the land. Suffer me to lay my head this night beneath thy roof and thou shalt be amply repaid».

Honest Peregil thus saw himself unexpectedly saddled with an infidel guest, but he was too humane to refuse a night's shelter to a fellow-being in so forlorn a plight, so he conducted the Moor to his dwelling. The children who had sallied forth open-mouthed as usual on hearing the tramp of the donkey, ran back with affright when they beheld the turbaned stranger and hid themselves behind their mother. The latter stepped forth intrepidly, like a ruffling hen before her brood when a vagrant dog approaches.

«What infidel companion», cried she, «is this you have brought home at this late hour to draw upon us the eyes of the Inquisition?»

«Be quiet, wife», replied the *gallego,* «here is a poor sick stranger, without friend or home; wouldst thou turn him forth to perish in the streets?»

The wife would still have remonstrated, for although she lived in a hovel, she was a furious stickler for the credit of her house; the little water-carrier, however, for once was stiff-necked and refused to bend beneath the yoke. He assisted the poor Moslem to alight and spread a mat and a sheepskin for him on the ground in the coolest part of the house, being the only kind of bed that his poverty afforded.

In a little while the Moor was seized with violent convulsions which defied all the ministering skill of the simple water-carrier. The eye of the poor patient acknowledged his kindness. During an interval of his fits he called him to his side and addressing him in a low voice, «My end», said he, «I fear is at hand. If I die, I bequeath you this box as a reward for your charity». So saying, he opened his *albornoz* or cloak and showed a small box of sandal-wood, strapped round his body. «God grant, my friend», replied the worthy little *gallego,* «that you may live many years to enjoy your treasure, whatever it may be». The Moor shook his head; he laid his hand upon the box and would have said something more concerning it, but his convulsions returned with increased violence and in a little while he expired.

The water-carrier's wife was now as one distracted. «This comes», said she, «of your foolish good-nature, always running into scrapes to oblige others. What will become of us when this corpse is found in our house? We shall be sent to prison as murderers and, if we escape with our lives, shall be ruined by notaries and *alguaciles*».

Poor Peregil was in equal tribulation and almost repented himself of having done a good deed. At length a thought struck him. «It is not yet day», said he, «I can convey the dead body out of the city and bury it in the sands on the banks of the Xenil. No one saw the Moor enter our dwelling and no one will know anything of his death».

So said, so done. The wife aided him; they rolled the body of the unfortunate Moslem in the mat on which he had expired, laid it across the ass and Peregil set out with it for the banks of the river.

As ill luck would have it, there lived opposite to the water-carrier a barber named Pedrillo Pedrugo, one of the most prying, tattling and mischief-making of his gossip tribe. He was a weasel-faced spider-legged varlet, supple and insinuating; the famous barber of Seville could not surpass him for his universal knowledge of the affairs of others and he had no more power of retention than a sieve. It was said that he slept but with one eye at a time and kept one ear uncovered, so that even in his sleep he might see and hear all that was going on. Certain it is, he was a sort of scandalous chronicle for the quidnuncs of Granada and had more customers than all the rest of his fraternity.

This meddlesome barber heard Peregil arrive at an unusual hour at night, and the exclamations of his wife and children. His head was instantly popped out of a little window which served him as a look-out and he saw his neighbour assist a man in Moorish garb into his dwelling. This was so strange an occurrence that Pedrillo Pedrugo slept not a wink that night. Every five minutes he was at his loophole, watching the lights that gleamed through the chinks of his neighbour's door and before daylight he beheld Peregil sally forth with his donkey unusually laden.

The inquisitive barber was in a fidget; he slipped on his clothes and, stealing forth silently, followed the water-carrier at a distance, until he saw him dig a hole in the sandy bank of the Xenil and bury something that had the appearance of a dead body.

The barber hied him home and fidgeted about his shop, setting everything upside down, until sunrise. He then took a basin under his arm and sallied forth to the house of his daily customer the *alcalde*.

The *alcalde* was just risen. Pedrillo Pedrugo seated him in a chair, threw a napkin round his neck, put a basin of hot water under his chin and began to mollify his beard with his fingers.

«Strange doings!» said Pedrugo, who played barber and newsmonger at the same time—«Strange doings! Robbery and murder and burial, all in one night!»

«Hey!—how— what is that you say?» cried the *alcalde*.

«I say», replied the barber, rubbing a piece of soap over the nose and mouth of the dignitary, for a Spanish barber disdains to employ a brush—«I say that Peregil the *gallego* has robbed and murdered a Moorish Mussulman and buried him this blessed night. *Maldita sea la noche*—accursed be the night for the same!»

«But how do you know all this?» demanded the *alcalde*.

«Be patient, *señor,* and you shall hear all about it», replied Pedrillo, taking him by the nose and sliding a razor over his cheek. He then recounted all that he had seen, going through both operations at the same time, shaving his beard, washing his chin and wiping him dry with a dirty napkin, while he was robbing, murdering and burying the Moslem.

Now it so happened that this *alcalde* was one of the most overbearing, and at the same time most griping and corrupt curmudgeons in all Granada. It could not be denied, however, that he set a high value upon justice, for he sold it at its weight in gold. He presumed the case in point to be one of murder and robbery; doubtless there must be rich spoil. How was it to be secured into the legitimate hands of the law? For as to merely entrapping the delinquent—that would be feeding the gallows, but entrapping the booty—that would be enriching the judge, and such according to his creed was the great end of justice. So thinking, he summoned to his presence his trustiest *alguacil,* a gaunt, hungry-looking varlet, clad according to the custom of his order in the ancient Spanish garb, a broad black beaver turned up at the sides, a quaint ruff, a small black cloak dangling from his shoulders, rusty black underclothes that set off his spare wiry frame, while in his hand he bore a slender white wand, the dreaded insignia of his office. Such was the legal bloodhound of the ancient Spanish breed that he put upon the traces of the unlucky water-carrier, and such was his speed and certainty, that he was upon the haunches of poor Peregil before he had returned to his dwelling, and brought both him and his donkey before the dispenser of justice.

The *alcalde* bent upon him one of his most terrific frowns. «Hark ye, culprit!» roared he, in a voice that made the knees of

the little *gallego* smite together—«hark ye, culprit! there is no need of denying thy guilt, everything is known to me. A gallows is the proper reward for the crime thou hast committed, but I am merciful and readily listen to reason. The man that has been murdered in thy house was a Moor, an infidel, the enemy of our faith. It was doubtless in a fit of religious zeal that thou hast slain him. I will be indulgent, therefore; render up the property of which thou hast robbed him and we will hush the matter up».

The poor water-carrier called upon all the saints to witness his innocence. Alas! not one of them appeared, and if they had, the *alcalde* would have disbelieved the whole calendar. The water-carrier related the whole story of the dying Moor with the straightforward simplicity of truth, but it was all in vain. «Wilt thou persist in saying», demanded the judge, «that this Moslem had neither gold nor jewels which were the object of thy cupidity?»

«As I hope to be saved, your worship», replied the water-carrier, «he had nothing but a small box of sandal-wood, which he bequeathed to me in reward for my services».

«A box of sandal-wood! a box of sandal-wood!» exclaimed the *alcalde,* his eyes sparkling at the idea of precious jewels. «And where is this box? Where have you concealed it?»

«An' it please your grace», replied the water-carrier, «it is in one of the panniers of my mule, and heartily at the service of your worship».

He had hardly spoken the words, when the keen *alguacil* darted off and reappeared in an instant with the mysterious box of sandal-wood. The *alcalde* opened it with an eager and trembling hand; all pressed forward to gaze upon the treasures it was expected to contain, when to their disappointment nothing appeared within, but a parchment scroll, covered with Arabic characters and an end of a waxen taper.

When there is nothing to be gained by the conviction of a

prisoner, justice even in Spain is apt to be impartial. The *alcalde* having recovered from his disappointment and found that there was really no booty in the case, now listened dispassionately to the explanation of the water-carrier, which was corroborated by the testimony of his wife. Being convinced, therefore, of his innocence, he discharged him from arrest; nay more, he permitted him to carry off the Moor's legacy, the box of sandal-wood and its contents as the well-merited reward of his humanity, but he retained his donkey in payment of costs and charges.

Behold the unfortunate little *gallego* reduced once more to the necessity of being his own water-carrier and trudging up to the well of the Alhambra with a great earthen jar upon his shoulder.

As he toiled up the hill in the heat of a summer noon, his usual good humour forsook him. «Dog of an *alcalde*!» would he cry, «to rob a poor man of the means of his subsistence, of the best friend he had in the world!» And then, at the remembrance of the beloved companion of his labours, all the kindness of his nature would break forth. «An, donkey of my heart!» would he exclaim, resting his burden on a stone and wiping the sweat from his brow—«Ah, donkey of my heart! I warrant me thou thinkest of thy old master! I warrant me thou missest the water-jars, poor beast!»

To add to his afflictions, his wife received him, on his return home, with whimperings and repinings; she had clearly the vantage-ground of him, having warned him not to commit the egregious act of hospitality that had brought on him all these misfortunes, and like a knowing woman, she took every occasion to throw her superior sagacity in his teeth. If ever her children lacked food or needed a new garment, she could answer with a sneer—«Go to your father—he is heir to king Chico of the Alhambra; ask him to help you out of the Moor's strong-box!»

Was ever poor mortal so soundly punished for having done a good action? The unlucky Peregil was grieved in flesh and spirit, but still he bore meekly with the railings of his spouse. At length one evening when after a hot day's toil she taunted him in the usual manner, he lost all patience. He did not venture to retort upon her, but his eye rested upon the box of sandal-wood, which lay on a shelf with the lid half open, as if laughing in mockery at his vexation. Seizing it, he dashed it with indignation to the floor: —«Unlucky was the day that I ever set eyes on thee», he cried, «or sheltered thy master beneath my roof!»

As the box struck the floor, the lid flew wide open and the parchment scroll rolled forth. Peregil sat regarding the scroll for some time in moody silence. At length rallying his ideas —«Who knows», thought he, «but this writing may be of some importance, as the Moor seems to have guarded it with such care?» Picking it up therefore he put it in his bosom, and the next morning, as he was crying water through the streets, he stopped at the shop of a Moor, a native of Tangiers, who sold trinkets and perfumery in the Zacatín, and asked him to explain the contents.

The Moor read the scroll attentively, then stroked his beard and smiled. «This manuscript» said he, «is a form of incantation for the recovery of hidden treasure that is under the power of enchantment. It is said to have such virtue that the strongest bolts and bars, nay the adamantine rock itself, will yield before it!»

«Bah!» cried the little *gallego,* «what is all that to me? I am no enchanter and know nothing of buried treasure». So saying, he shouldered his water-jar, left the scroll in the hands of the Moor and trudged forward on his daily rounds.

That evening, however, as he rested himself about twilight at the well of the Alhambra, he found a number of gossips assembled at the place, and their conversation, as is not unusual at that shadowy hour, turned upon old tales and traditions of a supernatural nature. Being all poor as rats, they dwelt with peculiar fondness upon the popular theme of enchanted riches left by the Moors in various parts of the Alhambra. Above all, they concurred in the belief that there were great treasures buried deep in the earth under the tower of the Seven Floors.

These stories made an unusual impression on the mind of honest Peregil, and they sank deeper and deeper into his thoughts as he returned alone down the darkening avenues. «If, after all, there should be treasure hid beneath that tower, and if the scroll I left with the Moor should enable me to get at it!» In the sudden ecstasy of the thought, he had well-nigh let fall his water-jar.

That night he tumbled and tossed, and could scarcely get a wink of sleep for the thoughts that were bewildering his brain. Bright and early, he repaired to the shop of the Moor and told him all that was passing in his mind. «You can read Arabic», said he, «suppose we go together to the tower and try the effect of the charm; if it fails, we are no worse off than before, but if it succeeds, we will share equally all the treasure we may discover».

«Hold», replied the Moslem; «this writing is not sufficient of itself; it must be read at midnight by the light of a taper singularly compounded and prepared, the ingredients of which are not within my reach. Without such a taper the scroll is of no avail»

«Say no more!» cried the little *gallego,* «I have such a taper at hand and will bring it here in a moment». So saying, he hastened home and soon returned with the end of yellow wax taper that he had found in the box of sandal-wood.

The Moor felt it and smelt it. «Here are rare and costly perfumes», said he, «combined with this yellow wax. This is the kind of taper specified in the scroll. While this burns, the strongest walls and most secret caverns will remain open. Woe to him, however, who lingers within until it be extinguished. He will remain enchanted with the treasure».

It was now agreed between them to try the charm that very night. At a late hour, therefore, when nothing was stirring but bats and owls, they ascended the woody hill of the Alhambra and approached that awful tower, shrouded by trees and rendered formidable by so many traditionary tales. By the light of a lantern, they groped their way through bushes and over fallen stones to the door of a vault beneath the tower. With fear and trembling they descended a flight of steps cut into the rock. It led to an empty chamber, damp and drear, from which another flight of steps led to a deeper vault. In this way they descended four several flights, leading into as many vaults, one below the other, but the floor of the fourth was solid; and though, according to tradition, there remained three vaults still below, it was said to be impossible to penetrate further, the residue being shut up by strong enchantment. The air of this vault was damp and chilly, and had an earthy smell, and the light scarce cast forth any rays. They paused here for a time in breathless suspense until they faintly heard the clock of the watch-tower strike midnight; upon this they lit the waxen taper which diffused an odour of myrrh and frankincense and storax.

The Moor began to read in a hurried voice. He had scarce finished when there was a noise as of subterraneous thunder. The earth shook and the floor, yawning open, disclosed a flight of steps. Trembling with awe, they descended and by the light of the lantern found themselves in another vault, covered with Arabic inscriptions. In the centre stood a great chest, secured with seven bands of steel, at each end of which sat an enchanted Moor in armour, but motionless as a statue, being controlled by the power of the incantation. Before the chest were several jars filled with gold and silver and precious stones. In the largest of these they thrust their arms up to the elbow

213

and at every dip hauled forth handfuls of broad yellow pieces of Moorish gold or bracelets and ornaments of the same precious metal, while occasionally a necklace of Oriental pearls would stick to their fingers. Still they trembled and breathed short while cramming their pockets with the spoils, and cast many a fearful glance at the two enchanted Moors who sat grim and motionless, glaring upon them with unwinking eyes. At length, struck with a sudden panic at some fancied noise, they both rushed up the staircase, tumbled over one another into the upper apartment, overturned and extinguished the waxen taper, and the pavement again closed with a thundering sound.

Filled with dismay, they did not pause until they had groped their way out of the tower and beheld the stars shining through the trees. Then seating themselves upon the grass, they divided the spoil, determining to content themselves for the present with this mere skimming of the jars, but to return on some future night and drain them to the bottom. To make sure of each other's good faith also, they divided the talismans between them, one retaining the scroll and the other the taper; this done, they set off with light hearts and well-lined pockets for Granada.

As they wended their way down the hill, the shrewd Moor whispered a word of counsel in the ear of the simple little water-carrier.

«Friend Peregil», said he, «all this affair must be kept a profound secret, until we have secured the treasure and conveyed it out of harm's way. If a whisper of it gets to the ear of the *alcalde*, we are undone!»

«Certainly!» replied the *gallego*, «nothing can be more true».

«Friend Peregil», said the Moor, «you are a discreet man, and I make no doubt can keep a secret, but you have a wife».

«She shall not know a word of it», replied the little water-carrier sturdily.

«Enough», said the Moor; «I depend upon thy discretion and thy promise».

Never was promise more positive and sincere, but, alas! what man can keep a secret from his wife? Certainly not such an one as Peregil the water-carrier who was one of the most loving and tractable of husbands. On his return home, he found his wife moping in a corner. «Mighty well», cried she as he entered, «you've come at last after rambling about until this hour of the night. I wonder you have not brought home another Moor as a housemate» Then bursting into tears, she began to wring her hands and smite her breast: «Unhappy woman that I am!» exclaimed she, «what will become of me? My house stripped and plundered by lawyers and *alguaciles;* my husband a do-no-good that no longer brings home bread for his family, but goes rambling about day and night with infidel Moors! O my children! my children! what will become of us? We shall all have to beg in the streets!»

Honest Peregil was so moved by the distress of his spouse, that he could not help whimpering also. His heart was as full as his pocket and not to be restrained. Thrusting his hand into the latter, he hauled forth three or four broad gold pieces, and slipped them into her bosom. The poor woman stared with astonishment and could not understand the meaning of this golden shower. Before she could recover her surprise, the little *gallego* drew forth a chain of gold and dangled it before her, capering with exultation, his mouth distended from ear to ear.

«Holy Virgin protect us!» exclaimed the wife. «What hast thou been doing, Peregil? Surely thou hast not been committing murder and robbery!»

The idea had scarce entered the brain of the poor woman than it became a certainty with her. She saw a prison and a gallows in the distance, and a little bandy-legged *gallego* hanging pendent from it, and, overcome by the horrors conjured up by her imagination, fell into violent hysterics.

What could the poor man do? He had no other means of pacifying his wife and dispelling the phantoms of her fancy than by relating the whole story of his good fortune. This, however, he did not do until he had exacted from her the most solemn promise to keep it a profound secret from every living being.

To describe her joy would be impossible. She flung her arms round the neck of her husband and almost strangled him with her caresses. «Now, wife», exclaimed the little man with honest exultation, «what say you now to the Moor's legacy? Henceforth never abuse me for helping a fellow creature in distress».

The honest *gallego* retired to his sheepskin mat and slept as soundly as if on a bed of down. Not so his wife; she emptied the whole contents of his pockets upon the mat and sat all night counting gold pieces of Arabic coin, trying on necklaces and earrings and fancying the figure she should one day make when permitted to enjoy her riches.

On the following morning the honest *gallego* took a broad golden coin, and repaired with it to a jeweller's shop in the Zacatín to offer it for sale, pretending to have found it among the ruins of the Alhambra. The jeweller saw that it had an Arabic inscription and was of the purest gold; he offered, however, but a third of its value, with which the water-carrier was perfectly content. Peregil now bought new clothes for his little flock and all kinds of toys, together with ample provisions for a hearty meal, and returning to his dwelling, set all his children dancing around him, while he capered in the midst, the happiest of fathers.

The wife of the water-carrier kept her promise of secrecy with surprising strictness. For a whole day and a half she went about with a look of mystery and a heart swelling almost to bursting, yet she held her peace, though surrounded by her gossips. It is true, she could not help giving herself a few airs, apologized for her ragged dress, and talked of ordering a new *basquiña* all trimmed with gold lace and bugles, and a new lace *mantilla*. She threw out hints of her husband's intention of leaving off his trade of water-carrying, as it did not altogether agree with his health. In fact she thought they should all retire to the country for the summer, that the children might have the benefit of the mountain air, for there was no living in the city in this sultry season.

The neighbours stared at each other and thought the poor woman had lost her wits, and her airs and graces and elegant pretensions were the theme of universal scoffing and merriment among her friends the moment her back was turned.

If she restrained herself abroad, however, she indemnified herself at home, and putting a string of rich Oriental pearls round her neck, Moorish bracelets on her arms and an aigrette of diamonds on her head, sailed backwards and forwards in her slattern rags about the room, now and then stopping to admire herself in a piece of broken mirror. Nay, in the impulse of her simple vanity, she could not resist, on one occasion, showing herself at the window, to enjoy the effect of her finery on the passers-by.

As the fates would have it, Pedrillo Pedrugo, the meddlesome barber, was at this moment sitting idly in his shop on the opposite side of the street, when his ever-watchful eye caught the sparkle of a diamond. In an instant he was at his loophole reconnoitring the slattern spouse of the water-carrier, decorated with the splendour of an Eastern bride. No sooner had he taken an accurate inventory of her ornaments, than he posted off with all speed to the *alcalde*. In a little while the hungry *alguacil* was again on the scent, and before the day was over, the unfortunate Peregil was again dragged into the presence of the judge.

«How is this, villain», cried the *alcalde,* in a furious voice. «You told me that the infidel who died in your house left nothing behind but an empty coffer, and now I hear of your wife flaunting in her rags decked out with pearls and diamonds. Wretch that thou art! prepare to render up the spoils of thy miserable victim and to swing on the gallows that is already tired of waiting for thee.»

The terrified water-carrier fell on his knees and made a full relation of the marvellous manner in which he had gained his wealth. The *alcalde,* the *alguacil* and the inquisitive barber listened with greedy ears to this Arabian tale of enchanted treasure. The *alguacil* was dispatched to bring the Moor who had assisted in the incantation. The Moslem entered, half frightened out of his wits at finding himself in the hands of the harpies of the law. When he beheld the water-carrier standing with sheepish looks and downcast countenance, he comprehended the whole matter. «Miserable animal», said he, as he passed near him, «did I not warn thee against babbling to thy wife?»

The story of the Moor coincided exactly with that of his colleague, but the *alcalde* affected to be slow of belief and threw out menaces of imprisonment and rigorous investigation.

«Softly, good *señor alcalde*», said the Mussulman who by this time had recovered his usual shrewdness and self-possession. «Let us not mar fortune's favours in the scramble for them. Nobody knows anything of this matter but ourselves; let us keep the secret. There is wealth enough in the cave to enrich us all. Promise a fair division and hall shall be produced; refuse, and the cave shall remain forever closed.»

The *alcalde* consulted apart with the *alguacil.* The latter was an old fox in his profession. «Promise anything», said he, «until you get posesion of the treasure. You may then seize

218

upon the whole and, if he and his accomplice dare to murmur, threaten them with the faggot and the stake as infidels and sorcerers.»

The *alcalde* relished the advice. Smoothing his brow and turning to the Moor, «This is a strange story», said he, «and may be true, but I must have ocular proof of it. This very night you must repeat the incantation in my presence. If there be really such treasure we will share it amicably among us and say nothing further of the matter; if ye have deceived me, expect no mercy at my hands. In the meantime you must remain in custody.»

The Moor and the water-carrier cheerfully agreed to these conditions, satisfied that the event would prove the truth of their words.

Towards midnight the *alcalde* sallied forth secretly attended by the *alguacil* and the meddlesome barber, all strongly armed. They conducted the Moor and the water-carrier as prisoners, and were provided with the stout donkey of the latter to bear off the expected treasure. They arrived at the tower without being observed and, tying the donkey to a fig-tree, descended into the fourth vault of the tower.

The scroll was produced, the yellow waxen taper lighted, and the Moor read the form of incantation. The earth trembled as before and the pavement opened with a thundering sound, disclosing the narrow flight of steps. The *alcalde,* the *alguacil* and the barber were struck aghast and could not summon courage to descend. The Moor and the water-carrier entered the lower vault and found the two Moors seated as before, silent and motionless. They removed two of the great jars, filled with golden coin and precious stones. The water-carrier bore them up one by one upon his shoulders, but though a strong-backed little man and accustomed to carry burdens, he staggered beneath their weight and found, when slung on each side of his donkey, they were as much as the animal could bear.

«Let us be content for the present», said the Moor, «here is as much treasure as we can carry off without being perceived and enough to make us all wealthy to our heart's desire».

«Is there more treasure remaining behind?» demanded the *alcalde*.

«The greatest prize of all», said the Moor, «a huge coffer bound with bands of steel and filled with pearls and precious stones».

«Let us have up the coffer, by all means», cried the grasping *alcalde*.

«I will descend for no more», said the Moor, doggedly, «enough is enough for a reasonable man; more is superfluous».

«And I», said the water-carrier, «will bring up no further burden to break the back of my poor donkey».

Finding commands, threats and entreaties equally vain, the *alcalde* turned to his two adherents. «Aid me», said he, «to bring up the coffer and its contents shall be divided among us». So saying, he descended the steps, followed with trembling reluctance by the *alguacil* and the barber.

No sooner did the Moor behold them fairly earthed, than he extinguished the yellow taper; the pavement closed with its usual crash and the three worthies remained buried in its womb.

He then hastened up the different flights of steps nor stopped until in the open air. The little water-carrier followed him as fast as his short legs would permit.

«What hast thou done?» cried Peregil, as soon as he could recover breath. «The *alcalde* and the other two are shut up in the vault.»

«It is the will of Allah!» said the Moor devoutly.

«And will you not release them?», demanded the *gallego*.

«Allah forbid!» replied the Moor, smoothing his beard. «It is written in the book of fate that they shall remain enchanted, until some future adventurer arrive to break the charm. The will of God be done!» So saying, he hurled the end of the waxen taper far among the gloomy thickets of the glen.

There was now no remedy; so the Moor and the water-carrier proceeded with the richly-laden donkey towards the city, nor could honest Peregil refrain from hugging and kissing his long-eared fellow-labourer thus restored to him from the clutches of the law, and, in fact, it is doubtful which gave the simple-hearted little man most joy at the moment, the gaining of the treasure or the recovery of the donkey.

The two partners in good luck divided their spoil amicably and fairly, except that the Moor who had a little taste for trinketry made out to get into his heap the most of the pearls and precious stones and other baubles, but then he always gave the water-carrier in lieu magnificent jewels of massy gold, of five times the size, with which the latter was heartily content. They took care not to linger within reach of accidents, but made off to enjoy their wealth undisturbed in other countries. The Moor returned to Africa to his native city of Tangiers, and the *gallego* with his wife, his children and his donkey made the best of his way to Portugal. Here, under the admonition and tuition of his wife, he became a personage of some consequence, for she made the worthy little man array his long body and short legs in doublet and hose with a feather in his hat and a sword by his side, and laying aside his familiar appellation of Peregil, assumed the more sonorous title of *Don Pedro Gil*. His progeny grew up a thriving and merry-hearted, though short and bandy-legged generation, while *Señora Gil*, befringed, belaced and betasselled from her head to her heels with glittering rings on every finger became a model of slattern fashion and finery.

As to the *alcalde* and his adjuncts, they remained shut up under the great tower of the Seven Floors, and there they remain spell-bound at the present day. Whenever there shall be a lack in Spain of pimping barbers, sharking *alguaciles* and corrupt *alcaldes,* they may be sought after, but if they have to wait until such time for their deliverance, there is danger of their enchantment enduring until doomsday.

LEGEND OF THE ROSE OF THE ALHAMBRA

OR

THE PAGE AND THE GER-FALCON

For some time after the surrender of Granada by the Moors, that delightful city was a frequent and favourite residence of the Spanish sovereigns, until they were frightened away by successive shocks of earthquakes which toppled down various houses, and made the old Moslem towers rock to their foundations.

Many, many years then rolled away, during which Granada was rarely honoured by a royal guest. The palaces of the nobility remained silent and shut up, and the Alhambra, like a slighted beauty, sat in mournful desolation among her neglected gardens. The Tower of the *Infantas,* once the residence of the three beautiful Moorish princesses, partook of the general desolation; the spider spun her web athwart the gilded vault, and bats and owls nestled in those chambers that had been graced by the presence of Zayda, Zorayda and Zorahayda. The neglect of this tower may partly have been owing to some superstitious notions of the neighbours. It was rumoured that the spirit of the youthful Zorahayda who had perished in that tower was often seen by moonlight seated beside the fountain in the hall or moaning about the battlements, and that the notes of her silver lute could be heard at midnight by wayfarers passing along the glen.

At length the city of Granada was once more welcomed by the royal presence. All the world knows that Philip V. was the first Bourbon that swayed the Spanish sceptre. All the world knows that he married in second nuptials Elizabetta or Isabella (for they are the same), the beautiful Princess of Parma, and all the world knows that by this chain of contingencies a French prince and an Italian princess were seated together on the Spanish throne. For the reception of this illustrious pair, the Alhambra was repaired and fitted up with all possible expedition. The arrival of the court changed the whole aspect of the lately deserted palace. The clangour of drum and trumpet, the tramp of steeds about the avenues and outer court, the glitter of arms and display of banners about barbican and battlement recalled the ancient and warlike glories of the fortress. A softer spirit, however, reigned within the royal palace. There was the rustling of robes and the cautious tread and murmuring voice of reverential courtiers about the antechambers; a loitering of pages and maids of honour about the gardens and the sound of music stealing from open casements.

Among those who attended in the train of the monarchs was a favourite page of the queen, named Ruiz de Alarcón. To say that he was a favourite page of the queen was at once to speak his eulogium, for every one in the suite of the stately Elizabetta was chosen for grace and beauty and accomplishments. He was just turned of eighteen, light and lithe of form and graceful as a young Antinous. To the queen he was all deference and respect, yet he was at heart a roguish stripling, petted and spoiled by the ladies about the court and experienced in the ways of women far beyond his years.

This loitering page was one morning rambling about the groves of the Generalife, which overlook the grounds of the Alhambra. He had taken with him for his amusement a favourite ger-falcon of the queen. In the course of his rambles,

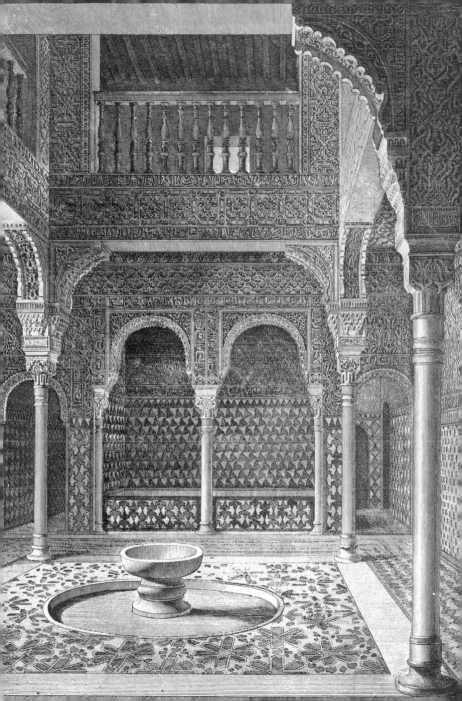

seeing a bird rising from a thicket, he unhooded the hawk and let him fly. The falcon towered high in the air, made a swoop at his quarry, but missing it, soared away, regardless of the calls of the page. The latter followed the truant bird with his eye in its capricious flight, until he saw it alight upon the battlements of a remote and lonely tower in the outer wall of the Alhambra, built on the edge of a ravine that separated the royal fortress from the grounds of the Generalife. It was in fact the «Tower of the Princesses».

The page descended into the ravine and approached the tower, but it had no entrance from the glen, and its lofty height rendered any attempt to scale it fruitless. Seeking one of the gates of the fortress, therefore, he made a wide circuit to that side of the tower facing within the walls.

A small garden, enclosed by a trellis-work of reeds over-hung with myrtle, lay before the tower. Opening a wicket, the page passed between beds of flowers and thickets of roses to the door. It was closed and bolted. A crevice in the door gave him a peep into the interior. There was a small Moorish hall with fretted walls, light marble columns and an alabaster fountain surrounded with flowers. In the centre hung a gilt cage containing a singing-bird; beneath it on a chair lay a tortoise-shell cat among reels of silk and other articles of female labour, and a guitar decorated with ribbons leaned against the fountain.

Ruiz de Alarcón was struck with these traces of female taste and elegance in a lonely and, as he had supposed, deserted tower. They reminded him of the tales of enchanted halls current in the Alhambra, and the tortoise-shell cat might be some spell-bound princess.

He knocked gently at the door. A beautiful face peeped out from a little window above but was instantly withdrawn. He waited, expecting that the door would be opened, but he wainted in vain; no footstep was to be heard within—all was silent. Had his senses deceived him or was this beautiful apparition the fairy of the tower? He knocked again and more loudly. After a little while the beaming face once more peeped forth; it was that of a blooming damsel of fifteen.

The page immediately doffed his plumed bonnet, and entreated in the most courteous accents to be permitted to ascend the tower in pursuit of his falcon.

«I dare not open the door, *señor*», replied the little damsel blushing, «my aunt has forbidden it».

«I do beseech you, fair maid; it is the favourite falcon of the queen. I dare not return to the palace without it».

«Are you then one of the cavaliers of the court?»

«I am, fair maid, but I shall lose the queen's favour and my place, if I lose this hawk.»

«¡*Santa María!* It is against you cavaliers of the court my aunt has charged me especially to bar the door.»

«Against wicked cavaliers doubtless, but I am none of these, but a simple harmless page who will be ruined and undonne if you deny me this small request».

The heart of the little damsel was touched by the distress of the page. It was a thousand pities he should be ruined for the want of so trifling a boon. Surely too he could not be one of those dangerous beings whom her aunt had described as a species of cannibal, ever on the prowl to make prey of thoughtless damsels; he was gentle and modest, and stood so entreatingly with cap in hand and looked so charming!

The sly page saw that the garrison began to waver and redoubled his entreaties in such moving terms that it was not in the nature of mortal maiden to deny him, so the blushing little warden of the tower descended and opened the door with a trembling hand. If the page had been charmed by a mere glimpse of her countenance from the window, he was ravished by the full-length portrait now revealed to him.

Her Andalusian bodice and trim *basquiña* set off the round

but delicate symmetry of her form which was as yet scarce verging into womanhood. Her glossy hair was parted on her forehead with scrupulous exactness and decorated with a fresh-plucked rose, according to the universal custom of the country. It is true her complexion was tinged by the ardour of a southern sun, but it served to give richness to the mantling bloom of her cheek and to heighten the lustre of her melting eyes.

Ruiz de Alarcón beheld all this with a single glance, for it became him not to tarry; he merely murmured his acknowledgements and then bounded lightly up the spiral staircase in quest of his falcon.

He soon returned with the truant bird upon his fist. The damsel in the meantime had seated herself by the fountain in the hall and was winding silk, but in her agitation she let fall the reel upon the pavement. The page sprang and picked it up, then dropping gracefully on one knee, presented it to her; but, seizing the hand extended to receive it, imprinted on it a kiss more fervent and devout than he had ever imprinted on the fair hand of his sovereign.

«¡Ave María, señor!» exclaimed the damsel, blushing still deeper with confusion and surprise, for never before had she received such a salutation.

The modest page made a thousand apologies, assuring her it was the way at court of expressing the most profound homage and respect.

Her anger, if anger she felt, was easily pacified, but her agitation and embarrassment continued, and she sat blushing deeper and deeper with her eyes cast down upon her work, entangling the silk which she attempted to wind.

The cunning page saw the confusion in the opposite camp and would fain have profited by it, but the fine speeches he would have uttered died upon his lips; his attempts at gallantry were awkward and ineffectual, and to his surprise, the adroit page who had figured with such grace and effrontery among the most knowing and experienced ladies of the court found himself awed and abashed in the presence of a simple damsel of fifteen.

In fact, the artless maiden in her own modesty and innocence had guardians more effectual than the bolts and bars prescribed by her vigilant aunt. Still, where is the female bosom proof against the first whisperings of love? The little damsel with all her artlessness instinctively comprehended all that the faltering tongue of the page failed to express, and her heart was flattered at beholding for the first time a lover at her feet—and such a lover!

The diffidence of the page, though genuine, was short-lived, and he was recovering his usual ease and confidence, when a shrill voice was heard at a distance.

«My aunt is returning from mass!» cried the damsel in affright, «I pray you, *señor,* depart».

«Not until you grant me that rose from your hair as a remembrance.»

She hastily untwisted the rose from her raven locks. «Take it», cried she, agitated and blushing, «but pray begone».

The page took the rose and at the same time covered with kisses the fair hand that gave it. Then, placing the flower in his bonnet and taking the falcon upon his fist, he bounded off through the garden, bearing away with him the heart of the gentle Jacinta.

When the vigilant aunt arrived at the tower, she remarked the agitation of her niece and an air of confusion in the hall, but a word of explanation sufficed. «A ger-falcon had pursued his prey into the hall.»

«Mercy on us! To think of a falcon flying into the tower. Did ever one hear of so saucy a hawk? Why, the very bird in the cage is not safe!»

The vigilant Fredegonda was one of the most wary of ancient spinsters. She had a becoming terror and distrust of what she denominated «the opposite sex», which had gradually increased through a long life of celibacy. Not that the good lady had ever suffered from their wiles, Nature having set up a safeguard in her face, that forbade all trespass upon her premises, but ladies who have least cause to fear for themselves are most ready to keep a watch over their more tempting neighbours.

The niece was the orphan of an officer who had fallen in the wars. She had been educated in a convent and had recently been transferred from her sacred asylum to the immediate guardianship of her aunt, under whose overshadowing care she vegetated in obscurity, like an opening rose blooming beneath a briar. Nor indeed is this comparison entirely accidental, for to tell the truth her fresh and dawning beauty had caught the public eye, even in her seclusion and, with that poetical turn common to the people of Andalusia, the peasantry of the neighbourbood had given her the appellation of «the Rose of the Alhambra».

The wary aunt continued to keep a faithful watch over her tempting little niece as long as the court continued at Granada and flattered herself that her vigilance had been successful. It is true the good lady was now and then discomposed by the tinkling of guitars and chanting of love ditties from the moonlit groves beneath the tower, but she would exhort her niece to shut her ears against such idle minstrelsy, assuring her that it was one of the arts of the opposite sex, by which simple maids were often lured to their undoing. Alas! What chance with a simple maid has a dry lecture against a moonlight serenade?

At length king Philip cut short his sojourn at Granada and suddenly departed with all his train. The vigilant Fredegonda watched the royal pageant as it issued forth from the Gate of Justice and descended the great avenue leading to the city. When the last banner disappeared from her sight, she returned exulting to her tower for all her cares were over. To her surprise a light Arabian steed pawed the ground at the wicket-gate of the garden. To her horror she saw through the thickets of roses a youth in gaily embroidered dress at the feet of her niece. At the sound of her footsteps he gave a tender adieu, bounded lightly over the barrier of reeds and myrtles, sprang upon his horse and was out of sight in an instant.

The tender Jacinta in the agony of her grief lost all thought of her aunt's displeasure. Throwing herself into her arms, she broke forth into sobs and tears.

«¡*Ay de mí!*» cried she, «he's gone! He's gone! He's gone! and I shall never see him more!»

«Gone! Who is gone? What youth is that I saw at your feet?»

«A queen's page, aunt, who came to bid me farewell.»

«A queen's page, child!» echoed the vigilant Fredegonda, faintly, «and when did you become acquainted with a queen's page?»

«The morning that the ger-falcon came into the tower. It was the queen's ger-falcon and he came in pursuit of it.»

«Ah, silly, silly girl! know that there are no ger-falcons half so dangerous as these young pranking pages and it is precisely such simple birds as thee that they pounce upon.»

The aunt was at first indignant at learning that, in despite of her boasted vigilance, a tender intercourse had been carried on by the youthful lovers almost beneath her eye, but when she found that her simple-hearted niece, though thus exposed without the protection of bolt or bar to all the machinations of the opposite sex, had come forth unsinged from the fiery ordeal, she consoled herself with the persuasion that it was owing to the chaste and cautious maxims in which she had, as it were, steeped her to the very lips.

While the aunt laid this soothing unction to her pride, the niece treasured up the oft-repeated vows of fidelity of the page. But what is the love of restless, roving man? A vagrant stream that dallies for a time with each flower upon its bank, then passes on and leaves them all in tears.

Days, weeks, months elapsed and nothing more was heard of the page. The pomegranate ripened, the vine yielded up its fruit, the autumnal rains descended in torrents from the mountains, the Sierra Nevada became covered with a snowy mantle and wintry blasts howled through the halls of the Alhambra— still he came not. The winter passed away. Again the genial spring burst forth with song and blossom and balmy zephyr; the snows melted from the mountains, until none remained but on the lofty summit of Nevada, glistening through the sultry summer air. Still nothing was heard of the forgetful page.

In the meantime the poor little Jacinta grew pale and thoughtful. Her former occupations and amusements were abandoned, her silk lay entangled, her guitar unstrung, her flowers were neglected, the notes of her bird unheeded and her eyes, once so bright, were dimmed with secret weeping. If any solitude could be devised to foster the passion of a love-lorn damsel, it would be such a place as the Alhambra, where everything seems disposed to produce tender and romantic reveries. It is a very paradise for lovers. How hard then to be alone in such a paradise —and not merely alone, but forsaken!

«Alas, silly child!» would the staid and immaculate Fredegonda say, when she found her niece in one of her desponding moods, «did I not warn thee against the wiles and deceptions of these men? What couldst thou expect, too, from one of a haughty and aspiring family—thou an orphan, the descendant of a fallen and impoverished line? Be assured, if the youth were true, his father who is one of the proudest nobles about the court, would prohibit his union with one so humble and portionless as thou. Pluck up thy resolution therefore and drive these idle notions from thy mind».

The words of the immaculate Fredegonda only served to increase the melancholy of her niece, but she sought to indulge it in private. At a late hour one midsummer night, after her aunt had retired to rest, she remained alone in the hall of the tower, seated beside the alabaster fountain. It was here that the faithless page had first knelt and kissed her hand: it was here that he had often vowed eternal fidelity. The poor little damsel's heart was overladen with sad and tender recollections, her tears began to flow and slowly fell drop by drop into the fountain. By degrees the crystal water became agitated and— bubble—bubble—bubble—boiled up and was tossed about until a female figure, richly clad in Moorish robes, slowly rose to view.

Jacinta was so frightened that she fled from the hall and did not venture to return. The next morning she related what she had seen to her aunt, but the good lady treated it as a phantasy of her troubled mind or supposed she had fallen asleep and dreamt beside the fountain. «Thou hast been thinking of the story of the three Moorish princesses that once inhabited this tower», continued she, «and it has entered into thy dreams».

«What story, aunt? I know nothing of it.»

«Thou hast certainly heard of the three princesses, Zayda, Zorayda and Zorahayda who were confined in this tower by the king their father and agreed to fly with three Christian cavaliers. The two first accomplished their escape but the third failed in her resolution and, it is said, died in this tower.»

«I now recollect to have heard of it», said Jacinta, «and to have wept over the fate of the gentle Zorahayda.»

«Thou mayest well weep over her fate», continued the aunt, «for the lover of Zorahayda was thy ancestor. He long bemoaned his Moorish love, but time cured him of his grief and he married a Spanish lady, from whom thou art descended».

Jacinta ruminated upon these words. «That what I have seen is no phantasy of the brain», said she to herself. «I am confident. If indeed it be the spirit of the gentle Zorahayda, which I have heard lingers about this tower, of what should I be afraid? I'll watch by the fountain to-night; perhaps the visit will be repeated».

Towards midnight, when everything was quiet, she again took her seat in the hall. As the bell in the distant watchtower of the Alhambra struck the midnight hour, the fountain was again agitated, and bubble—bubble—bubble—it tossed about the waters until the Moorish female again rose to view. She was young and beautiful, her dress was rich with jewels and in her hand she held a silver lute. Jacinta trembled and was faint, but was reassured by the soft and plaintive voice of the apparition and the sweet expression of her pale, melancholy countenance.

«Daughter of mortality», said she, «what aileth thee? Why do thy tears trouble my fountain and thy sighs and plaints disturb the quiet watches of the night?»

«I weep because of the faithlessness of man, and I bemoan my solitary and forsaken state.»

«Take comfort; thy sorrows may yet have an end. Thou beholdest a Moorish princess who like thee was unhappy in her love. A Christian knight, thy ancestor, won my heart and would have borne me to his native land and to the bosom of his church. I was a convert in my heart, but I lacked courage equal to my faith and lingered till too late. For this the evil genii are permitted to have power over me, and I remain enchanted in this tower until some pure Christian will deign to break the magic spell. Wilt thou undertake the task?»

«I will», replied the damsel, trembling.

«Come hither then and fear not; dip thy hand in the fountain, sprinkle the water over me and baptize me after the manner of thy faith; so shall the enchantment be dispelled and my troubled spirit have repose.»

The damsel advanced with faltering steps, dipped her hand in the fountain, collected water in the palm and sprinkled it over the pale face of the phantom.

The latter smiled with ineffable benignity. She dropped her silver lute at the feet of Jacinta, crossed her white arms upon her bosom and melted from sight, so that it seemed merely as if a shower of dewdrops had fallen into the fountain.

Jacinta retired from the hall filled with awe and wonder. She scarcely closed her eyes that night, but when she awoke at daybreak out of a troubled slumber, the whole appeared to her like a distempered dream. On descending into the hall, however, the truth of the vision was established, for beside the fountain she beheld the silver lute glittering in the morning sunshine.

She hastened to her aunt to relate all that had befallen her and called her to behold the lute as a testimonial of the reality of her story. If the good lady had any lingering doubts, they were removed when Jacinta touched the instrument, for she drew forth such ravishing tones as to thaw even the frigid bosom of the immaculate Fredegonda, that region of eternal winter, into a genial flow. Nothing but supernatural melody could have produced such an effect.

The extraordinary power of the lute became every day more and more apparent. The wayfarer passing by the tower was detained and, as it were, spellbound in breathless ecstasy. The very birds gathered in the neighbouring trees and, hushing their own strains, listened in charmed silence.

Rumour soon spread the news abroad. The inhabitants of Granada thronged to the Alhambra to catch a few notes of the trascendent music that floated about the tower of Las Infantas.

The lovely little minstrel was at length drawn forth from

her retreat. The rich and powerful of the land contended who should entertain and do honour to her, or rather who should secure the charms of her lute to draw fashionable throngs to their saloons. Wherever she went, her vigilant aunt kept a dragon watch at her elbow, awing the throngs of impassioned admirers, who hung in raptures on her strains. The report of her wonderful powers spread from city to city. Malaga, Seville, Cordova, all became successively mad on the theme; nothing was talked of throughout Andalusia but the beautiful minstrel of the Alhambra. How could it be otherwise among a people so musical and gallant as the Andalusians, when the lute was magical in its powers, and the minstrel inspired by love?

While all Andalusia was thus music mad, a different mood prevailed at the court of Spain. Philip V, as is well known, was a miserable hypochondriac and subject to all kinds of fancies. Sometimes he would keep to his bed for weeks together, groaning under imaginary complaints. At other times he would insist upon abdicating his throne, to the great annoyance of his royal spouse who had a strong relish for the splendours of a court and the glories of a crown, and guided the sceptre of her imbecile lord with an expert and steady hand.

Nothing was found to be so efficacious in dispelling the royal megrims as the powers of music; the queen took care therefore to have the best performers, both vocal and instrumental, at hand and retained the famous Italian singer Farinelli about the court as a kind of royal physician.

At the moment we treat of, however, a freak had come over the mind of this sapient and illustrious Bourbon, that surpassed all former vagaries. After a long spell of imaginary illness which set all the strains of Farinelli and the consultations of a whole orchestra of court fiddlers at defiance, the monarch fairly in idea gave up the ghost and considered himself absolutely dead.

This would have been harmless enough and even convenient both to his queen and courtiers, had he been content to remain in the quietude befitting a dead man, but to their annoyance he insisted upon having the funeral ceremonies performed over him and to their inexpressible perplexity began to grow impatient and to revile bitterly at them for negligence and disrespect in leaving him unburied. What was to be done? To disobey the king's positive commands was monstruous in the eyes of the obsequious courtiers of a punctilious court, but to obey him and bury him alive would be downright regicide!

In the midst of this fearful dilemma a rumour reached the court of the female minstrel who was turning the brains of all Andalusia. The queen dispatched missions in all haste to summon her to St. Ildefonso where the court at that time resided.

Within a few days, as the queen with her maids of honour was walking in those stately gardens, intended with their avenues and terraces and fountains to eclipse the glories of Versailles, the far-famed minstrel was conducted into her presence. The imperial Elizabetta gazed with surprise at the youthful and unpretending appearance of the little being that had set the world madding. She was in her picturesque Andalusian dress, her silver lute was in her hand and she stood with modest and downcast eyes, but with a simplicity, and freshness of beauty that still bespoke her «the Rose of the Alhambra».

As usual, she was accompanied by the ever-vigilant Fredegonda who gave the whole history of her parentage and descent to the inquiring queen. If the stately Elizabetta had been interested by the appearance of Jacinta she was still more pleased when she learnt that she was of a meritorious through impoverished line and that her father had brevely fallen in the service of the crown. «If thy powers equal their renown», said she, «and thou canst cast forth this evil spirit that possesses thy sovereign, thy fortunes shall henceforth be my care and honours and wealth attend thee».

Impatient to make trial of her skill, she led the way at once to the apartment of the moody monarch.

Jacinta followed with downcast eyes, through files of guards and crowds of courtiers. They arrived at length at a great chamber hung with black. The windows were closed to exclude the light of day, a number of yellow wax tapers in silver sconces diffused a lugubrious light and dimly revealed the figures of mutes in mourning dresses and courtiers who glided about with noiseless step and woe-begone visage. On the midst of a funeral bed or bier, his hands folded on his breast and the tip of his nose just visible, lay extended this would-be-buried monarch.

The queen entered the chamber in silence and pointing to a footstool in an obscure corner beckoned to Jacinta to sit down and commence.

At first she touched her lute with a faltering hand, but gathering confidence and animation as she proceeded, drew forth such soft aerial harmony that all present could scarce believe it mortal. As to the monarch who had already considered himself in the world of spirits, he set it down for some angelic melody or the music of the spheres. By degrees the theme was varied and the voice of the minstrel accompanied the instrument. She poured forth one of the legendary ballads treating of the ancient glories of the Alhambra and the achievements of the Moors. Her whole soul entered into the theme, for with the recollections of the Alhambra was associated the story of her love. The funeral chamber resounded with the animating strain. It entered into the gloomy heart of the monarch. He raised his head and gazed around; he sat up on his couch, his eye began to kindle. At length, leaping upon the floor, he called for sword and buckler.

The triumph of music or rather of the enchanted lute was complete; the demon of melancholy was cast forth and, as it were, a dead man brought to life. The windows of the apartment were thrown open; the glorious effulgence of Spanish sunshine burst into the late lugubrious chamber. All eyes sought the lovely enchantress, but the lute had fallen from her hand; she had sunk upon the earth and the next moment was clasped to the bosom of Ruiz de Alarcón.

The nuptials of the happy couple were shortly after celebrated with great splendour, but hold—I hear the reader ask, how did Ruiz de Alarcón account for his long neglect? Oh, that was all owing to the opposition of a proud, pragmatical old father. Besides, young people who really like one another soon come to an amicable understanding and bury all past grievances when once they meet.

But how was the proud, pragmatical old father reconciled to the match?

Oh, his scruples were easily overcome by a word or two from the queen, especially as dignities and rewards were showered upon the blooming favourite of royalty. Besides, the lute of Jacinta, you know, possessed a magic power and could control the most stubborn head and hardest breast.

And what came of the enchanted lute?

Oh, that is the most curious matter of all and plainly proves the truth of all this story. That lute remained for some time in the family, but was purloined and carried off, as was supposed, by the great singer Farinelli in pure jealousy. At his death it passed into other hands in Italy, who were ignorant of its mystic powers and, melting down the silver, transferred the strings to an old Cremona fiddle. The strings still retain something of their magic virtues. A word in the reader's ear, but let it go no further. That fiddle is now bewitching the whole world—it is the fiddle of Paganini!

THE VETERAN

AMONG the curious acquaintances I have made in my rambles about the fortress is a brave and battered old colo-
nel of Invalids, who is nestled like a hawk in one of the
Moorish towers. His history which he is fond of telling is a
tissue of those adventures, mishaps and vicissitudes that render
the life of almost every Spaniard of note as varied and
whimsical as the pages of Gil Blas.

He was in America at twelve years of age and reckons
among the most signal and fortunate events of his life his having seen General Washington. Since then he has taken a part
in all the wars of his country; he can speak experimentally of
most of the prisons and dungeons of the Peninsula, has been
lamed of one leg, crippled in his hands and so cut up and car-
bonadoed that he is a kind of walking monument of the troubles of Spain, on which there is a scar for every battle and
broil, as every year was notched upon the tree of Robinson
Crusoe. The greatest misfortune of the brave old cavalier, however, appears to have been his having commanded at Malaga during a time of peril and confusion, and been made a
general by the inhabitants to protect them from the invasion of
the French. This has entailed upon him a number of just
claims upon governement, that I fear will employ him until his
dying day in writing and printing petitions and memorials, to
the great disquiet of his mind, exhaustion of his purse and

penance of his friends, not one of whom can visit him without having to listen to a mortal document of half an hour in length and to carry away half a dozen pamphlets in his pocket. This, however, is the case throughout Spain; everywhere you meet with some worthy wight brooding in a corner and nursing up some pet grievance and cherished wrong. Besides, a Spaniard who has a lawsuit or a claim upon government may be considered as furnished with employment for the remainder of his life.

I visited the veteran in his quarters in the upper part of the *Torre del Vino,* or Wine Tower. His room was small but snug and commanded a beautiful view of the Vega. It was arranged with a soldier's precision. Three muskets and a brace of pistols, all bright and shining, were suspended against the wall with a sabre and a cane hanging side by side and above them two cocked hats, one for parade and one for ordinary use. A small shelf containing some half-dozen books formed his library, one of which, a little old mouldy volume of philosophical maxims was his favourite reading. This he thumbed and pondered over day by day, applying every maxim to his own particular case, provided it had a little tinge of wholesome bitterness and treated of the injustice of the world.

Yet he is social and kind-hearted, and provided he can be diverted from his wrongs and his philosophy is an entertaining companion. I like these old weather-beaten sons of fortune and enjoy their rough campaigning anecdotes. In the course of my visit to the one in question, I learnt some curious facts about an old military commander of the fortress, who seems to have resembled him in some respects and to have had similar forunes in the wars. These particulars have been augmented by inquiries among some of the old inhabitants of the place, particularly the father of Mateo Jiménez, of whose traditional stories the worthy I am about to introduce to the reader is a favourite hero.

THE GOVERNOR AND THE NOTARY

I N former times there ruled as governor of the Alhambra a doughty old cavalier who from having lost one arm in the wars was commonly known by the name of *el Gobernador Manco* or «the one-armed governor». He in fact prided himself upon being an old soldier, wore his moustaches curled up to his eyes, a pair of campaigning boots and a toledo as long as a spit with his pocket-handkerchief in the basket-hilt.

He was, moreover, exceedingly proud and punctilious and tenacious of all his privileges and dignities. Under his sway the immunities of the Alhambra as a royal residence and domain were rigidly exacted. No one was permitted to enter the fortress with fire-arms or even with a sword or staff, unless he were of a certain rank, and every horseman was obliged to dismount at the gate and lead his horse by the bridle. Now as the hill of the Alhambra rises from the very midst of the city of Granada, being, as it were, an excrescence of the capital, it must at all times be somewhat irksome to the captain-general who commands the province to have thus an *imperium in imperio,* a petty independent post in the very centre of his domains. It was rendered the more galling in the present instance from the irritable jealousy of the governor, that took fire on the least question of authority and jurisdiction, and from the loose vagrant character of the people that had gradually nestled themselves within the fortress, as in a sanctuary,

241

and from thence carried on a system of roguery and depredation at the expense of the honest inhabitants of the city.

Thus there was a perpetual feud and heart-burning between the captain-general and the governor, the more virulent on the part of the latter, inasmuch as the smallest of two neighbouring potentates is always the most captious about his dignity. The stately palace of the captain-general stood in the Plaza Nueva, immediately at the foot of the hill of the Alhambra, and here was always a bustle and parade of guards and domestics and city functionaries. A beetling bastion of the fortress overlooked the palace and public square in front of it, and on this bastion the old governor would occasionally strut backwards and forwards with his toledo girded by his side keeping a wary eye down upon his rival, like a hawk reconnoitring his quarry from his nest in a dry tree.

Whenever he descended into the city, it was in grand parade, on horseback, surrounded by his guards or in his state coach, an ancient and unwieldy Spanish edifice of carved timber and gilt leather, drawn by eight mules, with running footmen, out-riders and lackeys; on which occasions he flattered himself he impressed every beholder with awe and admiration as vicegerent of the king, though the wits of Granada, particularly those who loitered about the palace of the captain-general, were apt to sneer at his petty parade and in allusion to the vagrant character of his subjects to greet him with the appellation of «the king of the beggars». One of the most fruitful sources of dispute between these two doughty rivals was the right claimed by the governor to have all things passed free of duty through the city, that were intended for the use of himself or his garrison. By degrees this privilege had given rise to extensive smuggling. A nest of *contrabandistas* took up their abode in the hovels of the fortress and the numerous caves in its vicinity, and drove a thriving business under the connivance of the soldiers of the garrison.

The vigilance of the captain-general was aroused. He consulted his legal adviser and factotum, a shrewd meddlesome *escribano* or notary who rejoiced in an opportunity of perplexing the old potentate of the Alhambra and involving him in a maze of legal subtleties. He advised the captain-general to insist upon the right of examining every convoy passing through the gates of his city and he penned a long letter for him in vindication of the right. Governor Manco was a straightforward cut-and-thrust old soldier who hated an *escribano* worse than the devil and this one in particular worse than all other *escribanos*.

«What!» said he, curling up his moustaches fiercely, «does the captain-general set his man of the pen to practise confusions upon me? I'll let him see that an old soldier is not to be baffled by schoolcraft».

He seized his pen and scrawled a short letter in a crabbed hand, in which without deigning to enter into argument he insisted on the right of transit free of search and denounced vengeance on any custom-house officer who should lay his unhallowed hand on any convoy protected by the flag of the Alhambra. While this question was agitated between the two pragmatical potentates, it so happened that a mule laden with supplies for the fortress arrived one day at the gate of Xenil, by which it was to traverse a suburb of the city on its way to the Alhambra. The convoy was headed by a testy old corporal who had long served under the governor and was a man after his own heart, as rusty and staunch as an old Toledo blade.

As they approached the gate of the city the corporal placed the banner of the Alhambra on the pack saddle of the mule and, drawing himself up to a perfect perpendicular, advanced with his head dressed to the front, but with the wary side-glance of a cur passing through hostile ground and ready for a snap and a snarl.

««Who goes there?» said the sentinel at the gate.

«Soldier of the Alhambra», said the corporal, without turning his head.

«What have you in charge?»

«Provisions for the garrison.»

«Proceed.»

The corporal marched straight forward, followed by the convoy, but had not advanced many paces before a posse of custom-house officers rushed out of a small toll-house.

«Hallo there!» cried the leader. «Muleteer, halt and open those packages.»

The corporal wheeled round and drew himself up in battle array. «Respect the flag of the Alhambra», said he; «these things are for the governor».

«A *higo* for the governor and a *higo* for his flag. Muleteer, halt, I say.»

«Stop the convoy at your peril!» cried the corporal, cocking his musket; «Muleteer, proceed».

The muleteer gave his beast a hearty thwack, the custom-house officer sprang forward and seized the halter; whereupon the corporal levelled his piece and shot him dead.

The street was immediately in an uproar. The old corporal was seized and after undergoing sundry kicks and cuffs and cudgellings, which are generally given impromptu by the mob in Spain as a foretaste of the after penalties of the law, he was loaded with irons and conducted to the city prison, while his comrades were permitted to proceed with the convoy, after it had been well rummaged, to the Alhambra.

The old governor was in a towering passion when he heard of this insult to his flag and capture of his corporal. For a time he stormed about the Moorish halls and vapoured about the bastions, and looked down fire and sword upon the palace of the captain general. Having vented the first ebullition of his wrath, he despatched a message demanding the surrender of the corporal, as to him alone belonged the right of sitting in judgment on the offences of those under his command. The captain-general, aided by the pen of the delighted *escribano,* replied at great length, arguing that, as the offence had been committed within the walls of his city and against one of his civil officers, it was clearly within his proper jurisdiction. The governor rejoined by a repetition of his demand. The captain-general gave a surrejoinder of still greater length and legal acumen. The governor became hotter and more peremptory in his demands, and the captain-general cooler and more copious in his replies, until the old lion-hearted soldier absolutely roared with fury at being thus entangled in the meshes of legal controversy.

While the subtle *escribano* was thus amusing himself at the expense of the governor, he was conducting the trial of the corporal who, mewed up in a narrow dungeon of the prison, had merely a small grated window at which to show his iron-bound visage and receive the consolations of his friends.

A mountain of written testimony was diligently heaped up, according to Spanish form, by the indefatigable *escribano;* the corporal was completely overwhelmed by it. He was convicted of murder and sentenced to be hanged.

It was in vain the governor sent down remonstrance and menace from the Alhambra. The fatal day was at hand and the corporal was put *en capilla,* that is to say, in the chapel of the prison, as is always done with culprits the day before execution, that they may meditate on their approaching end and repent them of their sins.

Seeing things drawing to extremity, the old governor determined to attend to the affair in person. For this purpose he ordered out his carriage of state and, surrounded by his guards, rumbled down the avenue of the Alhambra into the city. Driving to the house of the *escribano,* he summoned him to the portal.

The eye of the old governor gleamed like a coal at beholding the smirking man of the law advancing with an air of exultation.

«What is this I hear», cried he, «that you are about to put to death one of my soldiers?»

«All according to law; all in strict form of justice», said the self-sufficient *escribano,* chuckling and rubbing his hands, «I can show your excellency the written testimony in the case.»

«Fetch it hither», said the governor. The *escribano* bustled into his office, delighted with having another opportunity of displaying his ingenuity at the expense of the hard-headed veteran.

He returned with a satchel full of papers and began to read a long deposition with professional volubility. By this time a crowd had collected listening with outstretched necks and gaping mouths.

«Prithee, man, get into the carriage, out of this pestilent throng, that I may the better hear thee», said the governor.

The *escribano* entered the carriage, when in a twinkling the door was closed, the coachman smacked his whip. Mules, carriage, guards and all dashed off at a thundering rate, leaving the crowd in gaping wonderment; nor did the governor pause until he had lodged his prey in one of the strongest dungeons of the Alhambra.

He then sent down a flag of truce in military style, proposing a cartel or exchange of prisoners—the corporal for the notary. The pride of the captain-general was piqued; he returned a contemptuous refusal and forthwith caused a gallows, tall and strong, to be erected in the centre of the Plaza Nueva for the execution of the corporal.

«Oho! is that the game?» said Governor Manco. He gave orders and immediately a gibbet was reared on the verge of the great beetling bastion that overlooked the Plaza. «Now», said he in a message to the captain-general, «hang my soldier when you please but at the same time that he is swung off in the square, look up to see your *escribano* dangling against the sky».

The captain-general was inflexible; troops were paraded in the square, the drums beat, the bell tolled. An immense multitude of amateurs had collected to behold the execution. On the other hand, the governor paraded his garrison on the bastion, and tolled the funeral dirge of the notary from the *Torre de la Campana,* or Tower of the Bell.

The notary's wife pressed through the crowd with a whole progeny of little embryo *escribanos* at her heels and, throwing herself at the feet of the captain-general, implored him not to sacrifice the life of her husband and the welfare of herself and her numerous little ones to a point of pride, «for you know the old governor too well», said she, «to doubt that he will put his threat in execution, if you hang the soldier».

The captain-general was overpowered by her tears and lamentations and the clamours of her callow brood. The corporal was sent up to the Alhambra under a guard in his gallows garb like a hooded friar, but with head erect and a face of iron. The *escribano* was demanded in exchange, according to the cartel. The once bustling and self-sufficient man of the law was drawn forth from his dungeon more dead than alive. All his flippancy and conceit had evaporated; his hair, it is said, had nearly turned grey with affright, and he had a downcast, dogged look, as if he still felt the halter round his neck.

The old governor stuck his one arm akimbo and for a moment surveyed him with an iron smile. «Henceforth, my friend», said he, «moderate your zeal in hurrying others to the gallows; be not too certain of your safety, even though you should have the law on your side, and above all take care how you play off your schoolcraft another time upon an old soldier».

GOVERNOR MANCO AND THE SOLDIER

W HEN Governor Manco or «the one-armed» kept up a show of military state in the Alhambra he became nettled at the reproaches continually cast upon his fortress of being a nestling-place of rogues and *contrabandistas*. On a sudden the old potentate determined on reform and, setting vigorously to work, ejected whole nests of vagabonds out of the fortress and the gypsy caves with which the surrounding hills are honey-combed. He sent out soldiers also to patrol the avenues and footpaths, with orders to take up all suspicious persons.

One bright summer morning a patrol, consisting of the testy old corporal who had distinguished himself in the affair of the notary, a trumpeter and two privates, was seated under the garden-wall of the Generalife beside the road which leads down from the Mountain of the Sun, when they heard the tramp of a horse and a male voice singing in rough, though not unmusical tones, an old Castilian campaigning song.

Presently they beheld a sturdy sunburnt fellow, clad in the ragged garb of a foot-soldier, leading a powerful Arabian horse caparisoned in the Morisco fashion.

Astonished at the sight of a strange soldier descending steed in hand from that solitary mountain, the corporal stepped forth and challenged him.

«Who goes there?»

«A friend.»

«Who and what are you?»

«A poor soldier just from the wars, with a cracked crown and an empty purse for a reward.»

By this time they were enabled to view him more narrowly. He had a black patch across his forehead, which with a grizzled beard added to a certain dare-devil cast of countenance, while a slight squint threw into the whole an occasional gleam of roguish good-humour.

Having answered the questions of the patrol, the soldier seemed to consider himself entitled to make others in return. «May I ask», said he, «what city is that which I see at the foot of the hill?»

«What city!» cried the trumpeter; «come, that's too bad. Here's a fellow lurking about the Mountain of the Sun and demands the name of the great city of Granada!»

«Granada! *¡Madre de Dios!* Can it be posible?»

«Perhaps not!» rejoined the trumpeter, «and perhaps you have no idea that yonder are the towers of the Alhambra?»

«Son of a trumpet», replied the stranger, «do not trifle with me; if this be indeed the Alhambra, I have some strange matters to reveal to the governor».

«You will have an opportunity», said the corporal, «for we mean to take you before him». By this time the trumpeter had seized the bridle of the steed, the two privates had each secured an arm of the soldier; the corporal put himself in front, gave the word, «Forward—march!» and away they marched for the Alhambra.

The sight of a ragged foot-soldier and a fine Arabian horse, brought in captive by the patrol, attracted the attention of all the idlers of the fortress and of those gossip groups that generally assemble about wells and fountains at early dawn. The wheel of the cistern paused in its rotations and the slip-shod servant-maid stood gaping with pitcher in hand, as the corporal passed by with his prize. A motley train gradually gathered in the rear of the escort.

Knowing nods and winks and conjectures passed from one to another. «It is a deserter», said one; «a *contrabandista*», said another; «a *bandolero*», said a third—until it was affirmed that a captain of a desperate band of robbers had been captured by the prowess of the corporal and his patrol. «Well, well», said the old crones, one to another, «captain or not, let him get out of the grasp of old Governor Manco if he can, though he is but one-handed».

Governor Manco was seated in one of the inner halls of the Alhambra, taking his morning's cup of chocolate in company with his confessor, a fat Franciscan friar from the neighbouring convent. A demure, dark-eyed damsel of Malaga, the daughter of his housekeeper, was attending upon him. The world hinted that the damsel who with all her demureness was a sly buxom baggage had found out a soft spot in the iron heart of the old governor, and held complete control over him. But let that pass. The domestic affairs of these mighty potentates of the earth should not be too narrowly scrutinised.

When word was brought that a suspicious stranger had been taken lurking about the fortress and was actually in the outer court in durance of the corporal, waiting the pleasure of his excellency, the pride and stateliness of office swelled the bosom of the governor. Giving back his chocolate-cup into the hands of the demure damsel, he called for his basket-hilted sword, girded it to his side, twirled up his moustaches, took his seat in a large high-backed chair, assumed a bitter and forbidding aspect, and ordered the prisoner into his presence. The soldier was brought in, still closely pinioned by his captors and guarded by the corporal. He maintained, however, a resolute self-confident air and returned the sharp, scrutinising look of the governor with an easy squint which by no means pleased the punctilious old potentate.

251

«Well, culprit», said the governor, after he had regarded him for a moment in silence, «what have you to say for yourself? Who are you?»

«A soldier, just from the wars, who has brought away nothing but scars and bruises.»

«A soldier—humph—a foot-soldier by your garb. I understand you have a fine Arabian horse. I presume you brought him too from the wars, besides your scars and bruises.»

«May it please your excellency, I have something strange to tell about that horse. Indeed I have one of the most wonderful things to relate; something too that concerns the security of this fortress, indeed of all Granada. But it is a matter to be imparted only to your private ear or in presence of such only as are in your confidence.»

The governor considered for a moment and then directed the corporal and his men to withdraw, but to post themselves outside of the door and be ready at a call. «This holy friar», said he, «is my confessor, you may say anything in his presence, and this damsel», nodding towards the handmaid who had loitered with an air of great curiosity, «this damsel is of great secrecy and discretion, and to be trusted with anything».

The soldier gave a glance between a squint and a leer at the demure handmaid. «I am perfectly willing», said he, «that the damsel should remain».

When all the rest had withdrawn, the soldier commenced his story. He was a fluent smooth-tongued varlet and had a command of language above his apparent rank.

«May it please your excellency» said he, «I am, as I before observed, a soldier and have seen some hard service, but my term of enlistment being expired, I was discharged not long since from the army at Valladolid, and set out on foot for my native village in Andalusia. Yesterday evening the sun went down as I was traversing a great dry plain of Old Castile».

«Hold», cried the governor, «what it this you say? Old Castile is some two or three hundred miles from this».

«Even so», replied the soldier coolly, «I told your excellency I had strange things to relate, but not more strange than true, as your excellency will find, if you will deign me a patient hearing».

«Proceed, culprit», said the governor, twirling up his moustaches.

«As the sun went down», continued the soldier, «I cast my eyes about in search of some quarters for the night, but as far as my sight could reach, there were no signs of a habitation. I saw that I should have to make my bed on the naked plain with my knapsack for a pillow, but your excellency is an old soldier and knows that to one who has been in the wars, such a night's lodging is no great hardship».

The governor nodded assent, as he drew his pocket-handkerchief out of the basket-hilt to drive away a fly that buzzed about his nose.

«Well, to make a long story short», continued the soldier, «I trudged forward for several miles until I came to a bridge over a deep ravine, through which ran a little thread of water, almost dried up by the summer heat. At one end of the bridge was a Moorish tower, the upper end all in ruins, but a vault in the foundation quite entire. Here, think I, is a good place to make a halt; so I went down to the stream, took a hearty drink, for the water was pure and sweet, and I was parched with thirst. Then, opening my wallet, I took out an onion and a few crusts which were all my provisions, and seating myself on a stone on the margin of the stream, began to make my supper intending afterwards to quarter myself for the night in the vault of the tower, and capital quarters they would have been for a campaigner just from the wars, as your excellency who is an old soldier may suppose».

«I have put up gladly with worse in my time», said the

governor, returning his pocket-handkerchief into the hilt of his sword.

«While I was quietly crunching my crust», pursued the soldier, «I heard something stir within the vault. I listened; it was the tramp of a horse. By-and-by, a man came forth from a door in the foundation of the tower close by the water's edge, leading a powerful horse by the bridle. I could not well make out what he was by the starlight. It had a suspicious look to me lurking among the ruins of a tower in that wild solitary place. He might be a mere wayfarer like myself; he might be a *contrabandista;* he might be a *bandolero!* What of that? Thank Heaven and my poverty, I had nothing to lose; so I sat still and crunched my crust.

«He led his horse to the water close by where I was sitting, so that I had a fair opportunity of reconnoitring him. To my surprise he was dressed in a Moorish garb with a cuirass of steel and a polished skull-cap that I distinguished by the reflection of the stars upon it. His horse too was harnessed in the Morisco fashion with great shovel stirrups. He led him, as I said, to the side of the stream, into which the animal plunged his head almost to the eyes and drank until I thought he would have burst.

«Comrade', said I, 'your steed drinks well; it's a good sign when a horse plunges his muzzle bravely into the water'.

«He may well drink' said the stranger, speaking with a Moorish accent, 'it is a good year since he had his last draught'.

«By *Santiago',* said, I, 'that beats even the camels that I have seen in Africa. But come, you seem to be something of a soldier. Will you sit down and take part of a soldier's fare?» In fact, I felt the want of a companion in this lonely place and was willing to put up with an infidel. Besides, as your excellency well knows, a soldier is never very particular about the faith of his company and soldiers of all countries are comrades on peaceable ground.»

The governor again nodded assent.

«Well, as I was saying, I invited him to share my supper, such as it was, for I could not do less in common hospitality. 'I have no time to pause for meat or drink', said he, 'I have a long journey to make before morning'.

«'In which direction?', said I.

«'Andalusia', said he.

«'Exactly my route', said I; 'so, as you won't stop and eat with me, perhaps you will let me mount and ride with you. I see your horse is of a powerful frame, I'll warrant he'll carry double'.

«'Agreed', said the trooper; and it would not have been civil and soldierlike to refuse, especially as I had offered to share my supper with him. So up he mounted and up I mounted behind him.

«'Hold fast', said he, 'my steed goes like the wind'.

«'Never fear me'», said I, and so off we set.

«From a walk the horse soon passed to a trot, from a trot to a gallop and from a gallop to a harum-scarum scamper. It seemed as if rocks, trees, houses, everything, flew hurry-scurry behind us.

«'What town is this?' said I.

«Segovia', said he; and before the word was out of his mouth, the towers of Segovia were out of sight. We swept up the Guadarrama mountains and down by the Escurial, and we skirted the walls of Madrid, and we scoured away across the plains of La Mancha. In this way we went up hill and down dale, by towers and cities, all buried in deep sleep, and across mountains and plains and rivers, just glimmering in the starlight.

«To make a long story short and not to fatigue your excellency, the trooper suddenly pulled up on the side of a mountain. 'Here we are' said he, 'at the end of our journey'. I looked about, but could see no signs of habitation; nothing but the mouth of a cavern. While I looked I saw multitudes of people in Moorish dress, some on horseback, some on foot, arriving as if borne by the wind from all points of the compass and hurrying into the mouth of the cavern, like bees into a hive. Before I could ask a question, the trooper struck his long Moorish spurs into the horse's flanks and dashed in with the throng. We passed along a steep winding way that descended into the very bowels of the mountain. As we pushed on, a light began to glimmer up by little and little like the first glimmerings of day, but what caused it I could not discern. It grew stronger and stronger, and enabled me to see everything around. I now noticed, as we passed along, great caverns, opening to the right and left, like halls in an arsenal. In some there were shields and helmets and cuirasses and lances and scimitars, hanging against the walls; in others there were great heaps of warlike munitions and camp-equipage, lying upon the ground.

«It would have done your excellency's heart good, being an old soldier, to have seen such grand provision for war. Then in other caverns there were long rows of horsemen armed to the teeth with lances raised and banners unfurled all ready for the field, but they all sat motionless in their saddles, like so many statues. In other halls were warriors sleeping on the ground beside their horses and footsoldiers in group ready to fall into the ranks. All were in old-fashioned Moorish dresses and armour.

«Well, your excellency, to cut a long story short, we at length entered an immense cavern, or I may say palace of grotto-work, the walls of which seemed to be veined with gold and silver, and to sparkle with diamonds and sapphires and all kinds of precious stones. At the upper end sat a Moorish king on a golden throne with his nobles on each side and a guard of African blacks with drawn scimitars. All the crowd that continued to flock in, and amounted to thousands and thousands, passed one by one before his throne, each paying homage as he passed. Some of the multitude were dressed in magnificent robes without stain or blemish and sparkling with jewels, others in burnished and enamelled armour, while others were in mouldered and mildewed garments and in armour all battered and dented and covered with rust.

«I had hitherto held my tongue, for your excellency well knows it is not for a soldier to ask many questions when on duty but I could keep silent no longer.

«'Prithee, comrade»' said I, 'what is the meaning of all this?'

«This', said the trooper, 'is a great and fearful mystery. Know, O Christian, that you see before you the court and army of Boabdil, the last king of Granada'.

«'What is this you tell me?' cried I. 'Boabdil and his court were exiled from the land hundreds of years agone and all died in Africa'.

«'So it is recorded in your lying chronicles», replied the Moor, 'but know that Boabdil and the warriors who made the last struggle for Granada were all shut up in the mountain by powerful enchantment. As for the king and army that marched forth from Granada at the time of the surrender, they were a mere phantom train of spirits and demons, permitted to assume those shapes to deceive the Christian sovereigns. And furthermore let me tell you, friend, that all Spain is a country under the power of enchantment. There is not a mountain cave, not a lonely watch-tower in the plains nor ruined castle on the hills, but has some spellbound warriors sleeping from age to age within its vaults, until the sins are expiated for which Allah permitted the dominion to pass for a time out of the hands of the faithful. Once every year on the eve of St. John they are released from enchantment from sunset to sunrise and permitted to repair here to pay homage to their sovereign, and the crowds which you beheld swarming into the cavern are

Moslem warriors from their haunts in all parts of Spain. For my own part, you saw the ruined tower of the bridge in Old Castile, where I have now wintered and summered for many hundred years, and where I must be back again by daybreak. As to the battalions of horse and foot which you beheld drawn up in array in the neighbouring caverns, they are the spellbound warriors of Granada. It is written in the book of fate that when the enchantment is broken, Boabdil will descend from the mountain at the head of this army, resume his throne in the Alhambra and his sway of Granada, and gathering together the enchanted warriors from all parts of Spain, will reconquer the Peninsula and restore it to Moslem rule'.

«'And when shall this happen?' said I.

«'Allah alone knows; we had hoped the day of deliverance was at hand, but there reigns at present a vigilant governor in the Alhambra, a staunch old soldier, well known as Governor Manco. While such a warrior holds command of the very outpost and stands ready to check the first irruption from the mountain, I fear Boabdil and his soldiery must be content to rest upon their arms.»'

Here the governor raised himself somewhat perpendicularly, adjusted his sword and twirled up his moustaches.

«To make a long story short and not to fatigue your excellency, the trooper, having given me this account, dismounted from his steed.

«'Tarry here', said he, 'and guard my steed while I go and bow the knee to Boabdil'. So saying, he strode away among the throng that pressed forward to the throne.

«'What's to be done?' thought I, when thus left to myself. 'Shall I wait here until this infidel returns to whisk me off on his goblin steed, the Lord knows where, or shall I make the most of my time and beat a retreat from this hobgoblin community?' A soldier's mind is soon made up, as your excellency well knows. As to the horse, he belonged to an avowed enemy of the faith and the realm, and was a fair prize according to the rules of war. So hoisting myself from the crupper into the saddle, I turned the reins, struck the Moorish stirrups into the sides of the steed and put him to make the best of his way out of the passage by which he had entered. As we scoured by the halls where the Moslem horsemen sat in motionless battalions, I thought I heard the clang of armour and a hollow murmur of voices. I gave the steed another taste of the stirrups, and doubled my speed. There was now a sound behind me like a rushing blast. I heard the clatter of a thousand hoofs. A countless throng overtook me. I was borne along in the press and hurled forth from the cavern, while thousands of shadowy forms were swept off in every direction by the four winds of heaven.

«In the whirl and confusion of the scene I was thrown senseless to the earth. When I came to myself, I was lying on the brow of a hill with the Arabian steed standing beside me, for in falling, my arm had slipped within the bridle which, I presume, prevented his whisking off to Old Castile.

«Your excellency may easily judge of my surprise on looking round, to behold hedges of aloes and Indian figs and other proofs of a southern climate and to see a great city below me, with towers and palaces and a grand cathedral.

«I descended the hill cautiously, leading my steed, for I was afraid to mount him again, lest he should play me some slippery trick. As I descended I met with your patrol who let me into the secret that it was Granada that lay before me, and that I was actually under the walls of the Alhambra, the fortress of the redoubted Governor Manco, the terror of all enchanted Moslems. When I heard this, I determined at once to seek your excellency to inform you of all that I had seen and to warn you of the perils that surround and undermine you, that you may take measures in time to guard your fortress, and the kingdom itself from this intestine army that lurks in the very bowels of the land».

«And prithee, friend, you who are a veteran campaigner, and have seen so much service», said the governor, «how would you advise me to proceed in order to prevent this evil?»

«It is not for a humble private of the ranks», said the soldier modestly, «to pretend to instruct a commander of your excellency's sagacity, but it appears to me that your excellency might cause all the caves and entrances into the mountain to be walled up with solid mason-work, so that Boabdil and his army might be completely corked up in their subterranean habitation. If the good father, too», added the soldier, reverently bowing to the friar and devoutly crossing himself, «would consecrate the *barricadas* with his blessing and put up a few crosses and relics and images of saints, I think they might withstand all the power of infidel enchantments».

«They doubtless would be of great avail», said the friar.

The governor now placed his arm akimbo with his hand resting on the hilt of his toledo, fixed his eye upon the soldier and gently wagging his head from one side to the other.

«So, friend», said he, «then you really suppose I am to be gulled with this cock-and-bull story about enchanted mountains and enchanted Moors? Hark ye, culprit!—not another word. An old soldier you may be, but you'll find you have an older soldier to deal with and one not easily outgeneralled. Ho! guards there! put this fellow in irons.»

The demure handmaid would have put in a word in favour of the prisoner, but the governor silenced her with a look.

As they were pinioning the soldier, one of the guards felt something of bulk in his pocket and, drawing it forth, found a long leathern purse that appeared to be well filled. Holding it by one corner, he turned out the contents upon the table, before the governor and never did freebooter's bag make more gorgeous delivery. Out tumbled rings and jewels and rosaries of pearls and sparkling diamond crosses and a profusion of ancient golden coin, some of which fell jingling to the floor and rolled away to the uttermost parts of the chamber.

For a time the functions of justice were suspended; there was an universal scramble after the glittering fugitives. The governor alone who was imbued with true Spanish pride maintained his stately decorum, though his eye betrayed a little anxiety until the last coin and jewel was restored to the sack.

The friar was not so calm; his whole face glowed like a furnace and his eyes twinkled and flashed at sight of the rosaries and crosses.

«Sacrilegious wretch that thou art!» exclaimed he, «what church or sanctuary hast thou been plundering of these sacred relics?»

«Neither one nor the other, holy father. If they be sacrilegious spoils, they must have been taken in times long past by the infidel trooper I have mentioned. I was just going to tell his excellency, when he interrupted me, that on taking possession of the trooper's horse, I unhooked a leathern sack which hung at the saddle-bow and which I presume contained the plunder of his campaignings in days of old, when the Moors overran the country».

«Mighty well; at present you will make up your mind to take up your quarters in a chamber of the Vermilion Towers, which, though not under a magic spell, will hold you as safe as any cave of your enchanted Moors.»

«Your excellency will do as you think proper», said the prisoner coolly. «I shall be thankful to your excellency for any accommodation in the fortress. A soldier who has been in the wars, as your excellency well knows, is not particular about his lodgings; provided I have a snug dungeon and regular rations, I shall manage to make myself comfortable. I would only entreat that, while your excellency is so careful about me, you would have an eye to your fortress, and think on the hint I dropped about stopping up the entrances to the mountain.»

Here ended the scene. The prisoner was conducted to a strong dungeon in the Vermilion Towers, the Arabian steed was led to his excellency's stable and the trooper's sack was deposited in his excellency's strong box. To the latter, it is true, the friar made some demur, questioning whether the sacred relics which were evidently sacrilegious spoils should not be placed in custody of the church, but as the governor was peremptory on the subject and was absolute lord in the Alhambra, the friar discreetly dropped the discussion, but determined to convey intelligence of the fact to the church dignitaries in Granada.

To explain these prompt and rigid measures on the part of old Governor Manco, it is proper to observe that about this time the Alpuxarra mountains in the neighbourhood of Granada were terribly infested by a gang of robbers, under the command of a daring chief named Manuel Borasco, who were accustomed to prowl about the country and even to enter the city in various disguises to gain intelligence of the departure of convoys of merchandise or travellers with well-lined purses, whom they took care to waylay in distant and solitary passes of their road. These repeated and daring outrages had awakened the attention of government and the commanders of the various posts had received instructions to be on the alert and to take up all suspicious stragglers. Governor Manco was particularly zealous in consequence of the various stigmas that had been cast upon his fortress and he now doubted not that he had entrapped some formidable desperado of this gang.

In the meantime the story took wind and became the talk, not merely of the fortress, but of the whole city of Granada. It was said that the noted robber Manuel Borasco, the terror of the Alpuxarras, had fallen into the clutches of old Governor

Manco and been cooped up by him in a dungeon of the Vermilion Towers, and every one who had been robbed by him flocked to recognize the marauder. The Vermilion Towers, as is well known, stand apart from the Alhambra on a sister hill, separated from the main fortress by the ravine down which passes the main avenue. There were no outer walls, but a sentinel patrolled before the tower. The window of the chamber in which the soldier was confined was strongly grated and looked upon a small esplanade. Here the good folks of Granada repaired to gaze at him, as they would at a laughing hyena, grinning through the cage of a menagerie. Nobody, however, recognized him for Manuel Borasco, for that terrible robber was noted for a ferocious physiognomy and had by no means the good humoured squint of the prisoner. Visitors came not merely from the city, but from all parts of the country, but nobody knew him and there began to be doubts in the minds of the common people whether there might not be some truth in his story. That Boabdil and his army were shut up in the mountain was an old tradition which many of the ancient inhabitants had heard from their fathers. Numbers went up to the Mountain of the Sun, or rather of St. Elena, in search of the cave mentioned by the soldier, and saw and peeped into the deep dark pit, descending, no one knows how far, into the mountain, and which remains there to this day—the fabled entrance to the subterranean abode of Boabdil.

By degrees the soldier became popular with the common people. A freebooter of the mountains is by no means the opprobious character in Spain that a robber is in any other country; on the contrary, he is a kind of chivalrous personage in the eyes of the lower classes. There is always a disposition also to cavil at the conduct of those in command, and many began to murmur at the high-handed measures of old Governor Manco and to look upon the prisoner in the light of a martyr.

The soldier, moreover, was a merry, waggish fellow that

had a joke for every one who came near his window and a soft speech for every female. He had procured an old guitar also and would sit by his window and sing ballads and love-ditties to the delight of the women of the neighbourhood, who would assemble on the esplanade in the evening and dance *boleros* to his music. Having trimmed off his rough beard, his sunburnt face found favour in the eyes of the fair, and the demure handmaid of the governor declared that his squint was perfectly irresistible. This kind-hearted damsel had from the first evinced a deep sympathy in his fortunes and, having in vain tried to mollify the governor, had set to work privately to mitigate the rigour of his dispensations. Every day she brought the prisoner some crumbs of comfort which had fallen from the governor's table or been abstracted from his larder, together with now and then a consoling bottle of choice Valdepeñas or rich Malaga.

While this petty treason was going on in the very centre of the old governor's citadel, a storm of open war was brewing up among his external foes. The circumstance of a bag of gold and jewels having been found upon the person of the supposed robber had been reported with many exaggerations in Granada. A question of territorial jurisdiction was immediately started by the governor's inveterate rival, the captain-general. He insisted that the prisoner had been captured without the precincts of the Alhambra and within the rules of his authority. He demanded his body therefore and the *spolia opima* taken with him. Due information having been carried likewise by the friar to the grand Inquisitor of the crosses and rosaries and other relics contained in the bag, he claimed the culprit as having been guilty of sacrilege and insisted that his plunder was due to the church, and his body to the next *auto de fe*. The feuds ran high, the governor was furious and swore rather than surrender his captive he would hang him up within the Alhambra as a spy caught within the purlieus of the fortress.

The captain-general threatened to send a body of soldiers to transfer the prisoner from the Vermilion Towers to the city. The Grand Inquisitor was equally bent upon despatching a number of the familiars of the Holy Office. Word was brought late at night to the governor of these machinations. «Let them come», said he, «they'll find me beforehand with them; he must rise bright and early who would take in an old soldier». He accordingly issued orders to have the prisoner removed at daybreak to the donjon-keep within the walls of the Alhambra. «And d'ye hear, child», said he to his demure hand-maid, «tap at my door and wake me before cock-crowing, that I may see to the matter myself».

The day dawned, the cock crowed, but nobody tapped at the door of the governor. The sun rose high above the mountain-tops and glittered in at his casement, ere the governor was awakened from morning dreams by his veteran corporal who stood before him with terror stamped upon his iron visage.

«He's off! he's gone!» cried the corporal, gasping for breath.

«Who's off—who's gone?»

«The soldier—the robber—the devil, for aught I know. His dungeon is empty, but the door locked; no one knows how he has escaped out of it.

«Who saw him last?»

«Your handmaid; she brought him his supper.»

«Let her be called instantly.»

Here was new matter of confusion. The chamber of the demure damsel was likewise empty, her bed had not been slept in; she had doubtless gone off with the culprit, as she had appeared for some days past to have frequent conversations with him.

This was wounding the old governor in a tender part, but he had scarce time to wince at it, when new misfortunes broke upon his view. On going into his cabinet he found his strong box open, the leather purse of the trooper abstracted and with it a couple of corpulent bags of doubloons.

But how, and which way had the fugitives escaped? An old peasant who lived in a cottage by the road-side, leading up into the Sierra, declared that he had heard the tramp of a powerful steed just before daybreak, passing up into the mountains. He had looked out at his casement and could just distinguish a horseman with a female seated before him.

«Search the stables!» cried Governor Manco. The stables were searched; all the horses were in their stalls, excepting the Arabian steed. In his place was a stout cudgel tied to the manger and on it a label bearing these words: «A Gift to Governor Manco from an Old Soldier».

LEGEND
OF THE TWO DISCREET STATUES

THERE lived once in a waste apartment of the Alhambra, a merry little fellow named Lope Sánchez who worked in the gardens and was as brisk and blithe as a grasshopper, singing all day long. He was the life and soul of the fortress; when his work was over, he would sit on one of the stone benches of the esplanade and strum his guitar and sing long ditties about the Cid and Bernardo del Carpio and Fernando del Pulgar and other Spanish heroes for the amusement of the soldiers of the fortress or would strike up a merrier tune and set the girls dancing *boleros* and *fandangos*.

Like most little men, Lope Sánchez had a strapping buxom dame for a wife who could almost have put him in her pocket, but he lacked the usual poor man's lot—instead of ten children he had but one. This was a little black eyed girl about twelve years of age, named Sanchica, who was as merry as himself and the delight of his heart. She played about him as he worked in the gardens, danced to his guitar as he sat in the shade and ran as wild as a young fawn about the groves and alleys and ruined halls of the Alhambra.

It was now the eve of the blessed St. John and the holiday-loving gossips of the Alhambra, men, women and children, went up at night to the Mountain of the Sun which rises above the Generalife to keep their midsummer vigil on its level summit. It was a bright moonlight night and all the mountains

267

were grey and silvery, and the city with its domes and spires lay in shadows below and the Vega was like a fairy land with haunted streams gleaming among its dusky groves. On the highest part of the mountain they lit up a bonfire according to an old custom of the country, handed down from the Moors. The inhabitants of the surrounding country were keeping a similar vigil, and bonfires here and there in the Vega and along the folds of the mountains blazed up palely in the moonlight.

The evening was gaily passed in dancing to the guitar of Lope Sánchez who was never so joyous as when on a holiday revel of the kind. While the dance was going on, the little Sanchica with some of her playmates sported among the ruins of an old Moorish fort that crowns the mountain [1] when, in gathering pebbles in the fosse, she found a small hand curiously carved of jet, the fingers closed and the thumb firmly clasped upon them. Overjoyed with her good fortune, she ran to her mother with her prize. It immediately became a subject of sage speculation and was eyed by some with superstitious distrust. «Throw it away», said one, «it's Moorish—depend upon it; there's mischief and witchcraft in it». «By no means», said another, «you may sell it for something to the jewellers of the Zacatín». In the midst of this discussion an old tawny soldier drew near who had served in Africa and was as swarthy as a Moor. He examined the hand with a knowing look. «I have seen things of this kind», said he, «among the Moors of Barbary. It is a great virtue to guard against the evil eye and all kinds or spells and enchantments. I give you joy, friend Lope, this bodes good luck to your child».

Upon hearing this, the wife of Lope Sánchez tied the little hand of jet to a ribbon and hung it round the neck of her daughter.

[1] *i. e.* the Moor's Seat (*Silla del Moro*).

The sight of this talisman called up all the favourite super-stitions about the Moors. The dance was neglected and they sat in groups on the ground, telling old legendary tales handed down from their ancestors. Some of their stories turned upon the wonders of the very mountain upon which they were seated, which is a famous hobgoblin region. One ancient crone gave a long account of the subterranean palace in the bowels of that mountain, where Boabdil and all his Moslem court are said to remain enchanted. «Among yonder ruins», said she pointing to some crumbling walls and mounds of earth on a distant part of the mountain, «there is a deep black pit that goes down, down into the very heart of the mountain. For all the money in Granada I would not look down into it. Once upon a time a poor man of the Alhambra, who tended goats upon this mountain, scrambled down into that pit after a kid that had fallen in. He came out again all wild and star-ing, and told such things of what he had seen that every one thought his brain was turned. He raved for a day or two about the hobgoblin Moors that had pursued him in the cavern and could hardly be persuaded to drive his goats up again to the mountain. He did so at last, but, poor man, he never came down again. The neighbours found his goats browsing about the Moorish ruins, and his hat and mantle lying near the mouth of the pit, but he was never more heard of».

The little Sanchica listened with breathless attention to this story. She was of a curious nature and felt immediately a great hankering to peep into this dangerous pit. Stealing away from her companions, she sought the distant ruins and after groping for some time among them came to a small hollow or basin near the brow of the mountain, where it swept stee-ply down into the valley of the Darro. In the centre of this basin yawned the mouth of the pit. Sanchica ventured to the verge and peeped in. All was black as pitch and gave an idea of immeasurable depth. Her blood ran cold; she drew back, then peeped in again, then would have run away, then took another peep—the very horror of the thing was delightful to her. At length she rolled a large stone and pushed it over the brink. For some time it fell in silence, then struck some rocky projection with a violent crash, then rebounded from side to side, rumbling and tumbling with a noise like thunder, then made a final splash into water, far, far below, and all was again silent.

The silence, however, did not long continue. It seemed as if something had been awakened within this dreary abyss. A murmuring sound gradually rose out of the pit like the hum and buzz of a be-hive. It grew louder and louder; there was the confusion of voices as of a distant multitude, together with the faint din of arms, clash of cymbals and clangour of trumpets, as if some army were marshalling for battle in the very bowels of the mountain.

The child drew off with silent awe and hastened back to the place where she had left her parents and their companions. All were gone. The bonfire was expiring and its last wreath of smoke curling up in moonshine. The distant fires that had blazed along the mountains and in the Vega were all extinguished, and everything seemed to have sunk to repose. Sanchica called her parents and some of her companions by name, but received no reply. She ran down the side of the mountain and by the gardens of the Generalife, until she arrived in the alley of trees leading to the Alhambra, when she seated herself on a bench of a woody recess to recover breath. The bell from the watch-tower of the Alhambra tolled midnight. There was a deep tranquillity, as if all nature slept, excepting the low tinkling sound of an unseen stream that ran under the covert of the bushes. The breathing sweetness of the atmosphere was lulling her to sleep, when her eye was caught by something glittering at a distance, and to her surprise she beheld a long cavalcade of Moorish warriors pouring down the mountain-side and along the leafy avenues. Some were armed with lances and shields, others with scimitars and battle-axes and with polished cuirasses that flashed in the moonbeams. Their horses pranced proudly and champed upon their bits but their tramp caused no more sound than if they had been shod with felt and the riders were all as pale as death. Among them rode a beautiful lady with a crowned head and long golden locks entwined with pearls. The housings of her palfrey were of crimson velvet embroidered with gold and swept the earth; but she rode all disconsolate with her eyes ever fixed upon the ground.

Then succeeded a train of courtiers magnificently arrayed in robes and turbans of diverse colours, and amidst them on a cream-coloured charger rode King Boabdil el Chico, in a royal mantle covered with jewels and a crown sparkling with diamonds. The little Sanchica knew him by his yellow beard and his resemblance to his portrait which she had often seen in the picture-gallery of the Generalife. She gazed in wonder and admiration at this royal pageant, as it passed glistening among the trees, but though she knew these monarchs and courtiers and warriors, so pale and silent, were out of the common course of nature, and things of magic and enchantment, yet she looked on with a bold heart, such courage did she derive from the mystic talisman of the hand which was suspended about her neck.

The cavalcade having passed by, she rose and followed. It continued on to the great Gate of Justice which stood wide open; the old invalid sentinels on duty lay on the stone benches of the barbican, buried in profound and apparently charmed sleep, and the phantom pageant swept noiselessly by them with flaunting banner and triumphant state. Sanchica would have followed, but to her surprise she beheld an opening in the earth, within the barbican, leading down beneath the foundations of the tower. She entered for a little distance and was encouraged to proceed by finding steps rudely hewn in the rock and a vaulted passage here and there lit up by a silver lamp, which, while it gave light, diffused likewise a grateful fragance. Venturing on, she came at last to a great hall, wrought out of the heart of the mountain, magnificently furnished in the Moorish style and lighted up by silver and crystal lamps. Here on an ottoman sat an old man in Moorish dress with a long white beard, nodding and dozing with a staff in his hand which seemed ever to be slipping from his grasp; while at a little distance sat a beautiful lady in ancient Spanish dress, with a coronet all sparkling with diamonds and her hair entwined with pearls, who was softly playing on a silver lyre. The little Sanchica now recollected a story she had heard among the old people of the Alhambra, concerning a Gothic princess confined in the centre of the mountain by an old Arabian magician, whom she kept bound up in magic sleep by the power of music.

The lady paused with surprise at seeing a mortal in that enchanted hall. «Is it the eve of the blessed St. John?» said she.

«It is», replied Sanchica.

«Then for one night the magic charm is suspended. Come hither, child, and fear not. I am a Christian like thyself, though bound here by enchantment. Touch my fetters with the talisman that hangs about thy neck and for this night I shall be free.»

So saying, she opened her robes and displayed a broad golden band round her waist and a golden chain that fastened her to the ground. The child hesitated not to apply the little hand of jet to the golden band and immediately the chain fell to the earth. At the sound the old man woke and began to rub his eyes, but the lady ran her fingers over the chords of the lyre and again he fell into a slumber and began to nod and his staff to falter in his hand. «Now», said the lady, «touch his staff with the talismanic hand of jet.» The child did so

and it fell from his grasp and he sunk in a deep sleep on the ottoman. The lady gently laid the silver lyre on the ottoman, leaning it against the head of the sleeping magician, then touching the chords until they vibrated in his ear: «O potent spirit of harmony», said she, «continue thus to hold his senses in thraldom till the return of day. Now follow me, my child», continued she, «and thou shalt behold the Alhambra as it was in the days of its glory, for thou hast a magic talisman that reveals all enchantments.» Sanchica followed the lady in silence. They passed up through the entrance of the cavern into the barbican of the Gate of Justice and thence to the *Plaza de los Aljibes* or esplanade within the fortress.

This was all filled with Moorish soldiery, horse and foot, marshalled in squadrons with banners displayed. There were royal guards also at the portal and rows of African blacks with drawn scimitars. No one spoke a word and Sanchica passed on fearlessly after her conductor. Her astonishment increased on entering the royal palace, in which she had been reared. The broad moonshine lit up all the halls and courts and gardens almost as brightly as if it were day, but revealed a far different scene from that to which she was accustomed. The walls of the apartments were no longer stained and rent by time. Instead of cobwebs, they were now hung with rich silks of Damascus, and the gildings and arabesque paintings were restored to their original brilliancy and freshness. The halls, instead of being naked and unfurnished, were set out with divans and ottomans of the rarest stuffs, embroidered with pearls and studded with precious gems, and all the fountains in the courts and gardens were playing.

The kitchens were again in full operation; cooks were busy preparing shadowy dishes and roasting and boiling the phantoms of pullets and partridges; servants were hurrying to and fro with silver dishes heaped up with dainties and arranging a delicious banquet. The Court of Lions was thronged with guards and courtiers and alfaquis, as in the old times of the Moors, and at the upper end in the saloon of judgment sat Boabdil on his throne, surrounted by his court and swaying a shadowy sceptre for the night. Notwithstanding all this throng and seeming bustle, not a voice nor a footstep was to be heard; nothing interrupted the midnight silence but the splashing of the fountains. The little Sanchica followed her conductress in mute amazement about the palace, until they came to a portal opening to the vaulted passages beneath the great tower of Comares. On each side of the portal sat the figure of a nymph, wrought out of alabaster. Their heads were turned aside and their regards fixed upon the same spot within the vault. The enchanted lady paused and beckoned the child to her. «Here», said she, «is a great secret which I will reveal to thee in reward for thy faith and courage. These discreet statues watch over a mighty treasure hidden in old times by a Moorish king. Tell thy father to search the spot on which their eyes are fixed and he will find what will make him richer than any man in Granada. Thy innocent hands alone, however, gifted as thou art also with the talisman, can remove the treasure. Bid thy father use it discreetly and devote a part of it to the performance of daily masses for my deliverance from this unholy enchantment».

When the lady had spoken these words, she led the child onward to the little garden of Lindaraxa, which is hard by the vault of the statues. The moon trembled upon the waters of the solitary fountain in the centre of the garden and shed a tender light upon the orange and citron trees. The beautiful lady plucked a branch of myrtle and wreathed it round the head of the child. «Let this be a memento», said she, «of what I have revealed to thee and a testimonial of its truth. My hour is come; I must return to the enchanted hall. Follow me not, lest evil befall thee —farewell. Remember what I have said and have masses performed for my deliverance», So saying, the lady entered a dark passage leading beneath the tower of Comares and was no longer seen.

The faint crowing of a cock was now heard from the cottages below the Alhambra in the valley of the Darro and a pale streak of light began to appear above the eastern mountains. A slight wind arose, there was a sound like the rustling of dry leaves through the courts and corridors and door after door shut to with a jarring sound.

Sanchica returned to the scenes she had so lately beheld thronged with the shadowy multitude, but Boabdil and his phantom court were gone. The moon shone into empty halls and galleries stripped of their transient splendour, stained and dilapidated by time and hung with cobwebs. The bat flitted about in the uncertain light and the frog croaked from the fish-pond.

Sanchica now made the best of her way to a remote staircase that led up to the humble apartment occupied by her family. The door as usual was open, for Lope Sánchez was too poor to need bolt or bar; she crept quietly to her pallet and, putting the myrtle wreath beneath her pillow, soon fell asleep.

In the morning she related all that had befallen her to her father. Lope Sánchez, however, treated the whole as a mere dream and laughed at the child for her credulity. He went forth to his customary labours in the garden, but had not been there long when his little daughter came running to him almost breathless. «Father! father!» cried she, «behold the myrtle wreath which the Moorish lady bound round my head!»

Lope Sánchez gazed with astonishment, for the stalk of the myrtle was of pure gold and every leaf was a sparkling emerald! Being not much accustomed to precious stones, he was ignorant of the real value of the wreath, but he saw enough to convince him that it was something more substantial than the stuff that dreams are generally made of, and that at any rate the child had dreamt to some purpose. His first care was to enjoin the most absolute secrecy upon his daughter; in this respect, however, he was secure, for she had discretion far beyond her years or sex. He then repaired to the vault, where stood the statues of the two alabaster nymphs. He remarked that their heads were turned from the portal and that the regards of each were fixed upon the same point in the interior of the building. Lope Sánchez could not but admire this most discreet contrivance for guarding a secret. He drew a line from the eyes of the statues to the point of regard, made a private mark on the wall, and then retired.

All day, however, the mind of Lope Sánchez was distracted with a thousand cares. He could not help hovering within distant view of the two statues and became nervous from the dread that the golden secret might be discovered. Every footstep that approached the place made him tremble. He would have given anything could he but have turned the heads of the statues, forgetting that they had looked precisely in the same direction for some hundreds of years without any person being the wiser.

«A plague upon them», he would say to himself, «they'll betray all. Did ever mortal hear of such a mode of guarding a secret?» Then on hearing any one advance, he would steal off, as though his very lurking near the place would awaken suspicion. Then he would return cautiously and peep from a distance to see if everything was secure, but the sight of the statues would again call forth his indignation. «Aye, there they stand», would he say, «always looking and looking and looking just where they should not. Confound them! they are just like all their sex: if they have not tongues to tattle with, they'll be sure to do it with their eyes.»

At length to his relief the long anxious day drew to a close. The sound of footsteps was no longer heard in the echoing halls of the Alhambra; the last stranger passed the threshold, the great portal was barred and bolted, and the bat and the frog and the hooting owl gradually resumed their night-ly vocations in the deserted palace.

Lope Sánchez waited, however, until the night was far ad-vanced, before he ventured with his little daughter to the hall of the two nymphs. He found them looking as knowingly and mysteriously as ever at the secret place of deposit. «By your leaves, gentle ladies», thought Lope Sánchez, as he passed between them, «I will relieve you from this charge that must have set so heavy in your minds for the last two or three cen-turies». He accordingly went to work at the part of the wall which he had marked and in a little while laid open a con-cealed recess, in which stood two great jars of porcelain. He attempted to draw them forth, but they were immovable, until touched by the innocent hand of his little daughter. With her aid he dislodged them from their niche and found to his great joy that they were filled with pieces of Moorish gold, mingled with jewels and precious stones. Before daylight he managed to convey them to his chamber and left the two guardian sta-tues with their eyes still fixed on the vacant wall.

Lope Sánchez had thus on a sudden become a rich man, but riches as usual brought a world of cares to which he had hitherto been a stranger. How was he to convey away his wealth with safety? How was he even to enter upon the enjoy-ment of it without awakening suspicion? Now, too, for the first time in his life the dread of robbers entered into his mind. He looked with terror at the insecurity of his habitation and went to work to barricade the doors and windows; yet after all his precautions he could not sleep soundly. His usual gaiety was at an end, he had no longer a joke or a song for his neigh-bours and in short became the most miserable animal in the Alhambra. His old comrades remarked this alteration, pitied him heartily and began to desert him, thinking he must be falling into want and in danger of looking to them for assistance. Little did they suspect that his only calamity was riches.

The wife of Lope Sánchez shared his anxiety, but then she had ghostly comfort. We ought before this to have mentioned that Lope, being rather a light inconsiderate little man, his wife was accustomed in all grave matters to seek the counsel and ministry of her confessor Fray Simón, a sturdy broad-shouldered blue-bearded, bullet-headed friar of the neighbouring covent of San Francisco, who was in fact the spiritual comforter of half the good wives of the neighbourhood. He was moreover in great esteem among diverse sisterhoods of nuns who requited him for his ghostly services by frequent presents of those little dainties and knick-knacks manufactured in convents, such as delicate confections, sweet biscuits and bottles of spiced cordials, found to be marvellous restoratives after fasts and vigils.

Fray Simón thrived in the exercise of his functions. His oily skin glistened in the sunshine as he toiled up the hill of the Alhambra on a sultry day. Yet notwithstanding his sleek condition, the knotted rope round his waist showed the austerity of his self-discipline; the multitude doffed their caps to him as a mirror of piety and even the dogs scented the odour of sanctity that exhaled from his garments and howled from their kennels as he passed.

Such was Fray Simón, the spiritual counsellor of the comely wife of Lope Sánchez and, as the father confessor is the domestic confidant of women in humble life in Spain, he was soon made acquainted in great secrecy with the story of the hidden treasure.

The friar opened eyes and mouth, and crossed himself a dozen times at the news. After a moment's pause, «Daughter of my soul!» said he, «know that thy husband has committed a double sin—a sin against both state and church! The treasure he hath thus seized upon for himself, being found in the royal domains, belongs of course to the crown, but being infidel wealth, rescued as it were from the very fangs of Satan, should be devoted to the church. Still, however, the matter may be accommodated. Bring hither the myrtle wreath».

When the good father beheld it, his eyes twinkled more than ever with admiration of the size and beauty of the emeralds. «This», said he, «being the first fruits of this discovery, should be dedicated to pious purposes. I will hang it up as a votive offering before the image of San Francisco in our chapel, and will earnestly pray to him this very night that your husband be permitted to remain in quiet possession of your wealth».

The good dame was delighted to make her peace with heaven at so cheap a rate, and the friar, putting the wreath under his mantle, departed with saintly steps towards his convent.

When Lope Sánchez came home, his wife told him what had passed. He was excessively provoked, for he lacked his wife's devotion and had for some time groaned in secret at the domestic visitations of the friar. «Woman», said he, «what hast thou done?

«What!» cried the good woman, «would you forbid my disburdening my conscience to my confessor?»

«No, wife! Confess as many of your own sins as you please, but as to this money-digging, it is a sin of my own and my conscience is very easy under the weight of it.»

There was no use, however, in complaining; the secret was told and like water spilled on the sand, was not again to be gathered. Their only chance was that the friar would be discreet.

The next day, while Lope Sánchez was abroad, there was a humble knocking at the door and Fray Simón entered with meek and demure countenance.

«Daughter», said he, «I have prayed earnestly to San Francisco and he has heard my prayer. In the dead of the night

279

the saint appeared to me in a dream, but with a frowning aspect. 'Why', said he, 'dost thou pray to me to dispense with this treasure of the Gentiles, when thou seest the poverty of my chapel? Go to the house of Lope Sánchez, crave in my name a portion of the Moorish gold to furnish two candlesticks for the main altar, and let him possess the residue in peace'».

When the good woman heard of this vision, she crossed herself with awe and, going to the secret place where Lope had hid the treasure, she filled a great leathern purse with pieces of Moorish gold and gave it to the friar. The pious monk bestowed upon her in return benedictions enough, if paid by Heaven, to enrich her race to the latest posterity; then slipping the purse into the sleeve of his habit, he folded his hands upon his breast and departed with an air of humble thankfulness.

When Lope Sánchez heard of this second donation to the church, he had well-nigh lost his senses. «Unfortunate man», cried he, «what will become of me? I shall be robbed by piecemeal; I shall be ruined and brought to beggary!»

It was with the utmost difficulty that his wife could pacify him, by reminding him of the countless wealth that yet remained, and how considerate it was for San Francisco to rest contented with so very small a portion.

Unluckily, Fray Simón had a number of poor relations to be provided for, not to mention some half-dozen sturdy bullet-headen orphan children and destitute foundlings, that he had taken under his care. He repeated his visits therefore from day to day with solicitations on behalf of Saint Dominic, Saint Andrew, Saint James, until poor Lope was driven to despair and found that unless he got out of the reach of this holy friar, he should have to make peace-offerings to every saint in the calendar. He determined therefore to pack up his remaining wealth, beat a secret retreat in the night and make off to another part of the kingdom.

280

Full of his project, he bought a stout mule for the purpose and tethered it in a gloomy vault underneath the tower of the Seven Floors, the very place from whence the *Belludo* or goblin horse without a head is said to issue forth at midnight and to scour the streets of Granada, pursued by a pack of hellhounds. Lope Sánchez had little faith in the story but availed himself of the dread occasioned by it, knowing that no one would be likely to pry into the subterranean stable of the phantom steed. He sent off his family in the course of the day with orders to wait for him at a distant village of the Vega. As the night advanced, he conveyed his treasure to the vault under the tower and, having loaded his mule, he led it forth and cautiously descended the dusky avenue.

Honest Lope had taken his measures with the utmost secrecy, imparting them to no one but the faithful wife of his bosom. By some miraculous revelation, however, they became known to Fray Simón. The zealous friar beheld these infidel treasures on the point of slipping forever out of his grasp and determined to have one more dash at them for the benefit of the church and San Francisco. Accordingly, when the bells had rung for *ánimas* and all the Alhambra was quiet, he stole out of his convent and, descending through the Gate of Justice, concealed himself among the thickets of roses and laurels that border the great avenue. Here he remained, counting the quarters of hours as they were sounded on the bell of the watchtower and listening to the dreary hootings of owls and the distant barking of dogs from the gypsy caverns.

At length he heard the tramp of hoofs, and through the gloom of the overshadowing trees imperfectly beheld a steed descending the avenue. The sturdy friar chuckled at the idea of the knowing turn he was about to serve honest Lope.

Tucking up the skirts of his habit and wriggling like a cat watching a mouse, he waited until his prey was directly before him, when darting forth from his leafy covert and putting one hand on the shoulder and the other on the crupper, he made a vault that would not have disgraced the most experienced master of equitation and alighted well-forked astride the steed. «Ah ha!» said the sturdy friar, «we shall now see who best understands the game». He had scarce uttered the words, when the mule began to kick and rear and plunge and then set off full speed down the hill. The friar attempted to check him, but in vain. He bounded from rock to rock and bush to bush; the friar's habit was torn to ribbons and fluttered in the wind, his shaven poll received many a hard knock from the branches of the trees, and many a scratch from the brambles. To add to his terror and distress, he found a pack of seven hounds in full cry at his heels and perceived too late that he was actually mounted upon the terrible *Belludo!*

Away they went, according to the ancient phrase «pull devil, pull friar», down the great avenue, across the Plaza Nueva, along the Zacatín, around the Bibarrambla—never did hunstman and hound make a more furious run or more infernal uproar. In vain did the friar invoke every saint in the calendar and the holy Virgin into ┬he bargain; every time he mentioned a name of the kind it was like a fresh application of the spur and made the *Belludo* bound as high as a house. Through the remainder of the night was the unlucky Fray Simón carried hither and thither and whither he would not, until every bone in his body ached and he suffered a loss of leather too grievous to be mentioned. At length the crowing of a cock gave the signal of returning day. At the sound the goblin steed wheeled about and galloped back for his tower. Again he scoured the Bibarrambla, the Zacatín, the Plaza Nueva and the avenue of fountains, the seven dogs yelling and barking and leaping up and snapping at the heels of the terrified friar. The first streak of day had just appeared as they reached the tower; here the goblin steed kicked up his heels, sent the friar a summerset through the air, plunged into the dark vault followed by the infernal pack and a profound silence succeeded to the late deafening clamour.

Was ever so diabolical a trick played off upon a holy friar? A peasant going to his labours at early dawn found the unfortunate Fray Simón lying under a fig-tree at the foot of the tower, but so bruised and bedevilled that he could neither speak nor move. He was conveyed with all care and tenderness to his cell and the story went that he had been waylaid and maltreated by robbers. A day or two elapsed before he recovered the use of his limbs; he consoled himself in the meantime with the thoughts that, though the mule with the treasure had escaped him, he had previously had some rare pickings at the infidel spoils. His first care on being able to use his limbs, was to search beneath his pallet, where he had secreted the myrtle wreath and the leathern pouches of gold extracted from the piety of dame Sánchez. What was his dismay at finding the wreath, in effect, but a withered branch of myrtle and the leathern pouches filled with sand and gravel!

Fray Simón with all his chagrin had the discretion to hold his tongue, for to betray the secret might draw on him the ridicule of the public and the punishment of his superior; it was not until many years afterwards on his death-bed that he revealed to his confessor his nocturnal ride on the *Belludo*.

Nothing was heard of Lope Sánchez for a long time after his disappearance from the Alhambra. His memory was always cherished as that of a merry companion, though it was feared from the care and melancholy observed in his conduct shortly before his mysterious departure that poverty and distress had driven him to some extremity. Some years afterwards one of his old companions, an invalid soldier, being at Malaga was knocked down and nearly run over by a coach and six. The carriage stopped, an old gentleman magnificently dressed with a bagwig and sword stepped out to assist the poor invalid. What was the astonishment of the latter to behold in this grand cavalier his old friend Lope Sánchez who was actually celebrating the marriage of his daughter Sanchica with one of the first grandees in the land.

The carriage contained the bridal party. There was dame Sánchez, now grown as round as a barrel and dressed out with feathers and jewels and necklaces of pearls and necklaces of diamonds and rings on every finger and altogether a finery of apparel that had not been seen since the days of Queen Sheba. The little Sanchica had now grown to be a woman and for grace and beauty might have been mistaken for a duchess, if not a princess outright. The bridegroom sat beside her, rather a withered, spindle-shanked little man, but this only proved him to be of the true blood, a legitimate Spanish grandee being rarely above three cubits in stature. The match had been of the mother's making.

Riches had not spoiled the heart of honest Lope. He kept his old comrade with him for several days, feasted him like a king, took him to plays and bull-fights and at length sent him away rejoicing with a big bag of money for himself and another to be distributed among his ancient messmates of the Alhambra.

Lope always gave out that a rich brother had died in America and left him heir to a copper mine, but the shrewd gossips of the Alhambra insist that his wealth was all derived from his having discovered the secret guarded by the two marble nymphs of the Alhambra. It is remarked that these very discreet statues continue even unto the present day with their eyes fixed most significantly on the same part of the wall, which leads many to suppose there is still some hidden treasure remaining there well worthy the attention of the enterprising traveller, though others and particularly all female visitors regard them with great complacency as lasting monuments of the fact that women can keep a secret.

MUHAMED ABU ALAHMAR,
THE
FOUNDER OF THE ALHAMBRA

HAVING dealt so freely in the marvellous legends of the Alhambra, I feel as if bound to give the reader a few facts concerning its sober history or rather the history of those magnificent princes, its founder and finisher, to whom the world is indebted for so beautiful and romantic an Oriental monument. To obtain these facts I descended from this region of fancy and fable, where everything is liable to take an imaginative tint, and carried my researches among the dusty tomes of the old Jesuits' library in the University. This once boasted repository of erudition is now a mere shadow of its former self, having been stripped of its manuscripts and rarest works by the French, when masters of Granada. Still it contains among many ponderous tomes of polemics of the Jesuit fathers several curious tracts of Spanish literature, and above all a number of those antiquated, dusty, parchment-bound chronicles, for which I have a peculiar veneration.

In this old library I have passed many delightful hours of quiet, undisturbed literary foraging, for the keys of the doors and book-cases were kindly entrusted to me and I was left alone to rummage at my leisure—a rare indulgence in these sanctuaries of learning which too often tantalize the thirsty student with the sight of sealed fountains of knowledge.

In the course of these visits, I gleaned the following particulars concerning the historical characters in question.

The Moors of Granada regarded the Alhambra as a miracle of art and had a tradition that the king who founded it dealt in magic, or at least was versed in alchemy, by means whereof he procured the immense sums of gold expended in its erection. A brief view of his reign will show the real secret of his wealth.

The name of this monarch, as inscribed on the walls of some of the apartments, was Abu Abd'allah (*i. e.* the father of Abdallah), but he is commonly known in Moorish history as Muhamed Abu Alahmar (or Mahomed, son of Alahmar) or simply, Abu Alahmar for the sake of brevity.

He was born in Arjona in the year of the Hejira 591, of the Christian era 1195 of the noble family of the Beni Nasar or children of Nasar, and no expense was spared by his parents to fit him for the high station to which the opulence and dignity of his family entitled him. The Saracens of Spain were greatly advanced in civilization, every principal city was a seat of learning and the arts, so that it was easy to command the most enlightened instructors for a youth of rank and fortune. Abu Alahmar, when he arrived at manly years, was appointed *alcaide* or governor of Arjona and Jaén, and gained great popularity by his benignity and justice. Some years afterwards on the death of Aben Hud the Moorish power in Spain was broken into factions, and many places declared for Muhamed Abu Alahmar. Being of a sanguine spirit and lofty ambition, he seized upon the occasion, made a circuit through the country and was everywhere received with acclamations. It was in the year 1238, that he entered Granada amidst the enthusiastic shouts of the multitude. He was proclaimed king with every demonstration of joy and soon became the head of the Moslems in Spain, being the first of the illustrious line of Beni Nasar that had sat upon the throne. His reign was such as to render him a blessing to his subjects. He gave the command of his various cities to such as had distinguished themselves by valour and prudence, and who seemed most acceptable to the people. He organized a vigilant police and established rigid rules for the administration of justice. The poor and the distressed always found ready admission to his presence, and he attended personally to their assistance and redress. He erected hospitals for the blind, the aged and infirm and all those incapable of labour, and visited them frequently not on set days with pomp and form, so as to give time for everything to be put in order and every abuse concealed, but suddenly and unexpectedly, informing himself by actual observation and close inquiry of the treatment of the sick and the conduct of those appointed to administer to their relief. He founded schools and colleges which he visited in the same manner, inspecting personally the instruction of the youth. He established butcheries and public ovens, that the people might be furnished with wholesome provisions at just and regular prices. He introduced abundant streams of water into the city, erecting baths and fountains, and constructing aqueducts and canals to irrigate and fertilize the Vega. By these means prosperity and abundance prevailed in this beautiful city; its gates were thronged with commerce and its warehouses filled with luxuries and merchandise of every clime and country.

While Muhamed Abu Alahmar was ruling his fair domains thus wisely and prosperously, he was suddenly menaced by the horrors of war. The Christians at that time, profiting by the dismemberment of the Moslem power, were rapidly regaining their ancient territories. James the Conqueror had subjected all Valencia and Ferdinand the Saint was carrying his victorious arms into Andalusia. The latter invested the city of Jaén, and swore not to raise his camp until he had gained possession of the place. Muhamed Abu Alahmar was conscious of the insufficiency of his means to carry on a war with the potent sovereign of Castile. Taking a sudden resolution therefore he repaired privately to the Christian camp, and made his unexpected appearance in the presence of King Ferdinand. «In me», said he, «you behold Muhamed, king of Granada; I confide in your good faith and put myself under your protection. Take all I possess and receive me as your vassal». So saying, he knelt and kissed the king's hand in token of submission.

King Ferdinand was touched by this instance of confiding faith and determined not to be outdone in generosity. He raised his late rival from the earth, and embraced him as a friend, nor would he accept the wealth he offered, but received him as a vassal, leaving him sovereign of his dominions, on condition of paying a yearly tribute, attending the Cortes as one of the nobles of the empire and serving him in war with a certain number of horsemen.

It was not long after this that Muhamed was called upon for his military services to aid King Ferdinand in his famous siege of Seville. The Moorish king sallied forth with five hundred chosen horsemen of Granada, than whom none in the world knew better how to manage the steed or wield the lance. It was a melancholy and humiliating service, however, for they had to draw the sword against their brethren of the faith.

Muhamed gained a melancholy distinction by his prowess in this renowned conquest, but more true honour by the humanity which he prevailed upon Ferdinand to introduce into the usages of war. When in 1248, the famous city of Seville surrendered to the Castilian monarch, Muhamed returned sad

and full of care to his dominions. He saw the gathering ills that menaced the Moslem cause; and uttered an ejaculation often used by him in moments of anxiety and trouble: «How straitened and wretched would be our life, if our hope were not so spacious and extensive!» «*¡Qué angosta y miserable sería nuestra vida, si no fuera tan dilatada y espaciosa nuestra esperanza!*»

When the melancholy conqueror approached his beloved Granada, the people thronged forth to see him with impatient joy, for they loved him as a benefactor. They had erected arches of triumph in honour of his martial exploits, and wherever he passed he was hailed with acclamations as *El Ghalib* or the conqueror. Muhamed shook his head when he heard the appellation. «*Wa la ghalib ila Alá!*», exclaimed he. (There is no conqueror but God!) From that time forward he adopted this exclamation as a motto. He inscribed it on an oblique band across his escutcheon, and it continued to be the motto of his descendants.

Muhamed had purchased peace by submission to the Christian yoke, but he knew that where the elements were so discordant and the motives for hostility so deep and ancient, it could not be secure or permanent. Acting therefore upon an old maxim, «Arm thyself in peace and clothe thyself in summer», he improved the present interval of tranquility by fortifying his dominions and replenishing his arsenals, and by promoting those useful arts which give wealth and real power to an empire. He gave premiums and privileges to the best artizans, improved the breed of horses and other domestic animals, encouraged husbandry and increased the natural fertility of the soil twofold by his protection, making the lovely valleys of his kingdom to bloom like gardens. He fostered also the growth and fabrication of silk, until the looms of Granada surpassed even those of Syria in the fineness and beauty of their productions. He moreover caused the

289

mines of gold and silver and other metals, found in the mountainous regions of his dominions, to be diligently worked, and was the first king of Granada who struck money of gold and silver with his name, taking great care that the coins should be skilfully executed.

It was about this time, towards the middle of the thirteenth century and just after his return from the siege of Seville, that he commenced the splendid palace of the Alhambra; superintending the building of it in person, mingling frequently among the artists and workmen, and directing their labours.

Though thus magnificent in his works and great in his enterprises, he was simple in his person and moderate in his enjoyments. His dress was not merely void of splendour, but so plain as not to distinguish him from his subjects. His harem boasted but few beauties, and these he visited but seldom, though they were entertained with great magnificence. His wives were daughters of the principal nobles and were treated by him as friends and rational companions. What is more, he managed to make them live as friends with one another. He passed much of his time in his gardens, especially in those of the Alhambra, which he had stored with the rarest plants and the most beautiful and aromatic flowers. Here he delighted himself in reading histories or in causing them to be read and related to him, and sometimes, in intervals of leisure employed himself in the instruction of his three sons, for whom he had provided the most learned and virtuous masters.

As he had frankly and voluntarily offered himself a tributary vassal to Ferdinand, so he always remained loyal to his word, giving him repeated proofs of fidelity and attachment. When that renowned monarch died in Seville in 1254, Muhamed Abu Alahmar sent ambassadors to condole with his successor Alfonso X, and with them a gallant train of a hundred Moorish cavaliers of distinguished rank, who were to attend each bearing a lighted taper round the royal bier during the funeral ceremonies. This grand testimonial of respect was repeated by the Moslem monarch during the remainder of his life on each anniversary of the death of King Fernando el Santo, when the hundred Moorish knights repaired from Granada to Seville and took their stations with lighted tapers in the centre of the sumptuous cathedral, round the cenotaph of the illustrious deceased.

Muhamed Abu Alahmar retained his faculties and vigour to an advanced age. In his seventy-ninth year he took the field on horseback, accompanied by the flower of his chivalry, to resist an invasion of his territories. As the army sallied forth from Granada, one of the principal *adalides* or guides who rode in the advance, accidentally broke his lance against the arch of the gate. The councillors of the king, alarmed by this circumstance which was considered an evil omen, entreated him to return. Their supplications were in vain. The king persisted and at noontide the omen, say the Moorish chroniclers, was fatally fulfilled. Muhamed was suddenly struck with illness and had nearly fallen from his horse. He was placed on a litter and borne back towards Granada, but his illness increased to such a degree that they were obliged to pitch his tent in the Vega. His physicians were filled with consternation, not knowing what remedy to prescribe. In a few hours he died vomiting blood and in violent convulsions. The Castilian prince Don Philip, brother of Alfonso X, was by his side when he expired. His body was embalmed, enclosed in a silver coffin and buried in the Alhambra in a sepulchre of precious marble, amidst the unfeigned lamentations of his subjects who bewailed him as a parent.

Such was the enlightened patriot prince who founded the Alhambra, whose name remains emblazoned among its most delicate and graceful ornaments and whose memory is calculated to inspire the loftiest associations in those who tread these fading scenes of his magnificence and glory. Though his undertakings were vast and his expenditures immense, yet his treasury was always full, and this seeming contradiction gave rise to the story that he was versed in magic art and possessed of the secret for transmuting baser metals into gold. Those who have attended to his domestic policy, as here set forth, will easily understand the natural magic and simple alchemy which made his ample treasury to overflow.

YUSEF ABUL HAGIG,
THE
FINISHER OF THE ALHAMBRA

B ENEATH the governor's apartment in the Alhambra is the royal mosque, where the Moorish monarchs performed their private devotions. Although consecrated as a Catholic chapel, it still bears traces of its Moslem origin; the Saracenic columns with their gilded capitals and the latticed gallery for the females of the Harem may yet be seen, and the escutcheons of the Moorish kings are mingled on the walls with those of the Castilian sovereigns.

In this consecrated place perished the illustrious Yusef Abul Hagig, the high-minded prince who completed the Alhambra, and who for his virtues and endowments deserves almost equal renown with its magnanimous founder. It is with pleasure I draw forth from the obscurity in which it has too long remained the name of another of those princes of a departed and almost forgotten race, who reigned in elegance and splendour in Andalusia, when all Europe was in comparative barbarism.

Yusef Abul Hagig (or, as it is sometimes written, Haxis), ascended the throne of Granada in the year 1333, and his personal appearance and mental qualities were such as to win all hearts and to awaken anticipations of a beneficent and prosperous reign. He was of a noble presence and great bodily strength, united to manly beauty; his complexion was exceeding fair and, according to the Arabian chronicles, he heightened the gravity and majesty of his appearance by suffering his beard to grow to a dignified length and dyeing it black. He had an excellent memory, well stored with science and erudition; he was of a lively genius and accounted the best poet of his time, and his manners were gentle, affable and urbane. Yusef possessed the courage common to all generous spirits. but his genius was more cultivated for peace than war and though obliged to take up arms repeatedly in his time, he was generally unfortunate. He carried the benignity of his nature into warfare, prohibiting all wanton cruelty and enjoining mercy and protection towards women and children, the aged and infirm and all friars and persons of holy and recluse life. Among other ill-starred enterprises, he undertook a great campaign in conjunction with the king of Morocco against the kings of Castile and Portugal, but was defeated in the memorable battle of Salado, a disastrous reverse which had nearly proved a death-blow to the Moslem power in Spain.

Yusef obtained a long truce after this defeat, during which time he devoted himself to the instruction of his people and the improvement of their morals and manners. For this purpose he established schools in all the villages with simple and uniform systems of education; he obliged every hamlet of more than twelve houses to have a mosque and prohibited various abuses and indecorums that had been introduced into the ceremonies of religion and the festivals and public amusements of the people. He attended vigilantly to the police of the city, establishing nocturnal guards and patrols and superintending all municipal concerns. His attention was also directed towards finishing the great architectural works commenced by his predecessors and erecting others on his own plans. The Alhambra, which had been founded by the good Abu Alahmar, was now completed. Yusef constructed the beautiful Gate of Justice, forming the grand entrance to the fortress, which he finished in 1348. He likewise adorned many of the courts and halls of the palace, as may be seen by the inscriptions on the walls in which his name repeatedly occurs. He built also the noble *Alcázar* or citadel of Malaga, now unfortunately a mere mass of crumbling ruins, but which most probably exhibited in its interior similar elegance and magnificence with the Alhambra.

The genius of a sovereign stamps a character upon his time. The nobles of Granada, imitating the elegant and graceful taste of Yusef, soon filled the city of Granada with magnificent palaces, the halls of which were paved with mosaic, the walls and ceilings wrought in fret-work, and delicately gilded and painted with azure, vermilion and other brilliant colours or minutely inlaid with cedar and other precious woods, specimens of which have survived, in all their lustre the lapse of several centuries. Many of the houses had fountains which threw up jets of water to refresh and cool the air. They had lofty towers also of wood or stone curiously carved and ornamented and covered with plates of metal that glittered in the sun. Such was the refined and delicate taste in architecture that prevailed among this elegant people, insomuch that, to use the beautiful simile of an Arabian writer, «Granada in the days of Yusef was as a silver vase filled with emeralds and jacynths».

One anecdote will be sufficient to show the magnanimity of this generous prince. The long truce which had succeeded the battle of Salado was at an end, and every effort of Yusef to renew it was in vain. His deadly foe, Alfonso XI of Castille, took the field with great force and laid siege to Gibraltar. Yusef reluctantly took up arms and sent troops to the relief of the place; when in the midst of his anxiety, he received tidings that his dreaded foe had suddenly fallen a victim to the plague. Instead of manifesting exultation on the occasion,

Yusef called to mind the great qualities of the deceased, and was touched with a noble sorrow. «Alas» cried he, «the world has lost one of its most excellent princes, a sovereign who knew how to honour merit, whether in friend or foe!»

The Spanish chroniclers themselves bear witness to his magnanimity. According to their accounts, the Moorish cavaliers partook of the sentiment of their king and put on mourning for the death of Alfonso. Even those of Gibraltar, who had been so closely invested, when they knew that the hostile monarch lay dead in his camp, determined among themselves that no hostile movement should be made against the Christians. The day on which the camp was broken up and the army departed bearing the corpse of Alfonso, the Moors issued in multitudes from Gibraltar and stood mute and melancholy, watching the mournful pageant. The same reverence for the deceased was observed by all the Moorish commanders on the frontiers, who suffered the funeral train to pass in safety, bearing the corpse of the Christian sovereign from Gibraltar to Seville [1].

Yusef did not long survive the enemy he had so generously deplored. In the year 1354, as he was one day praying in the royal mosque of the Alhambra, a maniac rushed suddenly from behind and plunged a dagger in his side. The cries of the king brought his guards and courtiers to his assistance. They found him weltering in his blood and in convulsions. He was borne to the royal apartments, but expired almost immediately. The murderer was cut to pieces and his limbs burnt in public to gratify the fury of the populace.

---

[1] «Y los moros que estaban en la Villa y Castillo de Gibraltar después que sopieron que el Rey Don Alfonso era muerto, ordenaron entresí que ninguno fuese osado de fazer ningún movimiento contra los Christianos nin mover pelea contra ellos; estovieron todos quedos y dezian entre ellos que aquel día muriera un noble rey y gran príncipe del mundo.» (Author's note.)

The body of the king was interred in a superb sepulchre of white marble; a long epitaph in letters of gold upon an azure ground recorded his virtues. «Here lies a king and martyr of an illustrious line, gentle, learned and virtuous, renowned for the graces of his person and his manners, whose clemency, piety and benevolence were extolled throughout the kingdom of Granada. He was a great prince, an illustrious captain, a sharp sword of the Moslems, a valiant standard-bearer among the most potent monarchs», etc.

The mosque still remains which once resounded with the dying cries of Yusef, but the monument which recorded his virtues has long since disappeared. His name, however, remains inscribed among the ornaments of the Alhambra and will be perpetuated in connexion with this renowned pile, which it was his pride and delight to beautify.

THE AUTHOR'S FAREWELL TO GRANADA

M Y serene and happy reign in the Alhambra was suddenly
brought to a close by letters which reached me, while
indulging in Oriental luxury in the cool hall of the baths, sum-
moning me away from my Moslem elysium to mingle once
more in the bustle and business of the dusty world. How was
I to encounter its toils and turmoils, after such a life of repose
and reverie? How was I to endure its commonplace, after the
poetry of the Alhambra?

But little preparation was necessary for my departure. A
two-wheeled vehicle, called a *tartana*, very much resembling
a covered cart, was to be the travelling equipage of a young
Englishman and myself through Murcia to Alicante and Valencia on our way to France, and a long-limbed varlet who
had been a *contrabandista* and, for aught I knew, a robber
was to be our guide and guard. The preparations were soon
made, but the departure was the difficulty. Day after day was it
postponed; day after day was spent in lingering about my
favourite haunts and day after day they appeared more
delightful in my eyes.

The social, and domestic little world also, in which I had
been moving, had become singularly endeared to me, and the
concern evinced by them at my intended departure convinced
me that my kind feelings were reciprocated. Indeed, when at
length the day arrived, I did not dare venture upon a leave-

taking at the good dame Antonia's; I saw the soft heart of
little Dolores at least was brim full and ready for an overflow.
So I bade a silent adieu to the palace and its inmates, and
descended into the city as if intending to return. There, however, the *tartana* and the guide were ready; so, after taking
a noon-day's repast with my fellow-traveller at the *posada,* I
set out with him on our journey.

Humble was the cortege and melancholy the departure of
El Rey Chico the Second! Manuel, the nephew of *Tía Antonia,*
Mateo, my officious but now disconsolate squire, and two or
three old invalids of the Alhambra with whom I had grown
into gossiping companionship, had come down to see me off,
for it is one of the good old customs of Spain to sally forth
several miles to meet a coming friend, and to accompany him
as far on his departure. Thus then we set out, our long-legged
guard striding ahead, with his *escopeta* on his shoulder, Manuel and Mateo on each side of the *tartana,* and the old invalids behind.

At some little distance to the north of Granada, the road
gradually ascends the hills; here I alighted and walked up slowly with Manuel who took this occasion to confide to me the
secret of his heart and of all those tender concerns between
himself and Dolores with which I had been already informed
by the all-knowing and all-revealing Mateo Jiménez. His doctor's diploma had prepared the way for their union and nothing
more was wanting but the dispensation of the Pope, on account
of their consanguinity. Then, if he could get the post of *mé-
dico* of the fortress, his happiness would be complete! I con-
gratulated him on the judgment and good taste he had shown
in his choice of a helpmate, invoked all possible felicity on
their union and trusted that the abundant affections of the
kind-hearted little Dolores would in time have more stable objects to occupy them than recreant cats and truant pigeons.

It was indeed a sorrowful parting when I took leave of

these good people and saw them slowly descend the hills, now and then turning round to wave me a last adieu. Manuel, it is true, had cheerful prospects to console him, but poor Mateo seemed perfectly cast down. It was to him a grievous fall from the station of prime minister and historiographer to his old brown cloak and his starveling mystery of ribbon-wearing, and the poor devil, notwithstanding his occasional officiousness, had somehow or other acquired a stronger hold on my sympathies than I was aware of. It would have really been a consolation in parting could I have anticipated the good fortune in store for him, and to which I had contributed; for the importance I had appeared to give to his tales and gossip and local knowledge, and the frequent companionship in which I had indulged him in the course of my strolls, had elevated his idea of his own qualifications and opened a new career to him, and the son of the Alhambra has since become its regular and well-paid cicerone, insomuch that I am told he has never been obliged to resume the ragged old brown cloak in which I first found him.

Towards sunset I came to where the road wound into the mountains and here I paused to take a last look at Granada. The hill on which I stood commanded a glorious view of the city, the Vega and the surrounding mountains. It was at an opposite point of the compass from *La cuesta de las Lágrimas* (the hill of tears) noted for the «last sigh of the Moor». I now could realize something of the feelings of poor Boabdil when he bade adieu to the paradise he was leaving behind and beheld before him a rugged and sterile road conducting him to exile.

The setting sun as usual shed a melancholy effulgence on the ruddy towers of the Alhambra. I could faintly discern the balconied window of the tower of Comares, where I had indulged in so many delightful reveries. The bosky groves and gardens about the city were richly gilded with the sunshine,

301

the purple haze of a summer evening was gathering over the Vega; everything was lovely, but tenderly and sadly so to my parting gaze.

«I will hasten from this prospect», thought I, «before the sun is set. I will carry away a recollection of it clothed in all its beauty».

With these thoughts I pursued my way among the mountains. A little further and Granada, the Vega and the Alhambra, were shut from my view and thus ended one of the pleasantest dreams of a life which the reader perhaps may think has been but too much made up of dreams.

INDEX

CONTENTS

INDEX OF ENGRAVINGS